THE
END
OF
MONEY

"A fascinating and enjoyable read, even though it is at times shocking to trace the roots of the collective loss of trust in banking. Interspersed with illuminating anecdotes from our recent financial history, *The End of Money* makes it clear that excessive debt and extreme money creation have eroded faith in the global financial system, perhaps best symbolised by the rise of cryptocurrencies."

– MICHAEL JORDAAN, BUSINESS LEADER & VENTURE CAPITALIST

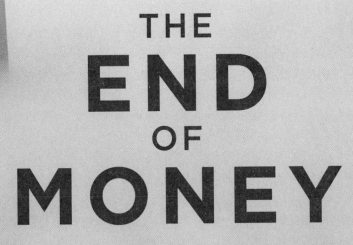

THE
END
OF
MONEY

THE GREAT EROSION OF TRUST IN BANKING, CHINA'S MINSKY MOMENT AND THE FALLACY OF CRYPTOCURRENCY

**DAVID BUCKHAM, ROBYN WILKINSON
& CHRISTIAAN STRAEULI**

Published in South Africa by Mercury
an imprint of Burnet Media

•

Burnet Media is the publisher of Mercury and Two Dogs books
www.burnetmedia.co.za
PO Box 53557, Kenilworth, 7745, South Africa

•

Published 2021
1 3 5 7 9 8 6 4 2

•

•

Cover design: Vanessa Wilson
Cover photograph: Shutterstock

•

•

Distributed by Jacana Media
www.jacana.co.za

•

Printed and bound by Tandym Print
www.tandym.co.za

•

ISBN 9781990956355

•

Set in Adobe Garamond Pro 11.5pt

ABOUT THE AUTHORS

David Buckham is the founder and CEO of Monocle, a management consulting firm specialising in banking and insurance. He has diverse experience within the banking and financial markets space, having guided regulatory implementation in banks around the world for two decades. He worked in Iceland, Denmark, Luxembourg, Singapore, Hong Kong, Malaysia, South Africa and the UK leading up to and during the Global Financial Crisis. Robyn Wilkinson is a professional writer, editor and analyst within the finance industry, with particular expertise in the areas of cryptocurrency, fintech and the history of the global financial system. Christiaan Straeuli is a professional writer, researcher and editor. He specialises in financial and economic research, particularly in the areas of monetary economics, the continued presence of corporate malfeasance and the Chinese banking system. All three authors hold master's degrees in English literature and are regular industry commentary writers.

To all those journalists who have swum against the tide, alone and of their own volition, and who have fought for freedom against the cold hand of totalitarianism.

CONTENTS

PROLOGUE

On the evening of the 13th of March 2008, Jamie Dimon, then CEO of JPMorgan Chase & Co, was at a restaurant in Midtown Manhattan celebrating his 52nd birthday with family and friends. At around 9pm, he received an unexpected phone call from Alan Schwartz, the CEO of Bear Stearns. Schwartz told Dimon that Bear needed $29 billion before the Asian markets opened in just a few hours, or else the 85-year-old investment bank would be forced to declare bankruptcy.

For about a week, rumours had been circulating through Wall Street that Bear Stearns was facing a liquidity crisis. The CEO's phone call was not only confirmation of the firm's precarious position, but also an obviously desperate plea for salvation – a plea that would go unanswered.

JPMorgan did not lend the money to Bear Stearns, and neither did anybody else. JPMorgan did, however, see an opportunity at hand. Three days after taking the call from Schwartz, Dimon made a deal to buy his crumbling competitor in a stock swap worth $2 a share, a discount of more than 90% on Bear's market value just a week before. Heavily supportive of the deal were US secretary of the Treasury Hank Paulson and chair of the Federal Reserve Ben Bernanke. Together, they arranged a $29-billion government loan via the Federal Reserve Bank of New York for Bear Stearns's toxic assets – effectively a bailout that facilitated the sale of its remaining, more stable assets to JPMorgan.

While those involved in the deal believed they had saved Bear Stearns from complete collapse – and in so doing prevented the collapse of the entire financial system – the American public saw the situation quite differently. The sale of one private financial institution to another made possible by a quasi-bailout orchestrated by the Federal Reserve sparked outrage in the public sphere. In the minds of people on the street, the government – advised by an ex-Wall Street suit in the form of Hank Paulson – had handed Jamie Dimon the deal of the century, while the US taxpayer had been stuck with a $29-billion bill. As protesters took to the streets, arranging marches and picketing outside Bear's headquarters in New York, the fury was palpable.

This was a moment in time that marked a tipping point in public opinion; when the us-versus-them mentality in the perception of Wall Street took firm hold; when the collective consciousness began outwardly acknowledging its loss of faith in banking and financial markets. It was a moment nearly four decades in the making, and it reflected a sentiment that has only worsened in the years since.

INTRODUCTION

There was a time not too long ago when people trusted banks. It was a time when banking was simple, when people believed in the integrity of money, and when banks were regarded as the best stewards of that money. A time when small-town banks were an integral part of each community, as familiar as the local, family-owned grocery store down the street. A time when everyone knew the bank tellers by name.

In the period that followed the end of World War II, banks were predominantly local and community-based, often family-run and usually with just a single branch to serve its immediate locality. When a bank was robbed in a town somewhere in Nevada or Texas, for example, it was the entire bank's cash reserves that were taken. Whereas the banking landscape today is dominated by a few powerful institutions, back in 1960 there were nearly 13,000 banks in America. These included thousands of small credit unions that served to make short-term loans to the working class, as well as thousands more savings and loan associations providing mortgages to ordinary Americans. Through the 1950s and '60s there was great stability in Western banking, a period during which interest rates virtually never changed.

The function of banks in society was also highly specific and easy to understand: banks took deposits and made loans.

At this time, banking wasn't glamorous. It wasn't a profession that attracted the best and the brightest from the finest institutions; they chose instead to become doctors or engineers or businessmen. In fact, until the 1970s banking was so safe that it verged on being dull – a sentiment best captured by what became known as the "3-6-3" rule. Bankers were said to pay 3% on deposits, write loans at 6%, and then, with their job done for the day, tee off at their local country club by 3pm.

A critical reason for this period of remarkable stability in the banking industry was the separation of investment banking and commercial banking as a result of the Glass-Steagall Act in 1933, which was introduced in response to the Wall Street Crash of 1929. Investment banking had become a particularly powerful force in 19th-century Europe, a practice that was deeply ingrained in the financing of imperial ambitions and in the progress of the Industrial Revolution. Private firms such as NM Rothschild & Sons, Kuhn, Loeb & Co and Lazard Frères helped to underwrite the equity and debt that financed the wave of progress in the rail, oil and logistics industries at the turn of the 20th century. Only two decades later, in the Roaring Twenties, these same firms created a booming trade in selling underwritten stock to retail investors on margin. This was the root cause of the collapse of the stock market in October 1929. By separating the two practices of commercial and investment banking, the Glass-Steagall Act ensured that investment banks – which were engaging in far riskier financial activities than commercial banks – could no longer take customer deposits.

The 1950s and '60s represented a simpler time in banking, but also a simpler time ideologically. World War II had brought with it an end to fascism. Continental Europe, Great Britain, the Soviet Union and Japan were economically and physically devastated, but at least the horrors were over – fascism was pronounced dead, along with Hitler and Mussolini. The post-war period ignited a spirit of reconstruction, of multilateralism, of creating a world order based on the ideals of liberal democracy. Japan and Germany were demilitarised. The United Nations was created, initially with 51 member states but growing eventually to more than 190 states, representing virtually the entire world. It seemed self-evident and undeniable that there should be a broad and sustained effort by all nation states to end war, to end poverty and essentially to eradicate evil. In this project, the outcome would be characterised by co-operation, harmonisation and international law.

For four decades after World War II, there were many internecine conflicts and several regional wars, but there was only one all-encompassing ideological battle. This was the showdown between the United States and the Soviet Union, between liberal democracy and communism – a battle that ended abruptly in 1989 with the fall of the Berlin Wall, signalling the end of the Cold War. At that moment it seemed truly to be "the end of history", as Francis Fukuyama famously put it in his 1989 essay and later his bestselling book of the same name. According to Fukuyama, the world had reached "the end-point of mankind's ideological evolution and the universalisation of Western liberal democracy as the final form of human government". It was the end of the struggle against European imperialism, and it was also the end of the ideological battle between the idea of individual freedom and its antithesis, communism. There would of course be conflicts to come but they would be fought on the fringes, fires to be put out at the edges of society. In the main, civilisation would advance with one underlying political model – democracy – and with the US leading the charge.

For a time, this is how it went. During the 1990s, following the advent of glasnost and perestroika in the USSR, the fall of communism and the release of Eastern Europe from Soviet control, it could be argued that the world took a holiday from history. Francis Fukuyama was right: on aggregate, the most fundamental ideological conflict was over and thus a time of advancement beckoned. World trade, globalisation, global banking, shared ideals, and co-operation in medicine, science and many other fields were all legitimate projects. It was a time of genuine optimism, coinciding with a great upliftment from poverty for hundreds of millions of people around the globe. The fundamental indicators predicted a time of real human progress.

It proved, however, to be a chimera. From the late 1990s onwards, the project of liberal democracy declined. Today it has been ground down, its energy dissipated. If, in retrospect, the year 1989 is seen as the zenith point of the project of liberal democracy, then we have declined substantially, both morally and ideologically, in the three decades since.

––––––––––

While the US, the UK and much of Western Europe were once politically oriented towards – and effectively obsessed with – overcoming communism and freeing the world of authoritarian rule, there exists now a general acceptance in the Western mindset of the rise of one-party nation states and the re-emergence of totalitarianism. Since the beginning of the 21st century, there has been a steady and undeniable decline in the potency of democratic ideals, with far less concern among both policy-makers and the general population for the loss of freedoms across the world.

The frightening speed with which Kabul was retaken by the Taliban after the hasty withdrawal of US troops from Afghanistan in mid-August 2021 served as stark evidence of just how deeply eroded the West's democratic ideals have become since the turn of the century. Accompanied by disturbing scenes of panic and mayhem as desperate Afghans clung to the sides of departing US aircraft, the fall of Kabul may prove to be a defining moment in the defence of the global democratic project – one more crack in an already significantly eroded dam wall that is on the brink of being overcome by a flood of totalitarianism. Writing in the immediate aftermath, French philosopher Bernard-Henri Lévy seemed to think as much. "The image of the liberal democracies, epitomised by the greatest among them, is tragically tarnished," he observed.

There is a stark contrast between the liberal rhetoric that characterised the anti-communist agenda of the 1980s and the myopia of the Western world towards the increasingly forceful and self-assured behaviour of, for example, China, North Korea, Myanmar, Turkey or Saudi Arabia in 2021. The momentum that the ideology of democracy once possessed has evidently been lost – mired by repeated failures within the political and economic systems of the West. An explosion of greed in the 1980s and '90s, validated by a set of radical economic theories, including monetary theory, saw the beginnings of an extreme version of capitalism taking hold. Mathematically complex and theoretically sophisticated, these theories drove a belief in the Western mindset that financial markets could be modelled and predicted and therefore more broadly understood, despite the fact that there existed little empirical evidence of the reliability of the models being used en masse in the financial industry. Simultaneously, there was a failure to regulate rapidly growing and dangerously opaque derivatives markets. Subsequent self-inflicted wounds in the financial markets were never properly diagnosed and dealt with. The result, in even the most liberal nations, has been a growing disillusionment with politicians and institutions, and ultimately with the democratic project and its associated economic system, free-market capitalism. The Western world has lost its way, which may well be the defining tragedy of our era.

Throughout the world, there is greater political polarisation than ever before. The political right has become radicalised and has appealed to a pre-Industrial Revolution state of mind, to a time of agrarian economics and fundamental rights, characterised by a complete and total distrust of government. The political left has become splintered, obsessed with academically inspired cultural and social minutiae, ignoring observable evils to rather ponder the almost limitless problem of the unrecognised rights embedded in identity politics. And during this period of polarisation, there has been a wilful ignorance shown towards the perpetuation and growth in power of authoritarian regimes. There has, in fact, been a greater acceptance over the past decade of the idea that state capitalism is a legitimate alternative to the free market and to liberal democracy – even when it exhibits paranoia, irrational censorship and retaliatory sanctions against its trade partners. Whereas in the 1980s it was the project of the West to defend democracy at all costs, today it is frowned upon to criticise what once would have been viewed as obvious behaviours of authoritarianism.

The root cause of the erosion of trust in democratic ideals is inherently political in nature, but it expresses itself economically and is intimately linked to the erosion of trust in banking and, more broadly, in financial markets. The causes of this erosion of trust in banking can be traced as far back as 1971, when US President Richard Nixon made a number of political decisions that became collectively known as the Nixon Shock. The most significant of these was to cancel the convertibility of the US dollar to gold, ultimately resulting in the failure of the Bretton Woods System of monetary exchange, which had been in existence since 1944. This decision, coupled with the shock of the 1973 OPEC Oil Crisis, began a period of significant turbulence in the global financial system and ultimately birthed a new type of hyper-capitalism. Indeed, as a direct result of these two events the financial world was plagued with extreme volatility in exchange rates, commodity prices, inflation and interest rates throughout the 1970s. These violent movements in rates and prices decimated small community-based banking and were the first signs that an era of distrust in the industry of banking, and even in money itself, had begun.

What followed in the next few decades can be summarily described as the financialisation of everything. After incremental deregulation throughout the 1980s and '90s, commercial banks were once again allowed to be amalgamated with investment banks through the undoing of the Glass-Steagall Act in 1999. For the first time since the end of the Great Depression, investment banks could again take customer deposits while continuing to engage in the risky activities of underwriting stocks and bonds, selling securities and trading. In turn, the relatively straightforward process of maturity intermediation – the process by which banks receive funding from the public in the form of deposits and provide funding to borrowers by "intermediating" the maturity of money; essentially borrowing short-term money and lending long-term money – was transformed. Investment banks began to engage in ever more complicated forms of financial engineering and risk intermediation to extract greater profits. Dangerous levels of leverage built up in these banks, and commercial banks were encouraged to lend with abandon, simply to feed the intermediation process.

Soon other industries were affected. Car manufacturers and furniture retailers became financial intermediaries. Telecommunications companies extended credit to customers. Insurance firms became derivatives traders, selling credit default swaps. Tax havens thrived and anonymity was ensured through the failure to regulate markets and financial institutions at a time when globalisation and increasing financial complexity were together driving massive change and growth in the financial industry. Money supply exploded, particularly after the 2007/2008 Global Financial Crisis, and this money had nowhere to go other than into the financial markets. As of 2021 this has driven stock markets to all-time highs at precisely the same time that the real economy has been brought to its knees by the Covid-19 pandemic and subsequent lockdowns. As a result, the rich have become even richer, and the chasm of inequality has widened significantly. The disconnect between Main Street and Wall Street has never been more glaring.

The world is now approaching the logical end point of this era of distrust. Today, to all intents and purposes, there are only mega-banks that remain – those banks that have survived the repeated financial crises over the fifty years that followed the Nixon Shock. These international corporations have become the antithesis of what they once were, no longer the stable, socially integrated entities at the heart of local communities. Where once upon a time customers might have thought of their bank as the local branch down the road, today's banks are symbolised by faceless skyscrapers that soar above the clouds, detached from the reality of the people below. And as the public in the West has lost faith in its financial institutions, two potentially catastrophic revolutions have taken place elsewhere – one in the East, and one in the digital realm.

First, the Chinese banking system has quietly grown to two and a half times the size of the US banking system. Between 2010 and 2020, Chinese banking assets grew at a faster rate than the official Chinese GDP growth rate, and at a much faster rate than those of banks in the Western world. This excess lending, if not being converted into economic growth, cannot be leaving China in significant quantities. It must therefore be flowing into assets within the nation and subsequently inflating the perceived value of those assets. This is a trend that has been ongoing for over twenty years now – and it must, logically, unravel. An analysis of Chinese banking today reveals numbers similar to those that should have warned us of the failure of the US housing market before 2007. Leverage is a dead giveaway.

Second, there are now thousands of different money replicants in circulation that are not backed by binding government declarations, but rather by essentially pointless, never-ending mathematical problems. That is to say, cryptocurrencies are here and they are more than a simple alternative to fiat money; they pose a grave risk to our functional societies. Countercultural and intrinsically anti-social, cryptocurrencies have encouraged a growing contingent of the public to consciously choose chaos over order, to dispense with global institutions in favour of what has become known as peer-to-peer transactions, cutting out the intermediary – the entire banking system – in favour of a world in which we need never trust each other again.

Thus the contemporary banking landscape is a space of ever-increasing complexity and ever-diminishing trust faced by twin threats. On the one hand, there has been an enormous explosion of debt in China, now the world's second-largest economy, which brings with it the potential for a repeat of the Global Financial Crisis. On the other hand, there exists a recent and widely adopted phenomenon that claims to be an alternative way to conduct financial transactions, called cryptocurrency, which undermines the idea of money itself. It is the economic version of the loosely organised and zombie-like storming of the US Capitol building. On the 6th of January 2021, an angry mob overran the seat of Congress, driven by an unfounded idea that the presidential election had been rigged, and galvanised by their complete and utter loss of faith in the most central institutions of democracy. This socio-political discontent is mirrored in the mania of cryptocurrency, a dangerous idea that will only accelerate chaos and disorder.

To some – perhaps many – the idea of a loss of trust in banking is no great tragedy, especially with the emergence of what they believe is a technical solution to replace it, cryptocurrencies. The naivety of this position is profound, but even those not in thrall to Bitcoin are likely to underestimate the importance of our financial institutions. Banking is an industry like no other. It is the mechanism by which money is kept safe and credit is extended. Over the course of centuries, it has been critical to human progress, the alleviation of poverty and the steady improvement of quality of life. Without banking, for example, the Industrial Revolution would never have happened on the scale and with the effect that it did. As a global industry, banking today makes possible international trade – essential to lifting entire nations out of obscurity and deterring violent appropriation of land and resources – and encourages multilateral diplomacy over protracted conflict. It also offers a set of internationally adopted standards of conduct, governing both capital and liquidity, that stabilise the international monetary system and ideally prevent money laundering, the financing of terrorism and crime, and tax evasion. In the strongest sense, banking, as it should be practised, enables the creation of a more just, peaceful and equal world.

This is no trivial point. If it is acknowledged that the international banking system is the "brain" that determines where capital and liquidity are best allocated to what could be called the body economic, then as an industry it cannot be treated as a passive participant in society. Because it is so fundamental to the functioning of the modern way of life, it has the power to either promote or erode social and humanist principles. It can starve authoritarianism or feed it. It can promote liberal democracy or fund totalitarianism – and it has proved in the 20th century to be capable of both.

It is distressing how much destruction had to occur for the world to take stock of itself in 1945. It is even more distressing that, having overcome communism in 1989, the world is now on a path of accelerating regression towards nationalism, extremism and total distrust in its institutions – including, perhaps most critically, banks. This book traces the key historical moments that have led to the steady erosion of trust in banking, and explains why it must be regained.

1

THE FINANCIAL CRISIS AND
THE PROBLEM OF LEVERAGE

On Monday the 10th of March 2008, three days before Bear Stearns CEO Alan Schwartz would make his Hail Mary dinnertime call to Jamie Dimon, senior executives from the investment bank scrambled to quell intensifying rumours about its financial position. Meanwhile, as the company's stock price tumbled to its lowest levels in five years, its chairman James Cayne was some 600 miles away from his Manhattan headquarters, playing in a multi-day bridge tournament in Detroit. It was a good day's play for Cayne and his bridge partner: they moved up to fourth place out of 130 overall in the "Imp Pairs" event of the North American Championship.

On the same day, Alan Schwartz was attending the company's annual four-day media conference in sunny Palm Beach, Florida. Wanting to get in a few extra days of golf, Schwartz had flown from New York to Palm Beach a week before the conference began. On his departure, there had been a few whispers about Bear Stearns's exposure to the faltering subprime mortgage market, but nothing serious enough to deter the CEO from enjoying his trip. By the time the conference commenced a few days later, however, speculation about a potential liquidity crisis had escalated. The media was hunting for a story, and with the chairman playing bridge in Detroit and the CEO playing golf in Palm Beach, a reporter from CNBC reached out for comment to the chairman of the executive committee, Alan "Ace" Greenberg. Caught off-guard, Greenberg snapped that the rumours were "ridiculous, totally ridiculous".

In the story that CNBC ran later that same day, Greenberg was made to sound hysterical and overly defensive. Readers were also reminded that Moody's had recently downgraded Bear Stearns's ALT-A Trust, which was related to subprime mortgage deals. The company's share price had been on a gradual decline since January, losing about 30% of its value in the two months to early March, but by the 10th the sell-off of its stock was accelerating significantly. Attempting to suppress the damaging rumours, Bear released an official statement quoting Schwartz. "Bear Stearns's balance sheet, liquidity and capital remain strong," he stated. Despite this – or perhaps because of it – the company's share price dropped 11% on the day.

To make matters worse, there was talk that an employee from the Office of the Comptroller of the Currency had in the past week been telephoning large financial institutions enquiring about their exposures to Bear Stearns. These calls, coupled with the increased press coverage related to its liquidity, severely spooked other Wall Street firms, and the cumulative effect of it all was a considerable increase in the cost of insuring Bear's debt on the credit default swaps (CDS) market. By 10 March, the cost of insuring $10 million of Bear's debt for five years had widened to as much as $650,000 per year compared to

$452,000 the week before – an incredibly wide margin for a CDS spread related to a multinational investment bank's debt, and ten to fifteen times greater than the spread on a AAA-rated instrument over a developed nation's government bond yield.

The market reacted quickly and decisively to these concerns, with the number of put options bought by options traders – betting that Bear Stearns's stock would soon devalue – rising sharply. On the day after the investment bank publicly stated that its financial position was "strong", the number of Bear put options sold was more than triple the twenty-day average – the market, on aggregate, strongly believed that its share price was going to continue to decline. While this was obviously concerning, even more telling was the type of option that most of the traders were buying. The most common contract being purchased gave traders the right, but not the obligation, to sell Bear stock for $30 a share before the end of the contract period on 21 March – just eight trading days from the start of the contract. A week earlier it had been trading at over $60 a share. Evidently, many market participants believed that Bear's share price would halve in less than two weeks, and they were willing to place significant bets on this conviction.

The rapid increase in the selling of put options can in part be explained by the actions of those large financial institutions that already had exposure to Bear Stearns's assets. After all, the best way for these institutions to hedge their positions was to buy put options, knowing that they could at least make some money on the other side of the trade if the investment bank's share price collapsed. Had the rumour about Bear's liquidity positions remained just a rumour, things might have turned out quite differently. Following phone calls from the Office of the

Comptroller of the Currency to every major financial institution both inside and outside Wall Street, however, what had started as a rumour became something of a self-fulfilling prophecy. At the close of the market on Tuesday the 11th, with its credit spreads widening drastically and the number of bets against it far outweighing those for it, Bear Stearns's fate appeared to be sealed.

————————

Despite everything that was happening that March, Bear Stearns had in fact made a profit in the first quarter of 2008. Anxious to suppress the damaging rumours that were circulating, the investment bank considered releasing its quarterly earnings early. Legally, however, it was not allowed to provide the public with any accounting details related to its balance sheet and liquidity until the official earnings call. The best the executives could do before then was to promise that everything was above board, and assure shareholders that when the financials were released the numbers would tell the same story. But a promise without proof was simply not good enough for some.

On the 11th of March, Dutch bank ING Group suspended its $500-million short-term funding facility with Bear Stearns. To compound the problem, an incident between traders from Hayman Capital and Goldman Sachs later that day raised a prominent red flag. Just after 5pm, the trader from Hayman sent an email to the derivatives desk at Goldman asking them to "please novate" a trade between Hayman's Subprime Credit Strategies Fund and its client Bear Stearns. Essentially, the trader was requesting that Goldman take over Hayman's $5-million derivatives position in the subprime mortgage market in a transaction with Bear. Not long after, the Goldman derivatives desk sent a simple and devastating reply: "GS does not consent to this trade." Even the mighty Goldman Sachs was refusing to step into trades for its clients when the transactions were related to Bear Stearns.

To make matters worse, a number of large clients requested to withdraw their funds from their accounts that same day, fearing that if Bear Stearns folded, their money would go down with it. The first was Renaissance Technologies, a hedge fund owned by Jim Simons, which held $20 billion with Bear. The second was Highbridge Capital Management, a hedge fund with about $35 billion under management. The loss of these major accounts was catastrophic, but Bear had no choice except to comply. Had it refused or even hesitated to fulfil the requests, panic would undoubtedly have spread, and every other client would have asked to withdraw their funds too. As it was, these were sizeable withdrawals to fulfil. How would Bear pull together the money required to pay back its clients?

To fund itself daily, Bear Stearns, like many other Wall Street investment banks, used short-term – often overnight – funding arrangements with other banks, called repurchase agreements or repos. In a typical repurchase agreement, a borrower, usually an investment bank, receives funds from a lender, usually a commercial bank, on a short-term basis. To secure the deal with the commercial bank, the investment bank provides assets, typically securities – either debt or equity – to be used as collateral for the agreement. In this agreement, the borrower commits itself to repurchasing its securities from the lender on a specified date and at a specified price, with an interest payment added to compensate for the lender's risk. At the time, Bear was borrowing in the region of $75 billion a day through various repo agreements with several large banks. Every day, staff on Bear's repo desk would call the banks they worked with to arrange their daily repo. They would likely speak to the same person on the other end of the phone, obtain a rate for the transaction, and lock in the funding. For any other business, having to borrow billions of dollars every day just to fund its daily operations would seem extremely risky, but for Bear Stearns – and indeed many other investment banks, including Goldman Sachs, Morgan Stanley and Lehman Brothers – this was simply the way that business was done.

Securing daily repo funds was usually a mundane exercise for Bear Stearns, but by the 11th of March the calls to the repo desks of large multinational banks to negotiate the terms of the deals had become distinctly more complicated. Witnessing the price of Bear's credit default swaps skyrocketing, its lenders were becoming increasingly wary, demanding more collateral and lending at far higher interest rates. By the following day many of the institutions that had previously lent to the investment bank on a daily basis simply refused to roll over funding.

It was only at this point that Alan Schwartz, the elusive CEO of Bear Stearns, finally made a public appearance in an interview with CNBC, broadcasting from the Breakers Hotel in Palm Beach. "None of these speculations are true," he said when asked whether other financial firms were no longer taking counterparty risk with Bear. "Our liquidity position has not weakened at all," he said when asked how its liquidity position had changed in the last few months, a time in which the American housing market had been in continuous decline. "We have many, many billions – $17 billion or so – in excess cash sitting on the balance sheet of the holding company as cushion. That's in addition to billions of dollars of cash and unpledged collateral that are at our subsidiaries. So, we don't see any pressure on our liquidity, let alone a liquidity crisis."

By that afternoon, most of the institutions that usually provided the investment bank with overnight funding had nonetheless decided not to re-engage in their repo transactions. Of the daily $75 billion that Bear Stearns required to fund its operations, only $20 billion had been secured for the next day's trading. Without this cash, Bear would effectively default on many of its obligations to its various lenders and, most critically, it would not be able to pay its clients who were requesting the withdrawal of their funds.

Company executives suggested selling off the bank's most liquid assets to boost cash reserves, but Schwartz refused, arguing that this would only signal that they were in more trouble than he had admitted. With few options remaining, and having finally realised the inevitability of the situation, Schwartz sought legal advice from Rodgin Cohen, a senior partner at Sullivan & Cromwell and a legal expert in the mergers and acquisitions of Wall Street financial firms. Cohen advised Schwartz that there was only one institution that could help Bear Stearns at this point: the Federal Reserve.

That night, Cohen phoned Timothy Geithner, president of the New York Federal Reserve. He pleaded with him to bring forward the loan programme that the Fed had announced the previous day for struggling financial institutions, but that would only officially launch in two weeks' time. Alternatively, Cohen asked Geithner to consider opening the discount window – a monetary tool used by the central bank to provide firms with liquidity, by exchanging troubled assets such as mortgage-backed securities for cash, usually on a short-term basis, in times of distress – so that the Fed could loan directly to Bear Stearns. This was not entirely unprecedented, with the central bank having provided this service to commercial banks in the past. But commercial banks were subject to closer and more stringent regulation than their investment bank counterparts, which were not considered *banks* at that time. It was only after the 2007/2008 Global Financial Crisis that investment banks would be forced to become bank holding companies, to be regulated under the same rules as commercial banks. Unconvinced, Geithner told Cohen that if the situation was as serious as it seemed, Schwartz should call him directly.

The next morning Schwartz did exactly that, and the two men debated Bear Stearns's options without coming to a definite answer as to how they could save the investment bank. By the middle of that day, several more clients had asked to withdraw their money, rapidly depleting Bear's available liquidity. By that afternoon, several of the banks that usually provided Bear with short-term funding decided they were not going to roll over their repo agreements without material and ultimately untenable alterations to the terms of the loans. Schwartz could no longer escape the reality that Bear Stearns would not be able to open the next morning for trading. With no other options remaining, he reached out to the only person who he believed could save the investment bank, JPMorgan CEO Jamie Dimon, calling him while he was out to dinner celebrating his birthday.

Jamie Dimon did not respond the way Alan Schwartz had hoped, and there was to be no lifeline for Bear Stearns. Instead, Dimon took the opportunity that presented itself, as presumably any banker in his position would have done. With Hank Paulson and Ben Bernanke stepping in to arrange a $29-billion New York Fed loan that would neutralise Bear's toxic assets, JPMorgan bought Bear Stearns at a 93% discount with a stock swap worth $2 a share. And it's here that the complex machinations of modern finance meet the practical reality of public perception. In the mind of the public at the time, these complexities were reduced to an essential truth: a reckless Wall Street investment bank had failed and taxpayer dollars had been used to bail it out, inadvertently benefiting an even more powerful bank, which was gifted the deal of the century.

In contemplating the Bear Stearns deal after the fact, Paulson believed that the failure of trust between government decision-makers and the public had been caused by a simple "communication issue". From his point of view, as he explained in an interview a decade after the Financial Crisis, bailing out the investment bank was necessary to prevent the total collapse of the American financial system. According to Paulson, the average person did not understand that if a gaping financial wound was not staunched at the source, then the whole system could bleed to death. What Paulson in turn did not realise at the time, however, was that the bailout of Bear was just the first of many emergency tourniquets that would need to be used to stop the financial system from collapsing in the coming months as the subprime mortgage crisis in America exploded into a full-blown global financial crisis.

Moreover, the idea that the average person didn't understand the inscrutable goings-on within the finance industry, as dictated by Wall Street and ex-Wall Street executives, had to a large degree become part of the reason the public was losing faith in the financial system. As the Crisis developed, it appeared that the government was simply pouring money back into Wall Street, saving the very same investment banks that had caused the problem in the first place. This money, the public believed, should rather have been used to support ordinary Americans who were being directly affected by a recession that had been directly caused by these firms. It could, they argued, have been used to alleviate the pain of the tens of thousands of blue-collar workers who had lost their homes to foreclosures as they failed to meet their mortgage payments, as well as the millions who had lost their jobs due to the dire economic conditions that the US now found itself in.

The 2008 presidential election for the successor to George W Bush, which took place amid the financial meltdown, only served to intensify public debate. Support for the two-term Bush administration, which had declined steadily following his decision to send US troops to Iraq, declined further as the Financial Crisis unfolded. The decision to grant federal funding to failing financial institutions, and particularly to non-bank institutions – the first act of its kind since the Great Depression – did not sit well with constituents on either side of party lines. For Democrats, the bailouts signalled that the government had an elitist agenda, favouring the powerful executives of Wall Street who paid for their political campaigns, while leaving ordinary Americans to fend for themselves. For many Republicans, the bailouts were something truly un-American: an action counter to the most fundamental tenets of free-market ideology.

The result of widespread dissatisfaction with the powers in office was the initiation of a populist movement in the US, which was tapped into by both the Obama and McCain presidential campaigns, though by the latter more than the former. Both candidates channelled the anger of the public to their benefit, promising that they would hold avaricious Wall Street bankers accountable for the mess they had created, while uplifting and supporting the average Joe on Main Street. With the markets in chaos and thousands losing their livelihoods each day, there was a whiff of revolution in the air.

On the left, commentators have argued that the beginnings of the Occupy Wall Street movement in 2011 can be traced to the early days of the Financial Crisis. The Crisis galvanised a belief that ever more power and wealth was being accumulated in the hands of a very few Americans, the 1%, while the average American, part of the 99%, was being left behind. Similarly, on the right, this populist strain of disgruntlement manifested in the Republican Tea Party movement, which advocated lower tax rates, less government intervention and a decrease in government expenditure.

Tracing back the development of these groups, we can consider the March 2008 protests outside the headquarters of Bear Stearns in the days following its acquisition by JPMorgan as the first skirmishes in a populist uprising – both on the side of the liberal anti-elitists and on the side of the conservative nationalists. The full force of these growing movements would not be felt, however, until after the collapse of the government-backed institutions Fannie Mae and Freddie Mac in late 2008. By this stage an increasing number of Americans were starting to believe that the government had in some way broken its social contract with its people. Those residing in the White House and those making billions on Wall Street, they believed, were becoming ever more detached from the plight of ordinary citizens.

———————

Five years after the Global Financial Crisis, in August 2013, US President Barack Obama visited the Desert Vista High School in Phoenix, Arizona. Phoenix had been right at the centre of the devastation that had unfolded when the housing market collapsed in the US, but rather than addressing the Crisis head-on, the president sought to divert attention from the dual failures of Wall Street and the government by taking a more optimistic line. Speaking to the crowd of thousands that had gathered at the school, Obama said, "The most tangible cornerstone that lies at the heart of the American Dream, at the heart of middle-class life – that's the chance to own your own home." The crowd roared. Despite the carnage of the Crisis, the white-picket-fence American Dream was still alive and well in the collective consciousness of the people.

Although the exact cause of the Crisis remains widely debated, the roots of the disaster can be found in what is perhaps one of the most fundamental aspects of modern capitalist culture: the idea of home ownership. This is an idea that extends far

THE END OF MONEY

beyond the physical purchase of a house. From John Locke's famous *Two Treatises of Government*, published in 1660 and advocating the God-given right to private property, to Thomas Jefferson's declaration that "a right to property is founded in our natural wants", the idea of property ownership is deeply ingrained in Western thinking. In more recent times, this sentiment has persisted, endorsed from the heights of political power by President Obama in Phoenix, and before him by President George W Bush, who was a fervent proponent of an "ownership society", and before *him* by President Bill Clinton, who promoted the idea of "a home for every American".

During his presidency from 1993 to 2001, Clinton's views on home ownership were propagated particularly through the revamping of the Community Reinvestment Act (CRA), which had been created by Ronald Reagan in 1977. The CRA was promulgated via the Department of Housing and Urban Development (HUD) to encourage banks to provide credit to struggling middle-to-low-income communities for the purpose of growing home ownership in America. To enforce the CRA, regulators would assess whether banks had taken the required portion of "credit-deprived" clients onto their books, with compliant institutions being favoured with approval for new branch applications and merger and acquisition requests. These low-income applicants were dubbed "subprime" borrowers due to their tarnished or limited credit histories, and to ensure they could afford their mortgages it became commonplace for banks to issue loans without any initial deposit required, and with borrowers not needing to pay any interest on the loan in the first few years of the contract. To make the sums work in the long run, the real financial pain was often simply deferred using adjustable interest rate terms, which increased repayment amounts as the loan matured, making it progressively more difficult for borrowers to fulfil their repayments as time went on.

Perhaps one of the most important developments in this regard came in 1992, when the political drive to expand the US home-ownership rate culminated in the passing of the Housing and Community Development Act. This Act introduced an affordable housing loan purchase mandate for the government-backed mortgage buyers Fannie Mae and Freddie Mac. The Federal National Mortgage Association, or Fannie Mae, was founded during the Great Depression in 1938 as part of President Roosevelt's New Deal. During this period, creating liquidity was a major concern for government, as severe economic conditions had made it almost impossible for the public to access credit, with banks unwilling or unable to create more loans in those uncertain times. Fannie Mae's express purpose was therefore to expand the secondary mortgage market by buying home loans from banks, effectively taking those loans off banks' balance sheets to create liquidity for the banks to make more loans. Decades later, the government created the Federal Home Loan Mortgage Corporation, or Freddie Mac, through the passing of the Emergency Home Finance Act of 1970. This piece of legislation aimed to extend and diversify the rapidly growing secondary mortgage market in which Fannie Mae had, until that point, been the only player.

With the introduction of the Housing and Community Development Act – overseen by the HUD department – it became law that affordable housing should make up at least 30% of Fannie Mae's and Freddie Mac's loan purchases. In 1996, the Clinton administration decided that their portfolio of subprime loans should be increased to at least 40%. In 2007 this was driven up to 55% by the Bush administration. There was, however, a fundamental problem with what may have been considered a noble ambition: while both Fannie Mae and Freddie Mac were created by government and had their operations broadly steered by political agendas, they were not technically government organisations. As so-called government-sponsored enterprises (GSEs), the two mortgage buyers operated with the backing of taxpayers' money and the implicit guarantee of government bailout in the event of bankruptcy, but they were also still publicly traded firms with profit-driving CEOs, who earned many millions of dollars a year in individual compensation. The drive to give as many Americans as possible the opportunity to own their own homes was thus being powered by contradictory political and economic forces.

The government-mandated increase in the approval of subprime mortgages has led many economists to conclude that the seeds of the Financial Crisis were sown during the Clinton era, fertilised under Bush, and ultimately tended by the government-backed institutions of Fannie Mae and Freddie Mac. Indeed, during the 1990s and early 2000s, business boomed for the two GSEs. Under the instruction of the American government through the Housing and Community Development Act, they rapidly increased the acquisition of middle- and low-income mortgages and made billions of dollars of profit in the process. During this time, they were consistently listed among the most profitable companies in the *Fortune* 500 list, with individuals such as Frank Raines – CEO of Fannie Mae from 1999 to 2004 – receiving tens of millions of dollars in salary and bonuses each year during their tenures. In hindsight, Fannie Mae and

Freddie Mac stand as the quintessential examples of free-market capitalist institutions that were operating according to distinctly socialist ideas. This strange combination of socialist thinking and capitalist zeal accelerated the rate of growth in the US property market, spurred on by low interest rates in the late 1990s and early 2000s.

This growth was further compounded as many Wall Street investment banks, then looking to recover from the effects of the 1997 Asian Financial Crisis, began radically increasing their exposure to the mortgage market. These firms were buying mortgage loans from banks and repackaging them into what appeared to be low-risk financial instruments, such as mortgage-backed securities and collateralised debt obligations, increasing their leverage substantially as they did so. And, technically, there was nothing wrong with what they were doing – at this point, while these firms were referred to as investment *banks*, they were not regulated in the same way as commercial banks. It was only post-Crisis that the very real need for oversight of these financial institutions was recognised.

Trouble began in 2004, when the Federal Reserve started to raise interest rates, which had been kept low to stimulate economic growth in the wake of the 2001 recession. Increasingly, many subprime borrowers found themselves unable to manage their repayments at the higher rates. Defaults on mortgage loans began to increase substantially, and by the end of 2007 more than twenty subprime lenders had filed for bankruptcy. The interbank market froze and global credit markets collapsed as asset prices fell and financial institutions struggled to ascertain the real value of trillions of dollars' worth of toxic mortgage-backed securities. By 2008, highly leveraged subprime mortgage and derivatives exposures had built up so drastically that the US faced its greatest financial crisis since the Great Depression.

When the subprime mortgage market collapsed in 2007, Fannie Mae and Freddie Mac held more than half of America's home loans in securities, with half of those being riskier HUD-mandated loans and a significant portion being subprime in nature. It is estimated that between them, the two giant GSEs had purchased $434 billion in securities backed by subprime loans between 2004 and 2006. By July 2008, with their stocks plummeting and their capital rapidly running out, and with half of the US's mortgage market at risk, there was little choice for the government but to take Fannie Mae and Freddie Mac into curatorship. The bailout of the two GSEs cost US taxpayers upwards of $187 billion, more than six times the cost of the New York Fed's quasi-bailout of Bear Stearns just four months earlier.

In October 2008, with the bankruptcy of many investment banks causing further devastation to financial markets, and as Obama and McCain battled it out to see who would succeed him, President Bush signed into law the Emergency Economic Stabilization Act. The Act essentially granted Treasury's request – via its secretary Hank Paulson, and justified in a formal document that in its entirety constituted less than three pages – for $700 billion to buy distressed mortgage-backed securities from private financial firms. This funding was made available through the Troubled Asset Relief Program, which facilitated the bailout of private institutions through the purchase of their troubled assets – a decision that formalised the Bear Stearns rescue process, and one that would lead to pronounced social fracturing in America, and indeed around the world, in subsequent years.

In contemplating the causes of the Global Financial Crisis it is undeniable that the elevation of free-market ideals in the Western world throughout the latter part of the 20th century introduced an untenable level of greed and moral hazard into the banking system, which grew ever more leveraged until the Crisis itself. The root of the problem, however, lay in a shift in political ideology. Following the failure of communism in the USSR, and in the absence of a defined external enemy, there was a notable pandering to American voters by politicians on both sides of the aisle. Democrats and Republicans alike appealed particularly to the twin concepts at the heart of capitalism: independence and individual ownership of property. In the aftermath of the Crisis it has become very easy to blame individual bad actors and Wall Street in general for the failure of the US banking system. But the real underlying driver was the political intervention that allowed the banking system to operate in a manner that was ultimately unsustainable – a phenomenon that is mirrored today in the build-up of leverage currently taking place in China.

2

IMPROBABLE PROFITS AND THE COST OF BANKING

Banks have lost their shine in the years since the 2007/2008 Global Financial Crisis. Plagued by regulatory requirements that severely hinder their ability to leverage themselves as they once did – which, while increasing capital buffers, limit their ability to make profits – banks generally make for much poorer investments than they did before the Crisis. Regularly beset by rogue trading, massive fines and internal misconduct that have led to congressional hearings and high-level dismissals, these institutions have also suffered enormous reputational damage, both individually and collectively, further diminishing public trust in the financial system as a whole. Since the Crisis, banking has transformed significantly from the exciting, alluring and superbly profitable business it once was. That, at least, is the case in the Western world.

In the East – and specifically in China – the biggest banks appear to be far more efficient, successful and profitable than the biggest banks in the West. A snapshot of the distinct shift in banking power that has taken place in recent years is provided by *The Banker* magazine's annual "Top 1000 World Banks" list, which has been ranking the world's largest international banks since 1970. In the ranking's first year of publication, Bank of America topped the list, recording $25 billion of assets on its balance sheet. In *The Banker's* 2021 list – based on 2020 financial year-end results – Bank of America's total assets were recorded at $2.8 trillion, having grown more than a hundred fold in half a century.

To put this growth in context, the GDP of the United States expanded at a compound annual growth rate of 4% from 1990 to 2020, while the top five American banks collectively increased their assets at a compound annual growth rate of 10% in the same period. This means that the largest banks in the US have, on average, grown at more than double the rate of GDP growth for thirty years. This is consistent with the fact that the financial services industry, and banking in particular, has become a greater contributor to GDP, owing to a tectonic shift in the global West away from industrialisation and towards tertiary services. As a result of this shift, just about everything has been financialised, a process epitomised by the explosion in the size and volume of derivatives trading from the 1980s onwards, with traders betting on every movement of every possible market, from gold to oranges to skimmed milk powder, and with each commodity's array of derivatives contracts becoming increasingly complex and abstract. In turn, this has created a need for a larger and more complex financial services industry capable of facilitating the transition from an industrial, manufacturing-led economy to a post-industrial, services-driven, tech-heavy, customer-centric economy.

Asset growth in the largest banks in developed Western nations has also been driven by significant consolidation within the global banking landscape over the last thirty years. This has resulted in many smaller, or large but distressed, banks being absorbed by the biggest and most powerful players in the industry. In fact, the biggest banks in the US by asset size at the end of 2020 – Citigroup, Wells Fargo, JPMorgan and Bank of America – can now be called "the big four" only because of the mergers and acquisitions of more than thirty separate companies in the last three decades. This trend of consolidation peaked during the Global Financial Crisis, when several large banks on the brink or in the process of collapse were acquired by more stable and liquid banks. Notable examples include JPMorgan's acquisition of Bear Stearns and Washington Mutual, Bank of America's acquisition of Countrywide Financial and Merrill Lynch, and Wells Fargo's acquisition of Wachovia. As a direct reaction to the carnage that occurred during the Crisis, competition regulation in the US slowed down these mega-mergers after 2008, though the largest players continued to accumulate market share in a far more concentrated banking industry.

There has been impressive growth and consolidation of power and assets among the largest US banks in the last few decades – and yet an American bank is no longer the largest in the world. The bank that took the top position on the inaugural list in 1970 doesn't even make it into the top five largest banks today. By asset size at year-end 2020, Bank of America now sits in a humble ninth place, some way behind its countrymate JPMorgan, which, with total assets of $3.4 trillion, sits in fifth. And that is as high as any American bank is placed by asset size.

Placed between Bank of America and JPMorgan are the UK's HSBC, France's BNP Paribas and Japan's Mitsubishi UFJ Financial Group. But when it comes to the top four largest banks, one nation now dominates the list. In fourth place is Bank of China (BOC), recording total assets of $3.7 trillion – 10% larger than JPMorgan. In third and second places are Agricultural Bank of China (ABC) and China Construction Bank (CCB), with $4.1 trillion and $4.3 trillion in total assets, respectively. And in first place, by a significant margin, is Industrial and Commercial Bank of China (ICBC), holding $5.1 trillion in assets on its balance sheet – more than 150% the size of JPMorgan, and larger than Bank of America and Citigroup combined.

A simple comparison of *The Banker*'s lists reveals just how significantly the banking landscape – and, indeed, the global economic landscape as a whole – has changed over the last half-century. More specifically, it reveals how dramatically it has changed in just the last decade alone. In the magazine's 2011 ranking, the top five largest banks in terms of asset size were all institutions residing in the West. In fact, they were all headquartered in Europe: BNP Paribas in France, Deutsche Bank in Germany, and HSBC, Barclays and Royal Bank of Scotland in the UK. In the same year, the majority of the top twenty banks by asset size were institutions from Western democratic nations, including the US, the UK, France, Germany, Spain and the Netherlands, while only four Chinese banks featured in the top twenty.

Today there are nine Chinese institutions in *The Banker*'s top twenty. A decade ago, in 2011, the combined assets of the four biggest Chinese banks represented 17% of the total combined assets of the top twenty, similar to the percentages for the UK, France and the US, which had respective total shares of 22%, 20% and 16%. The distribution of the world's largest banks by asset size was relatively diversified at that stage, with no single nation's banks holding more than a quarter of total assets. By 2021, however, Chinese banks held a dominant 47% share. The next largest proportion was held by US banks, with a 22% share, while banks from France and Japan each held total assets equivalent to 11%. Banks from the UK held just 5%, having topped the list a decade earlier.

From 1990 to 2010, the top five US banks grew their total assets at a rate of 14% per year. By contrast, that figure dropped to just 3% over the next decade – a clear demonstration of the significant effect that the Global Financial Crisis and subsequent regulations had on the US banking system. By comparison, from 2010 to 2020, the five largest Chinese banks grew their assets at a rate of 10% per year. In the same decade, Chinese GDP grew at a rate of 9% year-on-year – though, critically, averaging less than 7% in the last five years. What is plainly evident is that China's banking assets have grown at a staggering pace since the Crisis, while the growth of Western banks, especially in the US, has all but stalled. Perhaps even more importantly, China's banking assets have also grown at a considerably faster rate than their own GDP.

The top four Chinese banks are not just the biggest by asset size today; they are also the world's most profitable. As of 2021, ICBC was the most profitable bank in the world, recording pre-tax profits of $60 billion at year-end 2020. The next three most profitable banks were CCB, ABC and BOC, with figures of

$51 billion, $40 billion and $37 billion, respectively. In fifth place, at $35 billion, was JPMorgan.

When ranked against global companies *in every sector*, ICBC was the fourth most profitable company in the world according to *Fortune* magazine's "Global 2000" rankings for 2021. The only three firms above it were Apple, Microsoft and Saudi Aramco, making ICBC more profitable than enormous and ubiquitous multinational technology firms such as Alphabet (Google) and Facebook. This is surprising, given that, in the post-Financial Crisis era, banks have, on aggregate, become far less profitable than they once were. It thus seems illogical that Chinese banks could legitimately be so much more profitable than their Western counterparts, particularly considering their underlying economic and financial characteristics.

At first glance, the profits of these giant Chinese banks seem incongruent with the economic situation in which China exists – the country is, after all, considered a developing nation. For a deeper look, the relationship between economic output and bank profits of China and that of other countries, specifically the US, can be compared. To do this, the sum of the profits of the top five banks in China and that of the top five banks in the US is divided respectively by the GDPs of China and the US, to produce what could be called "banking profitability friction ratios". In simple terms, these ratios represent how much profit the top five banks are making per dollar of GDP generated in the same year. In making these calculations, it becomes clear that the economic cost of each dollar of bank profit is proportionally far greater in one country than the other.

When the 2020 profits of the top five banks in the US are divided by the nation's GDP, the US achieves a banking profitability friction ratio of 0.4%. In China, when the same calculation is performed, the ratio is some three and a half times greater at 1.4%. In China – an industrial nation driven primarily by manufacturing and exports – the top five banks' profits consume significantly more of the GDP pie than the top five banks' profits consume in the highly financialised, service-driven nation of the US.

This suggests a logical disconnect between the nature of the Chinese banking sector and the nature of the underlying industrial-driven economy. Not only are Chinese state-owned banks growing at a disproportionate rate compared to their economy, but they are also consuming a disproportionate amount of the GDP pie compared to banks in the US.

The extraordinary profitability of Chinese banks is largely driven by a combination of two factors. The first of these is the enormous year-on-year increases in the size of the largest Chinese banks' balance sheets over the last decade. The second is the fact that these institutions have achieved remarkably low cost-to-income ratios compared to the average cost-to-income ratios of banks around the world, and especially those residing in Western democratic nations.

The cost-to-income ratio is a commonly used measure of a bank's efficiency, as it indicates how effectively a bank can increase its revenue while keeping its costs down. These costs include salaries and bonuses, IT and property costs, and the costs associated with regulatory compliance, including the implementation of market conduct rules and the payment of potential regulatory fines. Banks strive to reduce all these costs while attempting to maximise revenue. In 2020 the simple average cost-to-income ratio of the largest five banks in China was 33%, while that of the five largest banks in the US was roughly double this figure at 65%. This enormous discrepancy could go a long way to explaining the phenomenal profitability of Chinese banks – though the question then still remains as to how it is possible for these banks to achieve such incredibly low costs while reporting such high revenues.

When comparing cost-to-income ratios from institutions around the world, Standard & Poor's (S&P) notes that "the economic, financial and regulatory environment of each country can affect cost-to-income ratios". This somewhat benign-sounding point could account for some of the differences between the ratios of Chinese banks and their Western counterparts, except for the fact that Chinese banks are subject to – and publicly assert that they comply with – the same rules and regulations followed by all other nations: the international banking regulations set by the Basel Committee on Banking Supervision (BCBS).

The BCBS – a subcommittee of the Bank for International Settlements (BIS) – was founded in 1974 with the express aim of achieving international convergence in banking standards. Since 1988, it has been responsible for the promulgation of a series of accords determining international standards for banking best practice, especially as it relates to capital adequacy requirements. As of 2021, the BCBS comprised 45 representatives from the central banks of 28 jurisdictions, including all countries in the EU, the UK, the US, Russia, Argentina, Brazil, India, South

Africa, Saudi Arabia, South Korea and, importantly, China. All members of the BCBS agree to implement the Basel standards within their own countries, which means that, in theory, Chinese banks are subject to the very same rules and regulations that have driven up cost-to-income ratios and driven down return on equity (ROE) in their Western counterparts. Yet, according to available data, Chinese banks have not been affected to nearly the same extent.

This point is particularly relevant to the rules relating to capital requirements, which have caused banks to deleverage, driving down ROEs because capital as a proportion of total liabilities is now higher than before. On the other hand, liquidity and market conduct rules have generally made banks less efficient, because these rules cost a significant amount to implement and make the intermediation process more expensive.

To make the point from another angle, banks in less democratic nations tend to record much lower simple unweighted average cost-to-income ratios than banks in more democratic countries. Consider, for example, Iran, Cuba, Turkmenistan, Egypt, Iraq, Tajikistan, Qatar, Saudi Arabia and the United Arab Emirates, each of which in 2019 reported a bank average cost-to-income ratio of between 20% and 35%. These nations were also all classified as authoritarian regimes in the Global Democracy Index published by *The Economist* that same year. This suggests that there exists a relationship between the level of democracy in a nation and the average cost-to-income ratio recorded by its banking industry. At the other end of the scale, according to the World Bank, banks in developed Western democratic nations – such as Germany, France, the Netherlands, the UK and the US – recorded average cost-to-income ratios of between 55%

and 80% in 2019. In most cases, the ratios of banks in Western democratic nations are at least double those of banks in nations classified as authoritarian regimes.

In the case of China – a nation classified by *The Economist* as an authoritarian regime with a democracy rating of 2.3 out of 10 – the average cost-to-income ratio across all Chinese banks in 2019 was 32%, ever so slightly lower than the average of the top five banks in China at the time. This placed China's banking system within the top ten lowest ratios in the world, sandwiched in the rankings between Qatar and the United Arab Emirates. Thus, while not the outright world leader, China is surpassed on this metric only by a handful of definitively undemocratic nations – none of which is a standing member of the BCBS. This makes China the nation with the lowest average cost-to-income ratios across its banking sector of any country that is presumed to comply with the many stringent rules and regulations set out by the BCBS – rules and regulations that have been specifically established to safeguard the safety and stability of the global financial system.

A close look at the income statements of specific banks – Bank of America and Bank of China, for example – reveals clear distinctions that can be made between the composition of each. This is especially true of these banks' revenues and costs, and the effect of these on their cost-to-income ratios, and ultimately their profits. In the case of Bank of America, at the end of 2019 – to examine a period before the onset of the Covid-19 pandemic – $91 billion worth of revenue and $55 billion worth of non-interest expenses were recorded. Dividing the total operating costs by the total revenue earned, Bank of America achieves a cost-to-income ratio of 60%. By comparison, Bank of China recorded $79 billion worth of revenue and $29 billion worth of non-interest expenses at the same point. Its revenue was thus smaller than Bank of America's but, critically, its expenses were about half. The resulting cost-to-income ratio for Bank of China is 36% – making expenses the clear differentiating factor between the Chinese bank and the American bank.

 Cost-to-income ratios and total bank assets are the significant differentiating factors today between Chinese banks and those from developed Western democratic nations – and, indeed, most banks around the world. China's enormous, and historically inefficient, state-owned banks appear to have become twice as efficient in the last decade while growing their balance sheets at over three times the rate of their Western counterparts. This fundamental revolution has occurred despite China being a member state of the BCBS, and having to comply with the same rules and regulations that have hampered Western banks' ability to leverage themselves and to consistently achieve double-digit returns on equity since the Global Financial Crisis.

3

FINANCIAL CRISES AND POLITICAL DIVERGENCE

When Jamie Dimon took the call from Alan Schwartz in March 2008 and listened as the Bear Stearns executive pleaded his case for a $29-billion loan to save his company, the CEO of JPMorgan may have experienced something akin to historical *déjà vu*. After all, a century before, in October 1907, the very first CEO of JP Morgan & Co, John Pierpont Morgan himself, had received a remarkably similar phone call from his partners.

At the time, JP Morgan was in his seventies and well established as one of the wealthiest and most powerful bankers in the world. When he took the call, he was enjoying a visit to Richmond, Virginia, for the triennial meeting of the Episcopal Church. But what he heard compelled him to abandon his plans in the countryside and race back to New York on the next available train. Panic had broken out on Wall Street, and the commercial centre of America was in dire need of a captain. In lieu of a central bank or a president – President Theodore Roosevelt was reportedly away on a hunting trip in Louisiana at the time – the plutocrats needed to take charge.

Several events occurred in the lead-up to the Panic of 1907. A year and a half earlier, the devastating San Francisco earthquake had triggered significant payouts from British insurers, and to stem the flow of money from the UK into the US, the Bank of England had raised its discount rate. As money started to flow back to the UK, the US stock market fell, and by May 1907 America was in a recession. Later that year, monetary conditions tightened even further when the country experienced its customary surge in demand for currency and credit from farmers over the autumn period, as they harvested and shipped their crops. Back then there existed no central bank in America to provide any alleviation during this seasonal rise in demand, and so it was common practice for banks to individually increase interest rates. With the US financial system already in a precarious position, a final, crippling blow was then dealt in October 1907. Two bankers, Charles W Morse and F Augustus Heinze, tried and failed to corner the stock of copper mining company United Copper, incurring a heavy loss. As news of the loss circulated, there was a run on all the banks and trusts that were associated with Morse and Heinze.

This panic was quickly contained within the banking sector, thanks to the role of the New York Clearing House Association. Prior to 1853, banks operating in New York had to perform their clearing processes manually; that is, a bank would record its exchanges with corresponding banks and then send porters to these banks to settle all transactions and exchange cheque for cash on a weekly basis. With the number of banks growing rapidly from 1849, the idea of a centralised clearing house was adopted, where certificates replaced the use of actual cash in the exchange process. This led, in 1853, to the establishment of the country's first clearing house, the New York Clearing House Association, which acted as a central bank and played a key role in preventing financial panics. It issued loan certificates that were backed by banknotes held by member banks, thus creating a quasi-currency that helped to stabilise the monetary system.

When the panic hit in 1907, the New York Clearing House Association acted as intended: it vouched for the solvency of its members, and bank runs were quickly halted. But the Clearing House provided no alleviation for US trusts, because trust companies were excluded from its membership. Instead, the panic intensified when news broke two days later that Morse had been associated with Charles T Barney, the president of the Knickerbocker Trust, the second-largest trust in the country.

Trust companies emerged in the US in the late 1800s, acting as executors and trustees for funds owned by individuals and companies. By the turn of the century, however, they increasingly found that there was insufficient demand for these services, and to survive, they began to engage in more general financial activities: taking deposits, providing loans and making investments. In doing so, trusts effectively began to operate like commercial banks, though they were far less regulated and often significantly more leveraged than banks. This had both positive and negative implications for the economy.

Trusts played a key role in providing liquidity by routinely extending short-term loans to New York equity markets, such as the New York Stock Exchange. At this time, nationally chartered commercial banks were prohibited from making uncollateralised loans or guaranteeing payment of cheques written by brokers on accounts with insufficient funds. But trusts didn't require collateral for the loans they extended in equity markets, which were repaid by the end of the business day. Brokers could therefore take a short-term loan from a trust and use it to purchase securities, which were then used as collateral for an overnight call loan from a bank, which was in turn used to purchase stock. The proceeds of these activities were then used to pay back the initial loan from the trust. This process supported daily transactions on exchanges, but it carried with it inherent risk. While trusts played an important role in the financial system, they generally had a low volume of cheque clearing compared to banks, and consequently held much lower cash reserves relative to deposits – usually around 5%, compared to 25% for commercial banks. As was the case with commercial banks, however, trust company deposit accounts were demandable in cash, making these institutions vulnerable to runs on deposits. And in October 1907, while the banks were saved by the safety net of the Clearing House, the trusts were in freefall.

Early in his career, JP Morgan had partnered with various prominent bankers to form his own company, and he had subsequently gained a significant share in all the largest industries in the US at the time, including rail, electricity and steel. He had also played an important role in reinstating order after the Panic of 1893, in which there had been a run on gold in the US Treasury. Fourteen years later, his influence was required once again.

Upon arriving back in New York, Morgan immediately assembled at his home the presidents of the largest banks, together with other prominent financiers, to devise a plan to quiet the panic. In his private study, he convinced them that there was only one thing to do: to stabilise the markets, they had to provide credit to those trusts deemed solvent, while insolvent trusts would be left to fail. With Morgan having already assembled a specialist team that was investigating each of the trusts in trouble, his plan was approved.

It didn't take long to conclude that Knickerbocker didn't pass the test, and on 22 October the trust was forced to close after more than $8 million had been withdrawn. Rather than containing the potential damage of the panic, the decision to let Knickerbocker collapse had the opposite effect: with the public's confidence in trusts now broken, a second wave of panic was ignited as depositors tried to access their money. With Morgan leading, the bank presidents, the US Treasury and the Clearing House worked together to implement further emergency measures to save the remaining trusts. While the US remained stuck in a recession until June the following year, a total financial collapse was averted.

The take-charge attitude of the leaders of the financial sector ultimately saved the country from economic disaster, and yet in the wake of the Panic of 1907, rather than applauding their efforts, the public began to view these men with great suspicion. For many, the fact that the bankers – and JP Morgan in particular – had possessed the power to rescue Wall Street from failure ignited concerns that a small, elite group of bankers and business leaders had gained altogether too much influence over the US financial system. Rumours began to circulate about the existence of a secret Illuminati-like group of bankers and financiers known as the "Money-trust", who were believed to be colluding to take full control of the nation's finances and future. These rumours became so widespread that in 1912 the chairman of the House Committee on Banking and Currency,

Arsène Pujo, was put in charge of investigating the Money-trust allegation, but no evidence was found of an actual secret society. In his report, Pujo did nonetheless highlight the fact that a relatively small group of individuals had undeniably gained control over some of the biggest markets in the US, including the manufacturing sector, the transportation sector, mining and telecommunications, and that several of the largest financial corporations were under the control of an even more concentrated group of financiers. Morgan was individually named in the report, together with other prominent bankers, including Paul Warburg, Jacob H Schiff, Felix M Warburg, Frank Peabody, William Rockefeller and Benjamin Strong Jr.

Trust in the financial system had, it seemed, reached an all-time low, and the findings spurred public support for a wave of policy changes that would reform the financial system and go some way to limiting the degree to which wealth and power could collect in such a small pool of beneficiaries. These changes included the approval of the Sixteenth Amendment, which authorised federal income tax, and the Clayton Antitrust Act of 1914. Perhaps most importantly, they also resulted in the passing of the Federal Reserve Act of 1913.

––––––––––

On a fine autumn day in 1910, a train was forced to wait at a station in New Jersey as, one by one, several latecomers dressed for the outdoors boarded the front cart. They spoke loudly about the duck-hunting trip they were about to take on Jekyll Island, just off the coast of Georgia, and referred to one another using only their first names in a bid to conceal their identities. They were, in fact, some of America's most influential bankers and government officials at the time, among them Senator Nelson Aldrich, chairman of the Senate Finance Committee; his private secretary, Arthur Shelton; Henry Davison, a partner at JP Morgan & Co; Abram Piatt Andrew, assistant Treasury secretary; Frank Vanderlip, president of National City Bank; and Paul Warburg, a partner at the investment bank Kuhn, Loeb & Co. And they would not be duck hunting that weekend but rather meeting to devise a plan to reform the American financial system.

In the wake of the Panic of 1907, it was clear that the US was in desperate need of a central bank, but establishing such an entity was no straightforward matter. The idea of centralising banking powers had met with strong opposition ever since the US was founded in 1776. A number of the Founding Fathers had regarded England's desire to place the monetary systems of its colonies under the supervision of the Bank of England as an act of oppression that had contributed directly to the American Revolutionary War. A constant tug-of-war over the subject of a central bank in America ensued – attempts to establish such an institution succeeded in 1782, 1791 and 1816, but in each case it operated only for a relatively short period before being shut down. Lawmakers in the agricultural South were particularly suspicious of a central bank, which they believed would disproportionately benefit the urban commercial hubs in the North. The major banks in the North, meanwhile, wanted to ensure that they were supported by a lender of last resort – but they wanted to take charge of this entity themselves, rather than leave it in the hands of government. Although the American

Civil War had ended in 1865, long-standing tensions between the North and the South were reignited as arguments over the issue raged with no clear way to appease all parties.

After the Panic of 1907, the necessity of having an institution that could prevent repeated bank failures in the US became undeniable. In immediate response, the Aldrich-Vreeland Act was passed in 1908, enabling national banks to establish national currency associations to issue emergency currency. The Act also established the National Monetary Commission, which was led by Nelson Aldrich and made up of members of Congress who travelled to Europe to observe the banking systems there. The Commission was impressed with how well the central banks in European countries operated, though the challenge of trying to implement such a system in the US remained. Public trust in the financial system had been shaken and there was a great deal of suspicion that certain powerful individuals would use this opportunity to further their hold over all aspects of business and industry in America.

By 1910, lawmakers were still stuck in a stalemate on the issue of a central bank. It was at this point that Aldrich decided to assemble a small group of men whom he believed capable of developing a solution that would provide a compromise between the clear necessity for a central bank and the deeply ingrained distrust of such an institution. To avoid further inflaming the conspiratorial stories of a so-called Money-trust that were spreading widely among the public, the men left their homes under the guise of embarking on a duck-hunting trip and boarded the train for Jekyll Island.

It was at this meeting – which the attendees would deny ever took place for at least thirty years after the fact – that the foundations of the Federal Reserve system were laid. Instead of a single central bank, the Jekyll Island group's solution was to create a network of central banks, which would accept assurances of future customer payments to businesses as collateral for cash. A bank in the South that found that its cash supplies were running low when farmers made withdrawals during the harvest season could, for example, then go to its central bank and gain access to cash, with a loan to a farmer serving as collateral. A national board of directors would be appointed to set the interest rate and therefore have some control over credit for the entire country.

Aldrich presented the plan to Congress, but it was not as well received as he had predicted. Indeed, the idea that a new set of powerful institutions would be created and managed by the banks initially met with outright suspicion. The first draft of the plan did, at least, provide a base from which a more tolerable system could be developed. Lawmakers agreed that there was a need for a central bank to provide stability to the US banking system, that the idea of decentralised banks was the only way forward, and that the governance of these banks had to be shared between the government and bankers, who would consider both business and agricultural interests. Plans for the Federal Reserve system were modified several times, with an eventual agreement that between eight and twelve reserve banks should be created in areas that were deemed of economic or political importance. Furthermore, a board of directors would be appointed, made up of three groups: local bankers, businessmen appointed by those bankers, and a group of representatives of the public. The Board of Governors in Washington would also include both the Treasury secretary and Federal Reserve governors appointed by the US president and approved by Senate.

Arriving at the final version of the Federal Reserve Act was not an easy process: a long and aggressive battle was fought between the banks and government for control over the new system. Nonetheless, in December 1913 the Federal Reserve came into being, providing a key source of stability to the US banking system, which quickly became the dominant centre of the global financial system. To insulate decisions made regarding monetary policy from undue political influence, the Federal Reserve was structured in two parts: a centralised authority known as the Board of Governors, located in Washington, and a decentralised network of twelve Federal Reserve Banks, located in Boston, New York, Philadelphia, Cleveland, Richmond, Atlanta, Chicago, St Louis, Minneapolis, Kansas City, Dallas and San Francisco. These banks were chosen in 1913 by the Reserve Bank Organization Committee, based on technical criteria such as available bank capital – with a minimum threshold of $4 million – together with a consideration of the industrial and financial activities, availability of transportation and communication lines, and population size of the region in which the banks were based.

To this day, the Board of Governors and the presidents of the twelve Reserve Banks together oversee the American banking system. Critically, policy and operational decisions made by the Fed do not require approval from Congress or the US president, and the Fed's operations are self-funded through interest earned on US government securities, interest on loans to financial firms, and fees charged to banks. Congress does, however, retain the power to change the laws governing the Fed and its structure.

Pure capitalism as it was practised in America prior to 1910 was already benefiting from industrialisation but was muted somewhat by the absence of a central bank. The US version of central banking established after the Panic of 1907 provided a compromise between a fierce American sense of independence and the undeniable benefit of having a bank of last resort and the guiding hand of central command. This provided tremendous advantages throughout the remainder of the 20th century as America's economic growth accelerated, especially in the decades following the end of World War II. It has also served as an important counterweight at moments when the banking system has faced significant pressure to capitulate to politically motivated agendas.

Most importantly, the establishment of the Federal Reserve worked to restore trust in the financial system after the Panic of 1907. This trust would, however, be tested repeatedly through the years – in the Wall Street Crash of 1929 and the ensuing Great Depression, in the 1980s Savings and Loan Crisis, in the 1990s dotcom bubble and, most severely, during the Global Financial Crisis.

On the 17th of September 2011, an unlikely group of people arrived in Zuccotti Park, a publicly accessible but privately owned area in New York City's Wall Street financial district. These were not the besuited financiers typically seen in the area but rather a crowd of casually dressed youngsters who proceeded to set up a temporary encampment – complete with a food tent, medical tent, computer hub and drumming circle – in what would become known as the Occupy Wall Street movement.

Rallying behind the slogan "We are the 99%", the protesters found inspiration from the often-cited statistic that wealth in the US is concentrated within just 1% of the population. They used this as a springboard for a general criticism of capitalism and, more specifically, of the greed and corruption that the protesters believed had been at the heart of the 2007/2008 Global Financial Crisis.

Although the recession in America had officially come to an end in 2009, the economic fallout from the Crisis had nonetheless been immense, both within the US and further afield. Millions of Americans lost their homes or found themselves struggling to pay their mortgages, and volatility in the US economy spread through the interlinked and integrated financial markets of the UK and Europe, resulting in a decline in housing prices on the other side of the Atlantic, as well as a drop in the value of pension funds and equities. In addition, the upward trajectory of international trade that had been observable since the end of World War II was suddenly halted, with world trade decreasing by 12.2% between 2008 and 2009. This sharp decline – the sharpest in recorded history – was known as "the Great Trade Collapse" and was largely the result of a sudden synchronised postponement in the purchasing of non-essential goods, as people chose to save money in the face of global financial uncertainty. This was further aggravated on the supply side, as many firms struggled to secure working capital and trade finance.

The economic ramifications of the Crisis were, however, only one of its destructive outcomes. In the months and years to come, the general mood in America became one of suspicion and bitterness. The public's trust in the financial industry – the commercial banks, investment banks, mortgage brokers and external ratings agencies that had been at the centre of the Crisis – had been shattered. Worse still, public trust in the government had also been shattered owing to the role it had played in the creation of the mortgage crisis through certain legislation and its support of Fannie Mae and Freddie Mac. Perhaps the biggest point of contention was the government's decision to provide considerable bailouts to failing financial institutions through the Troubled Asset Relief Program (TARP). For people on the street, it appeared to be distinctly unjust that the firms that had caused the Crisis should be saved from failure, while the average person suffered financial distress. There was also a growing concern that a precedent had been set that would encourage moral hazard in the future. Large financial institutions had, after all, essentially been provided with the implicit assurance that they could engage in high-risk, profit-driven activity, safe in the knowledge that if things went wrong, they would be bailed out by the government.

Absent from this line of thinking was the acknowledgement that the government *had* tried to discourage moral hazard by allowing investment bank Lehman Brothers to fail in September 2008, as the US Treasury refused at the time to use taxpayers' money to save a publicly listed company. The negative impact of this failure on highly interconnected global financial markets was so significant, however, that to allow further failures in the same manner as an act of moral punishment would have made the already severe economic disruption far worse across the globe. Just two weeks after Lehman Brothers' collapse, other failing investment firms were therefore saved by Treasury through the TARP.

As difficult economic conditions persisted in the years directly following the Crisis, the issue of economic inequality became a central focus in a broader criticism of Western capitalism, which was amplified in the minds of the public through the populist rhetoric of the Occupy Wall Street movement. For those who supported the movement, the government's apparent protection of the financial industry – which had, as far as they were concerned, created a situation that had significantly aggravated existing income inequalities – undermined the fundamental ideals of democracy and communicated clear support for capitalism in its most extreme form. Occupy Wall Street quickly found a following in other countries around the world, with protests staged in Tokyo, Vancouver, Santiago, London, Brussels, Rome and other major cities. Many ended in violent confrontations with police.

Within two months, however, the group of protesters that had ignited the movement was evicted from Zuccotti Park by police, and Occupy Wall Street effectively ended. This has led many observers to dismiss the movement as a relatively inconsequential, poorly organised protest that fizzled out without achieving much. Indeed, the protesters appeared to have had no explicit set of goals beyond making their disgruntled presence felt by the financiers who continued about their daily business in the offices around them. Ultimately, the protests prompted no formal policy negotiations or institutional changes.

In one important sense, though, the Occupy Wall Street movement did prove significantly disruptive. While the even shorter-lived protests outside the headquarters of Bear Stearns back in March 2008 may have marked a tipping point for public trust in financial institutions, the protests of late 2011 escalated this sentiment dramatically. There emerged a general narrative of discontent, focused on the belief that liberal democracy was in steady and inexorable decline and that its way of economic expression – capitalism – had patently failed. Indeed, retrospectively, Occupy Wall Street should be seen as a critical starting point of a less well-defined but much larger and more tumultuous wave of disruption that has continued to gather momentum in the West since the Global Financial Crisis, creating deep social divides that have extended far beyond the streets of New York. This wave of social discontent has culminated in many protests, often driven and exacerbated by social media, over the multifaceted issue of inequality.

Alhough the specific achievements of Occupy Wall Street may be difficult to quantify, it has undoubtedly had a key part to play in the growing trend of political polarisation evident in America over the last decade and mirrored in Europe following the 2009 European Sovereign Debt Crisis. The social and political impact of the Global Financial Crisis, and the responses of the Federal Reserve and the US Treasury, had the unintended but directly attributable consequence of amplifying social distrust in, and in some cases even hatred for, the institution of banking and the government that had protected it in its worst moments.

In attempting to rebuild some measure of trust, the response from the various political administrations has been to constrain the financial industry with an ever-growing set of technical regulations and to levy extremely heavy monetary fines. This is the institutional compromise by which Western society continues to avoid criminally charging and imprisoning white-collar criminals – by punishing the industry or the institutions instead. Indeed, there have been virtually no criminal convictions of senior bankers in Western society despite a plethora of individual bank failures sometimes orchestrated, or at best ignored, by the most senior levels of leadership. An outlier in this respect is the small nation of Iceland, which in the wake of the financial crash of its entire banking system in 2008 sentenced 36 bankers, including CEOs, to a total of 96 years of prison time. Had more bankers in the US and elsewhere faced the same fate, this might have gone some way to offsetting the mood of public distrust. Instead, a lack of perceived punishment of individuals has driven further divisions, creating long-lasting discord over the question of whether banks should exist as free-market entities at all. Even post-Crisis, there has been no shortage of instances of individual bank failures, systemic manipulation of markets and ongoing financial fraud. And it is these activities that have undone any remaining moral argument for banking as an industry that should self-regulate, let alone operate free of mistrust and constraints.

In October 2016, world news channels reported that a horde of more than a thousand angry protesters had taken to the streets of Athens, holding banners and repeatedly chanting "Shame on you! Shame on you!" as they made their way towards the office of Greece's prime minister, Alexis Tsipras. Overcome with fury and frustration, some of the protesters banded together at one point, attempting to overturn a police car that stood in their path. The police responded by firing teargas and pepper spray into the crowd. As far as protests go, the scene was relatively unremarkable – except for the fact that the protesters were all pensioners. Earlier that year, the Greek government had imposed substantial cuts on pension payouts, fulfilling one of several commitments it had made to both the European Union (EU) and the International Monetary Fund (IMF), which had provided bailout money in what had become the biggest rescue of a bankrupt country in history.

The European Sovereign Debt Crisis began in 2009 when the impact of the Global Financial Crisis began to expose significant weaknesses in the Eurozone's economic structures. At the centre of this particular crisis was Greece, which reported in 2009 that its budget deficit had increased to 12.5% of GDP – more than four times the 3% of GDP threshold for all EU members that had been set in the 1997 Stability and Growth Pact (SGP).

The groundwork for the unacceptable rise of Greece's sovereign debt had been laid long before the Financial Crisis hit. The unusually high budget deficit hadn't ballooned overnight; it had been escalating for years, as Georgios Papandreou, Greek prime minister between 2009 and 2011, admitted. For over a decade, Greece had consistently manipulated official data to ensure it appeared to be operating within the limits of the SGP and other criteria of the 1992 Maastricht Treaty, when in fact its budget deficit was already growing above mandated levels. When this came to light, though, the EU did not impose any sanctions. Germany and France were both also running budget deficits above the 3% threshold, and calling attention to Greece's violation would require punishing all three nations, which could have in turn crippled the Eurozone. If the EU seriously considered expelling nations that didn't comply with the criteria of the SGP – especially countries as financially stable as Germany and France – the euro would be weakened and the EU's power in international markets would be compromised, greatly harming its bid to convince countries such as the UK, Denmark and Sweden to adopt the euro.

Greece's debt continued to mount, and by the end of 2009 things were coming to a head. The EU was forced to confront the growing debt problem when the country's credit rating was downgraded by all three major ratings agencies – Fitch, Standard & Poor's and Moody's. Greece promised that it would take steps to lower its budget deficit to the required 3% of GDP within two years, but by this point concerns that the country might default on its sovereign debt had begun to escalate. Financial markets responded by demanding higher rates on Greek bonds – ten-year bond yield spreads widened, reaching above 35% in 2012, having hovered just above 5% in 2009. This was an almost unbelievable increase of 3,000 basis points over three years. As investors became concerned about the implications of a Greek default for the entire Eurozone, the crisis started to spread to Italy, Portugal and Spain, which, like Greece, had comparatively weaker banking systems than other members of the EU and had also reported high budget deficits.

In April 2010 – just four months after Greece had announced its plan to reduce its budget deficit – the possibility of default became material when Greece made a formal request to the EU for financial assistance. Responses to this were mixed. Should the country be allowed to default on its debt, it could destabilise the entire Eurozone; indeed, economists warned that it could trigger another global crisis, even larger than that of 2007/2008. However, many EU nations resented the idea of simply bailing Greece out. In the end, a compromise was reached: financial assistance was provided to Greece and other struggling countries by those EU nations in financially stronger positions, such as Germany and France, in conjunction with bailout packages from the IMF and, later, the European Central Bank. In exchange, these countries were required to adopt strict austerity measures as a form of punishment, which broadly translated into reducing government spending while increasing taxation. Italy, for example, increased healthcare fees and reduced government subsidies, family tax benefits and pensions for the wealthy, while Portugal reduced wages for government workers, cut military and infrastructure spending, and raised VAT and taxes on the wealthy. The UK reduced government jobs, lowered budgets and increased the retirement age. France increased corporate taxes and taxes on the wealthy, and ensured that many loopholes in its tax policies were closed. Greece, among other measures, was required to significantly reform its pension system, which in 2010 accounted for 14% of GDP – more than any other EU nation. Pensions were reduced, employees were forced to make higher contributions to their pension funds, and early retirement was limited, with severe implications for a country in which almost half of all households relied on pension payouts to survive. Protests soon erupted in the streets of Greece and throughout Europe.

With the slowing of the European economy came increased levels of unemployment, prompting the development of an anti-austerity movement that was ideologically aligned with the Occupy Wall Street protests occurring in America. The movement included various demonstrations in Portugal, Spain, France, Italy, Germany, Ireland and the UK, as well as the *indignados* – or "Indignant Citizens Movement" – in Greece.

THE END OF MONEY

It was during this time that the catchphrase "Grexit" began to circulate, as the possibility of a Greek exit from the Eurozone was hotly debated by both the public and the nation's leaders. This idea was not economically feasible for Greece, however, and in 2015 the country accepted another bailout package from the EU, with its accompanying austerity terms. Just a year later, Britain did what Greece had balked at and voted to leave the EU forever. This was the apex point of the European project and perhaps the beginning of its unravelling.

With the benefit of hindsight, the European project undermined itself by adopting austerity rather than stimulus. Instead of helping to alleviate the financial distress of its poorer members, as morally repugnant as this may have felt to German voters, it punished its miscreants by starving them. The effect of this has been long-lasting. In 2020, during the Covid-19 pandemic, the Greek government even sold some of its islands to private buyers rather than suffer further stringencies from Brussels. It is almost impossible to imagine the US Federal government leaving Louisiana or Alabama to the same fate that the EU left Greece or, for that matter, Portugal.

The fundamental ideological difference in approach to the Global Financial Crisis taken by the US and the EU has led to radically different outcomes – each with its own particular mix of subsequent economic and moral problems. More importantly, however, it is against this backdrop of ideological divergence between the two Western power centres that there has been a continued erosion of the neoliberal pro-democracy agenda that would otherwise have acted as a powerful counterbalance to China's significant global ambitions.

Political polarisation following financial crises has been extensively researched, with scholars noting that a decrease in political centrists and an increase in political extremists after a disruptive financial event form a recurring trend across different countries over the last century. In one study, conducted in 2020, data relating to Germany's 1931 Banking Crisis were analysed, and it was found that in those towns most affected by the crisis there was a subsequent increase in support for the Nazi Party. This, the researchers believe, was the result of a combination of lowered wages and increased economic inequalities as a direct result of the banking crisis, as well as the Nazis' use of propaganda, through which blame for the financial crisis was laid squarely on the Jewish population. Considering the result of the Nazis' ascent to power, it's worth bearing in mind the extent to which populists are able to leverage public discontent during times of economic hardship.

Another 2020 study similarly found a connection between the Eurozone Crisis and a rise of right-wing populism in Europe, focusing particularly on Greece over the previous ten years. The researcher highlighted the prominent use of a clear in-group out-group bifurcation in the rhetoric of populist politicians: this division is used to assure the in-group that they are entitled to the resources of the state, and an emphasis is placed on the need for this group to "take back control" and restore national sovereignty after financial disruption. A hallmark of populists' rhetoric is the idea of collective decision-making; that all decisions should be made according to the will of the people, bypassing representative institutions or governing bodies. In opposing the role of societal institutions, this approach almost inevitably tends towards authoritarianism.

Another study, published in a 2015 edition of the academic journal *European Economic Review*, found that in developed nations the extreme right in particular benefits from the political polarisation that follows banking crises. Importantly, this trend has been observed only in the case of financial crises, and not during and after other forms of natural or social crises. The researchers suggest that this is because the former are usually regarded as man-made, with a clear culprit, usually from the wealthy or the political elite. In these circumstances, it appears that the economic middle class seeks out the promise of stability, security and legal justice promised by the right. Not only do right-wing politicians offer a clear person, institution, political party or industry to blame for financial crises, but they also often invoke the threat of foreigners increasing competition for jobs and financial security in the aftermath of a crisis. The researchers note that "voters seem to be systematically lured by the political rhetoric of the far right, with its frequently nationalistic or xenophobic tendencies".

In his 2018 book *Identity: The Demand for Dignity and the Politics of Resentment*, Francis Fukuyama provides further insight on how this shift to the political right and the surge of support for populist politicians promote a distinctly nationalist agenda. Fukuyama also links the increase in radical identity politics in Western democracies to the widening of economic inequalities since the Global Financial Crisis and the European Debt Crisis. He further notes that while one might have expected to see a surge in support for left-wing socialist policies seeking to redress the economic imbalance, these policies can often be seen prioritising the needs of minorities, immigrants and other "less deserving" or "outsider" groups over the national group. In this case, support tends to swell for nationalist populists, who instead encourage general feelings of rage and injustice among their supporters, and who make promises for significant change to improve their living conditions.

With a dataset spanning more than 140 years between 1870 and 2014 and covering nearly a hundred financial crises and more than 800 national elections in twenty democratic nations, the *European Economic Review* study further suggests that this post-financial crisis political trend towards right-wing nationalism has been intensifying over time. Thus, it should come as little surprise that within a decade of the Financial Crisis, Donald Trump won the US presidential elections with the promise to physically isolate the nation from "others" by building a wall to keep out immigrants, and further found support during his presidency for an explicitly protectionist agenda that involved inciting a trade war with China and withdrawing America from major international organisations and agreements. Within the same decade, following a nationwide referendum, Britain announced that it would be withdrawing from the European Union. Studies found that the most common reason cited for the "Leave" vote was the hope for stricter border controls. It was also in this decade that the nationalist Bharatiya Janata Party won elections in India, the right-wing Law and Justice Party won in Poland, Rodrigo Duterte won the Philippine presidential election, Recep Tayyip Erdoğan won a second term as president of Turkey, Viktor Orban triumphed in Hungary for the third time running, Jair Bolsonaro took the presidency in Brazil, the

Freedom Party joined a governing coalition in Austria, and the right-wing populist Lega Nord did the same in Italy. Meanwhile, China and Russia have strengthened their positions in the world order through an authoritarian model of leadership that is in marked contrast to the Western model of open societies and free markets.

Ideological differences in the period that immediately preceded the Global Financial Crisis were, in sum, significantly amplified during and after the Crisis, leading to political polarisation in the Western world. In the absence of a cohesive neoliberal ideology, a vacuum has been created in which China's increasingly strident political and global aspirations have gone largely ignored by Western powers, as has the fact that these aspirations have been funded by what has become the largest, and most indebted, banking system on earth.

The failure of the US banking system, whether influenced by systemic political interference or the result of idiosyncratic greed, has been the catalyst for more than a decade of increasingly anti-democratic outcomes. As a result, the silent majority in the West no longer cares as much as it once did for multilateralism, or for the spread of liberal politics and social agendas throughout the developing world. It cares more for immediate, local outcomes, both because its constituents have been personally disenfranchised and because they have been manipulated by leaders who leverage widespread feelings of discontent to further their own political aspirations.

4

A CENTURY OF HUMILIATION
- AND BEYOND

America's bid to strongly regulate its banking sector in the wake of the 2007/2008 Global Financial Crisis is in large part a reaction to what many people have seen as a failure of the free-market system. It is, in essence, an attempt to restore trust in a system that undeniably drove enormous economic growth prior to the Crisis, but that self-destructed when the commitment to hyper-capitalist ideals undermined its own ideological justifications. In direct contrast to the free-market system of the West is the communist ideology that underlies China's political structure and approach to economic management. This structure, Francis Fukuyama suggests, is strongly driven by the legacy of China's so-called Century of Humiliation and the subsequent desire to restore dignity within the nation.

The Century of Humiliation was heralded by Britain's victory over China in the First Opium War between 1839 and 1842. Under the subsequent Treaty of Nanking, China was forced to surrender Hong Kong to Britain. This was the first in a series of conflicts in which China ceded territories in unequal treaties to nations with stronger militaries, including the US, France, Russia and Japan. These treaties often forced China to accept trade agreements that favoured foreign merchants, enabling them to sell their goods in the country with few or no restrictions and low tariffs, with detrimental consequences for the local economy.

The idea of humiliation was no mere side effect of China's military losses; it was used intentionally and strategically by Britain to enforce psychological superiority over its enemy. In 1860, for example, the British attacked Beijing's Summer Palace, the primary residence of the Chinese imperial court, in retaliation for the murder of several British and French troops in a hostage crisis. With the emperor having escaped the palace beforehand, the attack held no military value but was instead used to weaken Chinese morale. Rather than inflicting bodily harm on the occupants of the palace, British troops were instructed to plunder it of priceless artefacts. This was a tactic that continued throughout the colonial occupation of China, with the systematic looting and destruction of several other palaces undertaken as deliberate acts of humiliation. Today, many of these stolen artefacts remain in foreign museums and private collections. The ruins of the Summer Palace, meanwhile, are preserved by the Chinese government as an important reminder of the country's humiliation and a powerful motivator for its aspirations to greatness.

In his 2014 essay, "Dealing with China", Fukuyama explains how China's desire to restore its dignity has undoubtedly been a powerful driving force behind its economic growth under the rule of the Chinese Communist Party (CCP). "The CCP has been very explicit about the fact that it alone is responsible for reversing the hundred years of humiliation and making China a great power again," he writes. "This is something that most Chinese seem to accept and take great pride in."

It was a process that began in 1949, when years of civil war culminated in the defeat of the nationalist Guomindang party of Chiang Kai-shek and the establishment of the People's Republic of China under the CCP. Led by Mao Zedong, the CCP had as its primary goal to rebuild the country and establish it as a global leader by modernising and strengthening the economy through industrialisation and the establishment of a successful socialist order. In practice, this translated into a high level of state control, with the government managing the country's economic output by setting production goals, dictating prices and determining the allocation of resources.

In 1953, the first Five Year Plan for rapid economic growth, based on the economic model of Soviet Russia, was introduced. It focused on industrial development over agriculture, investment in new technologies for heavy industry, and increased state ownership of businesses. Privately owned businesses were put under considerable pressure to sell to the state or form joint public-private enterprises. By 1956, roughly 70% of all modern industrial enterprises were state-owned and the remaining 30% were under joint public-private ownership. Individual farming households were organised into large communes, with income shared according to the amount of labour contributed by each family. By 1957, almost all farm households in China had joined a commune.

Although the first Five Year Plan yielded some economic improvements, these were deemed too modest by the Chinese government. As a result, the second Five Year Plan, intended as a continuation of the first, was abandoned in favour of the mass mobilisation of the population to produce a "Great Leap Forward" for the country's economy. The CCP hoped to realise within a very short timeframe the kind of economic growth that had taken other developed nations decades to achieve, and it believed this could be accomplished primarily through an increased focus on industrial production. Private food production was prohibited and most of the population was diverted to mining and industrial processing, while those who remained in the agricultural sector were forced to continue to work in mismanaged co-operatives. China's grain harvest rapidly declined, but rather than admit to a failing agricultural sector, the government released fabricated reports of record production and continued to export grain. In 1959, when famine ravaged the country, the lack of structural organisation and support for the agricultural sector proved a grave mistake, resulting in disastrously low crop yields. The famine endured until 1962, during which time it is estimated that more than 30 million people starved to death.

Under Liu Shaoqi, chairman of the CCP between 1959 and 1968, measures were taken to stabilise the economy. These were largely undone, however, when the country entered a period of great social and political turbulence in the late 1960s and early 1970s, which became known as the Great Proletarian Cultural Revolution. Believing that the CCP's new leader was sacrificing ideological purity for the sake of economic stability, former chairman Mao Zedong, together with a group of radical supporters within the CCP, removed Liu Shaoqi from power and imprisoned him until his death in 1969. In 1966, Mao shut down the country's schools and mobilised students to cleanse society of "impure" elements and to revive the revolutionary spirit. A period of violent countrywide anarchy followed, with students forming paramilitary groups known as the Red Guard, which harassed and attacked anyone who did not support Mao. It is estimated that 1.5 million people were killed during the Cultural Revolution, with many others suffering imprisonment, torture and seizure of property. During this period, the economy also suffered, with industrial production dropping by an estimated 12% between the years 1966 and 1968.

As power struggles broke out among members of the CCP in the late 1960s, the Chinese population became increasingly divided and disillusioned, and the Cultural Revolution lost momentum. In desperation, many poorer people abandoned the communal farming model and began to engage in subsistence farming and offer their services privately as labourers, thus generating quiet but defiant resistance from below. The revolution came to an end after Mao's death in 1976, when a civil, military and police coalition managed to unseat the most radical remaining members of the CCP. Under the leadership of Deng Xiaoping, the process of reforming the Chinese economy began.

Prior to this, nearly three-quarters of China's industrial production was generated by centrally controlled, state-owned enterprises, with private companies and foreign investment firms generally barred from operating in the country. The efficacy of this approach is difficult to estimate in real terms. Chinese government statistics suggest that GDP grew at an average annual rate of 6.7% from 1953 to 1978, but the accuracy of this data is debatable, and other sources suggest an average annual GDP growth rate for the period closer to 4.5%. Under Deng, the Chinese government began to gradually reform the economy according to free-market principles. The CCP shifted its focus to fostering growth through industrial modernisation and significantly increasing China's participation in the international economy. It established diplomatic relations with the US, increased exports, and implemented policy changes that would attract foreign investment to drive modernisation. A hybrid economic system began to emerge in which farmers were permitted to sell a percentage of their crops, and private enterprise was encouraged in the commercial and retail sectors. Special economic zones were established along the coast that offered tax and trade incentives to attract foreign investment, and economic policy-making was decentralised to provincial and local governments. This approach proved largely effective, so that China righted itself along a path of economic growth that would continue uninterrupted for the following forty years. Between 1979 and 2018, China managed to double the size of its economy in real terms roughly every eight years in what the World Bank has described as "the fastest sustained expansion by a major economy in history".

China's decision to embrace free-market principles in its economic strategies also provided an opportunity for strengthening its relationships with the West. In 1972, Richard Nixon became the first American president to visit China when he travelled to Beijing to begin the process of establishing diplomatic links between the two nations. This was both a defining moment that marked China's willingness to open up to the global market and a convergence between two major world powers. There was a great deal of international goodwill towards China at this point; however, the moment also marked the start of what would prove to be a dangerous political shift within China.

With the opening of their economy, the Chinese became increasingly exposed to the ideologies of other countries, and certain sectors of the population, such as university students and those working in the media, began to discuss, report on and generally criticise social and political issues far more openly than they had ever dared before. In the late 1970s, residents of Beijing began to write their political opinions on a long wall in the city's Xicheng District that became known as the "Democracy Wall", demonstrating a newfound freedom of thought and speech, especially regarding the growing economic disparities that were resulting from the economic reforms. Indeed, while many businesses in the formal sector were thriving, high levels of inflation were making life harder for citizens in the lower economic strata. Their plight was underscored by academics and students who were critical of the destruction that had been unleashed during the Cultural Revolution, as well as by the increased level of corruption that had accompanied the economic boom.

Disillusionment with the government led to ongoing protests throughout the 1980s, but this nascent civilian freedom was violently crushed, and the lingering terror and totalitarianism of the country's leadership was laid bare in a single episode at the decade's close. In 1989, the same year that the Berlin Wall fell – seemingly representing the triumph of democracy in the world – reports emerged of a massacre at Tiananmen Square in

Beijing. In the early hours of the morning of 4 June, fearing that the protests could ignite a full revolution, the CCP deployed military troops and tanks to the centre of the city and ordered them to open fire on a large group of demonstrators who had gathered there. In the days following the incident, the government worked to suppress all information and video footage that could be leaked to the outside world. According to the CCP – which maintains to this day that the military response was warranted to maintain stability in the country – 200 civilians were killed in what it referred to as "counter-revolutionary riots". The real number, however, is likely to have been far higher. Student leaders and journalists estimate the death toll to have been in the thousands, and the UK publicly released a report from a diplomat in China's main administrative body in 2017 that put the number of deaths at more than 10,000. The actual number remains unknown, and Chinese authorities continue to ban commemorations of those killed at Tiananmen Square and strictly regulate online content regarding the incident.

The democratic world condemned the massacre: the US imposed economic sanctions against China for human rights violations, and the European Economic Community cancelled all high-level contracts and loans and instituted an arms embargo against the country. Economic growth began to slow, and China found itself, once again, facing the same conundrum that had repeated itself throughout the country's history: loosen state control to achieve economic gains, knowing that social volatility will inevitably follow, or tighten state control to enforce social stability but stymie economic growth. In answer to this, the CCP laid out its vision of a socialist market economy, effectively negotiating a social contract with the population in which it was implicitly agreed that people would be free to pursue entrepreneurial activities and capitalist gains, as long as this occurred within the framework of state control. This led to the creation of what a former vice chairman of the CCP, Chen Yun, described as a "birdcage economy" – one in which citizens could spread their wings to better their economic circumstances but within strict state-imposed limitations.

In the years that followed, the Chinese economy flourished, gaining significant momentum in 2001 when the country joined the World Trade Organization (WTO) – a move that cemented a tacit acceptance by the international community of the authoritarian rule of the CCP. As a result, Chinese exports increased dramatically, foreign investment flowed into the country, and many multinationals relocated their manufacturing plants to China to take advantage of cheaper labour and less regulation. This caused major global disruption, notably in the US, as the Chinese model of using cheap labour to produce low-cost goods forced down international merchandise prices. In turn, this forced the closure of many manufacturing plants in other parts of the world. It is estimated that as many as two million jobs were lost in the manufacturing sector in the US alone, a fact that Donald Trump highlighted during his 2016 presidential campaign when he stated that "China's entrance into the World Trade Organization has enabled the greatest jobs theft in the history of our country".

China's entry into the WTO, and the nation's subsequent economic growth over the next two decades, must be recognised, at least partly, as an outcome of the Western liberal approach of adopting a far less strident tone towards the country's authoritarian, centrally governed control economy. Despite witnessing a growing intolerance for democratic sympathies and voices within China's borders, the US and Europe collectively opened up their multilateral organisations and economies to China and, in so doing, assisted China in achieving its economic goals. This involved a myopic view of human rights injustices and suppression of the media, and a wilful ignorance of the CCP's manipulation of well-established international trade norms.

In the name of globalisation, the West grew increasingly tolerant of China's theft of intellectual property, market manipulation through currency control, and unequal trade deals, including the taxing or outright barring of the import of foreign goods. It also chose to overlook Chinese state support for economically unviable export industries, from retail clothing to vehicle manufacturing to telecommunications equipment. Since the turn of the 21st century, Western democracies have made disproportionate allowances for Chinese market conduct that has been distinctly out of sync with the principles governing international trade since the end of World War II. This has been coupled with a tacit acceptance of China's unique version of capitalism, one that no longer requires liberal democracy as its ideological foundation, but is heavily reliant on the enormous growth of its government-owned banking system to fund its remarkable economic progress.

The differences between the ideological systems driving the Western and the Chinese banking systems become particularly pertinent when recalling *The Banker* magazine's list of "Top 1000 World Banks". In analysing the rankings in this list over the past two decades, a clear distinction emerges between the rate of asset growth among Chinese and among Western banks, the latter having grown on aggregate at a much slower pace since 2008. There exists one clear reason for this: the rampant proliferation of banking regulations throughout the Western democratic financial system. As a direct result of the carnage caused by the Global Financial Crisis, banking regulators based in the US and in Europe have imposed very strict, expensive, and somewhat inefficient laws on the banks that fall within their purview.

The plethora of regulations with which banks internationally are now expected to comply includes various forms of capital and liquidity constraints, strict loan provisioning requirements, and a host of market conduct regulations, which, if breached, often result in multi-billion-dollar fines. This new regulatory regime has significantly constrained banks' ability to leverage themselves and to expand their asset base, as they did in the two decades before the onset of the Financial Crisis. While this explains to a large extent why the growth of total assets of US and other Western banks has slowed significantly, it does not account for the remarkable growth experienced by Chinese banks over the same period. As an active member state of the Basel Committee on Banking Supervision (BCBS), China and its banks are, as has been previously articulated, regulated under the same BCBS directives as banks in the US and across the world. Yet Chinese banks have ostensibly managed to escape the most restrictive effects of this regulatory regime and have continued to grow their balance sheets at a remarkable rate over the past decade.

As was the case with all other nations across the globe, China was significantly affected by the Financial Crisis. In its aftermath, 20 million migrant workers returned home after losing their jobs, exports dropped and foreign markets froze. The Chinese government was swift to respond, however, releasing a four trillion yuan economic stimulus package, or about $580 billion at the time, to drive large internal infrastructure projects, such as the building of railways, highways and power lines. In addition, the central bank increased money supply, government-backed banks drastically increased lending, and state-owned companies were instructed to grow and invest. Although the total amount of funding injected into the economy by the CCP government in the years following the Crisis has never been officially disclosed, Chinese-American political scientist Minxin Pei estimates that, between 2009 and 2011, Chinese banks issued 35 trillion yuan, or about $5.4 trillion, in new loans – equivalent to over 70% of the country's GDP in 2011 – in what he called, at the time, "the mother of all debt bombs".

Following the Crisis, Chinese banks were compelled by the state to extend loans to troubled borrowers and to roll over their loans when required. Because the government controls the banking system in China, it could ignore the advice of global investors and institutions, such as the International Monetary Fund, that preached open markets and austerity, sometimes with devastating results. This represents a key point of divergence in terms of how the world's various financial systems have been managed over the past decade. Compare the Chinese response to that of the EU, for example, specifically in the case of the Greek 2009 Sovereign Debt Crisis. In exchange for emergency funding, Greece was, in effect, punished by the EU through the imposition of extreme austerity measures. The economic consequences of this were so severe that for a while Greece threatened to leave the EU altogether. While recession hit the US and Europe and belts were tightened to curb spending in those regions, China, in marked contrast, continued to spend and grow, closing the economic gap between itself and the incumbent leaders of the world economy at an accelerating pace. Between 2008 and 2010, as the rest of the world reeled, China maintained a compound annual GDP growth rate of roughly 10%, and by the end of 2010 it had overtaken Japan to become the world's second-largest economy. It also became the world's largest manufacturer, merchandise trader and holder of foreign exchange reserves. Nowhere, however, was China's post-Crisis growth-at-all-costs attitude more evident than in the immense expansion of its banking system.

The size of the Chinese banking sector, measured as total assets held by all commercial banks, grew at a thunderous pace between 2010 and 2020. At the start of the decade, China's total banking assets stood at $14.3 trillion, representing 235% of Chinese GDP at the time. In the same year, the US had $11.9 trillion in total banking assets, equal to 90% of its GDP. Ten years later, the total assets of the Chinese banking sector had grown to $49 trillion, equal to roughly 330% of GDP. In the US, by comparison, the banking assets-to-GDP ratio was almost unchanged: it had grown its total banking assets to $20.6 trillion, representing 89% of GDP. If Chinese GDP data are to be taken at face value, as of year-end 2020, the ratio of total banking assets to GDP in China is more than three and a half times the size of the corresponding ratio in the US.

China's banking system was not always as large and complex as it is today. Between the 1950s and 1980s it was relatively small and insular. The state-owned People's Bank of China – created in 1948 through the consolidation of all the existing national banks at the time – served as both the central bank and the only commercial bank in the newly formed People's Republic of China. In the early 1980s, reforms were implemented by the government to expand the banking system, introducing five new specialised state-owned banks that could take deposits and make loans to the public. These banks were Industrial & Commercial Bank of China, China Construction Bank, Bank of China, Bank of Communications and Agricultural Bank of China, each specialising in a specific sector of the economy. In 1994, three more specialised "policy banks" were introduced: Agricultural Development Bank of China, China Development Bank and Export-Import Bank of China. These banks took over the responsibility of directing government funding to economic and trade development projects from the commercial banks. While the five large commercial banks have each undergone their own initial public offerings, the government still holds a controlling stake in each and effectively controls how they operate.

Since expanding the banking landscape to allow for the participation of more banking institutions – albeit mostly state-owned institutions – the Chinese banking system has grown at an astonishing rate in both breadth and depth, especially since the mid-1990s, when the first city commercial banks were established. In the decade between 1990 and 2000, roughly 140 city banks emerged as primary deposit takers and lenders to the urban public, forming the sub-layer of the banking system beneath the five large national commercial banks. One level down from the city banks, hundreds of county banks or rural banks were created to supply banking facilities to the hundreds of millions of rural Chinese families and businesses across the country. In total, since the initial dispersion of responsibility from one state-owned bank in the early 1980s, the Chinese banking system has now evolved into a gigantic, sprawling, multi-layered web of banking institutions, both state-owned and private, with over 4,500 individual banks at different levels of the banking system's hierarchy in 2021. This is roughly equivalent to the number of banks in the US banking system. Chinese banks do serve a much larger population, however – in 2020, ICBC alone had over 680 million retail customers, which is more than twice the size of the entire population of the US.

In recent years, the growth of the Chinese banking system's assets – which in 2016 surpassed in size those of the entire EU – has continued to accelerate, while the rest of the world lags behind. From year-end 2019 to year-end 2020, despite the challenges posed by the Covid-19 pandemic, Chinese banks' pre-tax profits increased by roughly 5%, while pre-tax profits across banks globally fell roughly 20%. As a result of this growth, Chinese banks held more than a quarter of the world's banking assets and generated over a third of all banking profits for year-end 2020. Perplexingly, according to official figures, it appears that not only is the Chinese banking system largely unaffected by the strict regulatory regime that was imposed on banks globally after the Global Financial Crisis, but it is also counterintuitively immune to the devastating economic effects of the Covid-19 pandemic, which resulted in a severe reduction in the profitability of banks across the globe in 2020.

5

THE RISE OF THE FREE MARKET

To understand the effect of regulations on the banking sector in the Western world, it is important to consider the historical context in which these regulations were developed and have been applied. In particular, consideration must be given to the profound growth that took place in America's economy and its financial system in the decades prior to the Global Financial Crisis. In this respect, the 1970s were crucial.

Throughout the second half of the 20th century, the US dominated the world in terms of manufacturing output and exports, though the massive surge in growth it had experienced during the post-war period began to slow significantly in the 1970s – a decade of great disruption both within the US and internationally. This disruption began as Richard Nixon's first presidential term was drawing to a close in 1972. Wishing to placate the American voter base as elections drew near, the Republicans exerted pressure on the Federal Reserve to keep interest rates as low as possible to ensure that money stayed cheap, lending remained plentiful, and short-term economic growth was stimulated. Between December 1971 and December 1972, money supply – the total volume of money held by the public in an economy – grew rapidly from $228 billion to $249 billion in the most liquid instruments (M1). Growth was even steeper in less liquid instruments (M2), which include M1 plus savings deposits and other "near-money" equivalents; they increased from $710 billion to $802 billion. With this growth came an inevitable inflationary effect – but the president's attitude to this was clear. "We'll take inflation, if necessary, but we can't take unemployment," he declared. In the end, so long as the voting public felt the immediate positive effects of his cheap-money policies, Nixon was happy.

Nixon won the 1972 election in a landslide, taking 49 of 50 states, but it came at a great cost: inflation ballooned from about 3% in 1972, as measured by the consumer price index, to 11% in 1974 when Nixon, facing almost certain impeachment, left the White House. America had already entered a period of inflation growth, which had begun in 1965 – when inflation stood at 1.6% – as the Federal Reserve began to implement expansionary economic policies that it believed would radically boost employment levels in the US. At the time, moderate increases in inflation caused by expansionary monetary policy were deemed tolerable so long as these policies spurred economic growth and lowered unemployment. The Federal Reserve's decision to capitulate to Nixon in the lead-up to the 1972 election accelerated the rise in inflation to extremely high levels, however, miring America in an era that became known as "the Great Inflation". This period continued until 1982, with inflation peaking at around 14% in 1980.

In tandem with the rapid rise of inflation in the US came a significant destabilisation of the international monetary system through the dissolution of the Bretton Woods System and the subsequent decoupling of the dollar from the price of gold. In an attempt to ensure greater international economic stability at the end of World War II, the Bretton Woods Agreement was created at the UN's 1944 Monetary and Financial Conference under the guidance of esteemed British economist John Maynard Keynes and the chief international economist of the US Treasury, Harry Dexter White. The agreement introduced a regulated foreign exchange system to the world, based on fixed exchange rates. At the time, the US held three-quarters of the world's gold supply and so it was decided that the US dollar would be pegged to the price of gold – set at $35 per ounce – and that all other currencies would be pegged to the US dollar. Essentially what this meant was that central banks around the world agreed to maintain a fixed exchange rate between their currencies and the dollar, effectively replacing the gold standard with an international "dollar standard".

The Bretton Woods System supported significant growth in international trade in the post-war period, with countries settling their international payments in dollars. Initially, America dominated the export markets, but by the 1970s the country was facing increased competition from Europe and Japan. At the same time, the US had radically increased its military spending and foreign aid during the Vietnam War, and with fewer dollars flowing into America and more flowing out, soon US dollar reserves held by other countries exceeded the US's gold reserves. The danger of this situation became material when France and the UK announced their intention to exchange their dollars for gold, prompting Paul Volcker, then the Treasury undersecretary for monetary affairs, to observe that, "If the British, who had founded the system with us, and who had fought so hard to defend their own currency, were going to take gold for their dollars, it was clear the game was indeed over."

In response, Nixon announced a temporary suspension of the dollar's convertibility to gold, and though an attempt was made to preserve the Bretton Woods System, it was dissolved by March 1973 as governments opted instead for a system of floating exchange rates. This introduced foreign exchange volatility, interest rate volatility and commodity price volatility into the international monetary system, altering the economic landscape significantly. An examination of annual bank failures illustrates the profound effect this volatility had on the banking system: in the US, bank failures rarely exceeded single digits between 1940 and 1980, whereafter they rose rapidly, with over 200 occurring in 1988 alone. This volatility in the US was further compounded by the sudden and dramatic increase in the price of oil from 1973.

Until the 1900s, the US was the largest producer of oil in the world. This changed when significant reserves were discovered by British explorers in the Middle East in the first half of the 20th century. By 1960, 85% of the world's oil production was owned by the "Seven Sisters" – seven oil companies that would eventually be consolidated to become BP, Chevron, ExxonMobil and Royal Dutch Shell. With all these companies headquartered in the developed world, Middle Eastern countries came to the realisation that they were essentially supplying Western countries with the raw material to produce petrochemicals, which they were then buying back at highly inflated prices. To reclaim some control over their countries' natural resources, oil-producing nations in the Middle East – notably Iran, Iraq, Kuwait and Saudi

Arabia – formed the Organisation of the Petroleum Exporting Countries (OPEC) in 1960. Initially, the cartel wielded little influence over the price of oil, but in 1973 it unexpectedly found itself in a position of great geopolitical power.

There had long been tension between the Arab states that formed part of the cartel and Israel, which had been formally established in 1948 when the United Nations decided to partition Palestine into Jewish and Arab states. At the time, it was also decided that the area of religious significance surrounding Jerusalem would be placed under the control of the UN, but this proved futile in preventing further conflict in the region. What followed was a series of political clashes that included the First Arab-Israeli War in 1948, the Suez Canal Crisis in 1956 and the Six-Day War in 1967. Then came the Yom Kippur War in 1973, when an Arab coalition attacked Israel on the holiest day on the Jewish calendar, which also coincided with the Muslim holy month of Ramadan that year. Israel was quick to respond, aided materially by the supply of arms from the US, and held its own in attacks led by Egypt and Syria, which were in turn backed by the Soviets.

By the time a ceasefire was imposed on 25 October 1973, the US had made itself a dangerous enemy of the Arab states. OPEC imposed an embargo that banned oil exports to the US and any other country that had supported Israel, and cut oil production generally. In December of that year, OPEC further announced that its members would set their own prices for export for the first time in history. Subsequently, the oil price nearly quadrupled between 1973 and 1974.

This sharp jump in price was not simply the result of malignant greed; it was one side effect of a complex millennia-old geopolitical conflict that underscored the collective decision-making of the OPEC countries at the time. The results of OPEC's decision for the Western world were, however, profound. Oil price volatility had a direct effect on the price of all outputs of industrial processes, with severe implications for the global economy, which was already experiencing heightened levels of volatility owing to the failure of the Bretton Woods System. For an extended period, this system of artificially fixed exchange rates had obfuscated the variations in economic conditions that existed between countries, but these underlying differentials were laid bare as the world instead adopted a system of floating exchange rates. Together, the failure of the Bretton Woods System and the OPEC Oil Crisis introduced a level of complexity and volatility into the international monetary system that had never before been experienced. And it was during this period of volatility that the free-market ideals embedded in the very fabric of the Western world began to assert themselves and thrive.

———————

The US economy was already struggling under the weight of rising inflation by the time the twin disruptions of the Bretton Woods failure and the OPEC Oil Crisis took effect. Not long after Richard Nixon's re-election in 1972, industrial production began to decline, the stock market started cooling off, foreign investors became increasingly spooked by a destabilised dollar, and unemployment steadily rose. Following twenty years of unwavering economic growth and stability, Keynesian economists and central bankers were thoroughly perplexed by the simultaneous rise of inflation and unemployment.

In the world of simplified Keynesian economics, rising inflation was tolerable because it was seen as a direct result of rising demand; in other words, more market demand would logically push up the price of goods and services. This increased demand would theoretically allow companies to expand to meet the market's needs, allowing them to hire more workers and consequently decrease the unemployment rate. In this framework, inflation had always been linked to a healthy, growing economy and was not considered overly concerning; it was assumed that it would always self-correct as demand decreased and unemployment increased. In the 1970s this was upended: the simultaneous rise of inflation and the slowdown of economic growth in the US signalled a new phenomenon, which became known as stagflation.

At this point, the very fundamentals of the economics that underpinned central banking had to be reconsidered. With inflation continuing to rise, the Federal Reserve began to run out of ideas to curb accelerating price increases. By 1979, after almost a decade of poor monetary policy under the Nixon regime, Paul Volcker was brought in by President Jimmy Carter as the chairman of the Federal Reserve to save the US economy from runaway inflation. It took Volcker just over three years to correct a complex problem that today's economists believe had been building for fifteen years.

As soon as he stepped into his new position, Volcker had a clear plan: he needed to increase interest rates to combat inflation. Over a two-year period, the federal funds rate was ratcheted up sharply from around 10% in 1979 to double that in 1981.

A tough period of belt-tightening followed, putting a squeeze on the US economy. Companies were reluctant to borrow money from banks at such high interest rates, and aggregate investment in new equipment and stock subsequently slowed drastically, with many industries forced to lay off workers in what became a recession marked by an unemployment rate of over 10% – the highest rate in the post-war era, which would only be surpassed in 2020 with the onset of the Covid-19 pandemic.

Volcker's tight monetary policy and the subsequent economic recession fuelled public ire, culminating in widespread protests and a continuous barrage of attacks on the Fed during the 1980s. This wave of discontent reached its apex in a protest by struggling farmers who drove their tractors into the heart of Washington DC to blockade the route to the Eccles Building, which houses the Board of Governors for the Federal Reserve. Despite the fury of the American citizenry and extreme political pressure, Volcker persisted with his policies.

In the midst of the recession that he had caused, with trust in the Fed at an all-time low and with even his colleagues beginning to doubt the extremity of the policies he was implementing, Volcker displayed unique self-belief and a particular stubbornness of character. As detailed in his 2018 autobiography, he was at one point called to a secret meeting with Ronald Reagan in the White House library – a location known to have no recording devices – and asked by the president, through Chief of Staff James Baker, not to raise interest rates before the 1984 election. In the history of the Fed, much political pressure has been applied to it by various governments, both Democratic and Republican, yet legally the country's central bank is expected to stand independent of the government.

Presumably unwilling to yield to the same request that had been made by Nixon of the Fed in the early 1970s, which had begun the very period of inflation he was trying to combat, Volcker stuck to his guns, not allowing the president to intervene in monetary policy.

While Volcker's extreme policies remain controversial to this day, it is undeniable that he eventually succeeded in breaking the back of inflation. This was critical, in terms of both protecting the US economy and protecting the global financial system from the knock-on effects of a destabilised dollar. Perhaps even more importantly for the future of America, his approach also marked a significant shift in the economic principles by which central banks are able to influence the economy.

Paul Volcker's decision to increase interest rates, effectively decreasing the velocity of money to tame inflation, was closely aligned with the revolutionary economic ideas being proposed at the time by American economist Milton Friedman. Although Friedman had already made several important contributions to the study of economics, his theories were not widely accepted until the 1970s, when his theory of monetarism succeeded where conventional Keynesian wisdom had failed to provide a macroeconomic explanation for US stagflation. While Keynesian economics held that government-sponsored fiscal policy was the most effective way to ensure economic stability, Friedman argued that gradual and persistent changes in money supply have the power to influence economic activity in a much more immediate manner. With this school of thought providing newfound clarity on the economic circumstances of the time, Friedman was awarded the Nobel Prize in Economics in 1976. His work – and his core belief in the free market – soon spread beyond the academic sphere, informing important government policy decisions during the 1980s.

Friedman was critical of the social democratic approach to economic management that had dominated in the West since the end of World War II. For many, this approach had provided something of a middle ground between totalitarianism – especially as it manifested itself in the severe Soviet version of communism – and extreme capitalism, the failure of which was still strongly linked in most people's minds to the struggles endured during the Great Depression. Believing that the only way to avoid totalitarianism was through economic planning, most academics and policy-makers at the time supported the conventional wisdom of Keynes, who maintained that governments had a responsibility to manage their economies through periods of both recession and economic growth. In direct contrast, Friedman argued instead that the free market, unshackled from state intervention, was the only mechanism by means of which economic prosperity could be stimulated.

More than this, Friedman believed the only way to achieve personal freedom was through the free-market system, a belief that was shared by the man who won the Nobel Prize in Economics two years before him, Austrian-British economist and philosopher Friedrich von Hayek. This dimension of their economic philosophies was perhaps best articulated in Von Hayek's seminal work, *The Road to Serfdom*. Published in 1944, it argued that it was impossible for a government to undertake economic planning without imposing the set of ideological values underlying its decisions on society. The imposition of the beliefs of the ruling group on the public amounted to a violation of individual rights, which, Von Hayek argued, was the inevitable outcome of the state control at the heart of totalitarianism and communism. The only way to avoid this and to ensure individual freedom and true democracy was through a free-market system. Friedman echoed this argument, writing in a special introduction to the University of Chicago Press's 50th anniversary edition of Von Hayek's book that individual freedom could only be achieved "in a liberal order in which government activity is limited primarily to establishing the framework within which individuals are free to pursue their own objectives". The only order in which this was possible, Friedman maintained, was a free-market system – in his words, "the only mechanism that has ever been discovered for achieving participatory democracy".

Having weathered the economic disruptions of the 1970s, the US righted itself along a path of growth during the 1980s, spurred on by the ideological victory that accompanied the end of the Cold War. Communism, after all, had failed spectacularly to achieve economic prosperity where it had been applied, and this only seemed to confirm the validity of free-market capitalism as a mechanism for achieving both economic growth and increased social cohesion through the idea of the rising tide by which, theoretically, it would ultimately lift the economic circumstances of all sectors of society. Leading the way in terms of free-market economic policies were the US, under the leadership of President Ronald Reagan, and the UK, then under Prime Minister Margaret Thatcher. Reagan and Thatcher were closely aligned in their desire to rid the world of what they saw as the evils of communism, as well as in their belief in the efficiency of the free market. It was this intertwining of political and economic beliefs that undoubtedly influenced the radical changes implemented by both politicians during their tenures. This approach was arguably necessary, given that both leaders took office at a difficult time in their countries' economic histories: the UK, like the US, was also suffering from high inflation and high unemployment, which had led to widespread frustration among the public. Both Reagan and Thatcher were under significant pressure to make changes that would turn things around, but their commitment to the free market would produce distinctly different results.

In 1979, Margaret Thatcher – the first female prime minister of Britain – took office and immediately implemented an unpopular strategy to reduce inflation. At the time it had reached roughly 13%, according to the consumer price index. The plan was to streamline industries that had grown inefficient as a result of the power of trade unions and the socialist approach of the Labour Party, and to bring order after a series of labour strikes that had taken place during Britain's "Winter of Discontent" between 1978 and 1979. Thatcher's strategy aimed to reduce the interference of the state in the British economy by privatising state-owned industries, reducing state spending on social services, deregulating industries, limiting money supply and curbing the influence of the unions.

In practical terms this meant some harsh realities for the people of Britain. Tightening of government spending to reduce the public finance deficit meant higher taxes and reduced subsidies for faltering industries, leading to roughly 10,000 businesses declaring bankruptcy and unemployment climbing still further – to three million people by 1982. Meanwhile, tighter monetary policy pushed interest rates up to a peak of 17% in 1980. Inflation continued to climb, productivity declined, GDP fell, and the UK entered a recession.

Thatcher received widespread criticism from economists, who feared that her approach would continue to plunge Britain deeper into the economic mire, and riots broke out in the streets of London as people grew increasingly angry about the issue of growing unemployment. The prime minister's commitment to hard-line free-market policies earned her the title "the Iron Lady" – a moniker that failed to perturb her. "If you lead a country like Britain, a strong country, a country which has taken a lead in world affairs in good times and in bad, a country that is always reliable, then you have to have a touch of iron about you," she declared. By the end of 1982, inflation had begun to decrease, and increased productivity began to stimulate the economy.

Thatcher's policies further supported significant industrial growth over the following years, swelled the middle class in Britain and curbed the social unrest caused by the unions. More generally, her approach also forced the country to abandon its commitment to nationalised industry, redefined the role of the welfare state, and refocused economic policy on the centrality of the free market. Despite these successes, however, when Thatcher stepped down in 1990, the public finance deficit remained high, as did unemployment, leaving the success of her policies a much-debated topic. To this day, the argument is still made that she played a significant role in exacerbating economic and social divisions in Britain through the inadvertent favouring of wealthy elites over the working class, creating a chasm that still persists in the fabric of Britain's society and economy.

These mixed results were mirrored on the other side of the Atlantic, where President Reagan was taking a similar approach in an attempt to boost the American economy as it emerged from recession in the early 1980s. Reagan likewise aimed to reduce the intervention of the state in the American economy by decreasing government spending, reducing federal regulation of industry, slowing the expansion of money supply, and – perhaps most significantly – lowering income taxes and capital gains taxes. Applying the theory of trickle-down economics in an approach that would become known as "Reaganomics", the president convinced Congress to lower the income tax rate for the top income bracket from 70% to 50% through the passing of the Economic Recovery Tax Act. Five years later, in 1986, this was further lowered with the passing of the Tax Reform Act – something of an early warning sign of the turn being taken by free-market capitalism in the US. The following year, corporate tax rates were also significantly reduced.

There were pros and cons to this approach. While the US economy began to experience steady growth after 1982 and the stock market boomed, the increase in wages was not significant. As in Britain, the gap between the wealthy and the poor began to expand, with lower tax rates further exacerbating economic inequality. In addition, instead of seeing a decrease in government spending in line with the decrease in taxes, gross federal debt ballooned from $900 billion in 1980 to $2.7 trillion by 1988.

This was primarily due to frenzied defence spending in what was to be the climax of the arms race with the USSR, as well as to the government bailout of financial institutions during the Savings and Loan Crisis that occurred in the US in the early 1980s.

It would still be decades before the UK officially voted to leave the European Union, but the country had by this stage already begun to align itself, both politically and economically, more strongly with the US through its opposition to communism and embracing of free-market principles. However, despite the ideological drivers supposedly powering the progress of these two nations, in place of social democracy emerged a kind of ultra-capitalist democracy in which the free market was strongly championed from the highest levels of leadership but the egalitarian goals essential to social democracy remained elusive.

Rather than aligning perfectly in the way that policy-makers had envisioned, the ideals of social democracy and those of the free market found themselves in tension with one another under Thatcher and Reagan. It is this tension that effectively set the stage for the decades to come in the West, though its most destructive outcomes only became pronounced in the years leading up to the Global Financial Crisis. China, meanwhile, continued to grow in strength under communist rule.

6

CHINA'S NON-PERFORMING LOANS

China's bourgeoning economic growth in the two decades following its admission to the World Trade Organization in 2001 has been mirrored by the growth of the nation's rapidly expanding banking system. But this banking growth has not been accepted by all at face value. While it undoubtedly looks impressive on paper, many economic analysts from beyond the mainland have voiced their scepticism of the official numbers released by the Chinese authorities.

As a result of the formidable control that the CCP maintains over every part of the Chinese economy, it is almost impossible to gain a sense of the true underlying state of the banking system and the financial system as a whole from the outside. Financial reporting coming out of China is infamously difficult to authenticate, delivering as it does high-level figures but rarely revealing essential information at a more granular level. One such high-level figure, which is viewed with some reservation by various analysts from outside China – a figure that is critically important to the wellbeing of any bank and to any banking system in general – is the rate of non-performing loans (NPLs).

In *The Banker*'s ranking of the largest banks in the world for 2020, it is interesting to note that the top four banks on the list – ICBC, CCB, ABC and BOC – all recorded the same NPL ratio figure of 1.4% for year-end 2019. This figure represents the ratio between the value of all NPLs over the value of total loans, and the fact that it is identical for the top four state-owned commercial Chinese banks suggests the Chinese government is pursuing a form of co-ordinated NPL targeting policy. This is especially likely given that Dai Xianglong, the former governor of the People's Bank of China (PBOC), admitted in 2001 that the Chinese banking system had experienced alarmingly high NPLs since the mid-1990s, to the extent that the central bank was forced to become extensively involved in the operations of the top five state-owned banks to directly address the escalating NPL problem.

In 2003, official reports from PBOC estimated that NPLs in the top four Chinese banks were in the region of 2.4 trillion yuan (roughly $290 billion at the time), representing a 23% NPL ratio – which is to say that almost a quarter of their combined loan books were classified as NPLs. While this number is itself deeply concerning, credit rating agencies outside China estimated that the true value was closer to 3.5 trillion yuan ($423 billion), representing roughly a third of total loans owing. Realising the severity of the situation, the government embarked on a drastic programme to reduce NPLs in their largest banks, using what are known as asset management corporations (AMCs) to move substantial amounts of bad debt off their banks' balance sheets.

In 1999, the Chinese government established four state-owned AMCs to deal with the banking system's growing distressed debt situation, which had been exacerbated by the Asian Financial Crisis. Each of these four AMCs was matched to one of the large state-owned banks: Orient Asset Management to BOC, Great Wall Asset Management to ABC, Cinda Asset Management to CCB, and Huarong Asset Management to ICBC. They were created specifically to buy up bad debt from the nation's largest state-owned banks and to recover as much as possible from these NPLs. The majority of these loans originated in the two decades that followed the founding of the large state-owned banks in the early 1980s and the ensuing drive by the Chinese government to enact extensive "policy lending" under the principles of the country's command economy regime.

Since the founding of the People's Republic of China in 1949, the command economy, overseen by the ruling CCP, had dictated the nation's production and distribution of goods and services. In contrast to a free-market economy, which is guided by the market forces of supply and demand, the command economy is a system in which the government determines which goods should be produced, how much should be produced, and at what price these goods should be sold. A critical component of the command economy is the extension of loans from the banking system to government-selected corporations to fulfil government-mandated production quotas. Under this policy regime, until 1997 – when the government began to reform the banking industry to incentivise banks to make their lending decisions on a more commercial basis – banks had to legally fulfil lending quotas prescribed by government, irrespective of risk and commercial viability.

As a result of the government's lending policy, together with the inefficiency and weak financial performance of its state-owned enterprises, China's banking system became burdened by high rates of NPLs in the 1990s. In response, the plan for the four state-owned AMCs was to buy NPLs from the large state-owned banks and dispose of them over a ten-year period. This was a vital step in the government's plan to reform the banking system, as the state-owned banks' balance sheets had become bloated and inefficient, resulting in a deterioration in the quality of their assets. It would, they believed, solve the problem and facilitate growth in the banking system.

———————

In the first round of disposals between 1999 and 2000, $169 billion worth of NPLs was transferred from the four large state-owned banks to the four corresponding AMCs, equating to over 20% of the banks' combined assets. From 2001 to 2005, another $200 billion worth was transferred, and in 2007 the last of the big four banks to complete its restructure, ABC, sent another $112 billion worth of NPLs to its AMC. The total distressed debt moved from the balance sheets of the big four banks between 2000 and 2007 came to $481 billion. To put this in perspective, that was twice the size of Portugal's GDP in 2007.

To initially capitalise the four AMCs, the Chinese Ministry of Finance bought 10 billion yuan worth of special AMC bonds, totalling 40 billion yuan in equity capital ($6 billion at the time). But this initial injection was obviously not enough to acquire the hundreds of billions of dollars' worth of NPLs from the banks. To pay the banks for the acquisition of their bad loan portfolios, the AMCs therefore issued ten-year bonds, which the big four state-owned banks bought in exchange for their NPLs. For the banks, this was a win-win scenario. First win: the bonds would pay a periodic coupon over a ten-year period and ultimately pay back the principal at maturity. Second win: in terms of capital adequacy requirements, the bonds attracted a much lower risk weighting than the NPLs, since there was an implicit guarantee from the government. In sum, the big four state-owned banks could now hold less capital, having shifted the bad loans off their balance sheets by packaging them into bonds and selling them to the AMCs. Furthermore, they could continue to make potentially irresponsible new loans, safe in the knowledge that they too could be packaged and sold to the AMCs if required.

There was, however, a fundamental flaw in this plan: while the banks had removed the NPLs from their balance sheets and replaced them with AMC bonds, the underlying risk associated with the bad loans was still very much the same. For the AMCs to successfully repay the bond coupons and principal over the ten-year period, they would have to recover a significant portion of the bad loans they had bought. To make matters worse, the NPLs were sold to the AMCs at full book value, making it near impossible for these AMCs to be economically viable from the outset, as a full recovery of the amounts owed was never realistic.

The decision to price the NPLs at book value was, ultimately, a political one. Most of the NPLs in question originated from loans made to state-owned entities, and the state was concerned that if the loans were sold at a discounted rate, it would suggest that the SOEs from which the loans had originated – and the government itself – were perhaps not in a financial position to make their full loan repayments. This would make every future loan to these organisations questionable. By selling the NPLs at their full book value, several problems were avoided at once: no immediate write-downs of bad loans were required by the banks, the SOEs were spared any reputational damage, and the debt overhang was pushed out for a decade, when the first ten-year bonds would come due.

By 2006, however, the extent of the problem was becoming clear, with the recovery rate on the NPLs standing at just 20% – barely enough to cover the interest payments owed on the ten-year bonds. With the maturity date of the initial ten-year bonds approaching in 2009, it was clear that the AMCs would not be able to repay the principal amounts on the bonds without external assistance. The AMCs and the state faced a dilemma.

Having operated for a decade by this stage, the AMCs had also incurred extensive costs. They had thousands of staff members to pay and rent to cover for offices in some of China's most expensive financial districts, in addition to having to make the recurring coupon payments on the ten-year bonds. By 2008, the AMCs had collectively lost billions of dollars in total, mostly as write-downs from the unrecovered NPLs. When the bonds came due the following year, the government simply extended the bond maturity for another ten years. To appease auditors and for the bonds to maintain their full value on the banks' balance sheets, the Ministry of Finance also provided a notice that guaranteed support for the full repayment of the bonds' interest and principal if the AMCs were not able to do so for any reason. With a government guarantee in place, the NPL problem was effectively pushed out for yet another decade.

As a result of this process, the largest banks in China avoided the unpleasant reality of writing down any losses related to the huge pile of NPLs they had accumulated in the 1980s and '90s. If this had not been the case, the NPLs would have significantly eroded their capital base, potentially to such an extent that the government would have had to recapitalise the banks. Instead, with this disaster transferred a decade into the future, the banks' balance sheets appeared strong and healthy just in time for them to go public in the mid-2000s, drawing external investment that would bolster their capital reserves in line with international regulatory requirements.

In 2020, the four largest AMCs still dominated the NPL market, buying over 50% of the bad loans created by the Chinese banking system that year. Since the creation of the original four AMCs in 1999, however, the AMC landscape has expanded rapidly. In 2020, there were over 35 local AMCs in China to serve local lenders, and this number is only growing, aided by the government's relaxation of regulations in 2016 that allowed more than one AMC to exist per province.

The need for more AMCs is directly related to the increasing amount of bad debt being created in the Chinese banking system every year. As an example, between 2016 and 2019, the dollar amount of officially reported NPLs across the Chinese banking system increased from roughly $220 billion to $340 billion, which is equivalent to a compound annual growth rate of 15.6% over the three-year period. Although the official NPL ratio reported by China's banks may seem to remain relatively low at around 2%, the nominal amount of NPLs continues to grow at a rapid pace. This bad debt is offset in the NPL equation, however, by the equivalent or even greater rate of growth in the Chinese banking system's asset base – and when NPLs *do* begin to accumulate in the banking system, they are simply shifted to a corresponding AMC at full book value, accompanied by an explicit government guarantee.

———————————

In the twenty years following the introduction of the AMCs in China, the simple average NPL ratio across the entire Chinese banking system dropped dramatically from 29.8% in 2001 to 0.95% in 2015, before slowly starting to creep up again to 1.96% in 2020. Despite this seemingly successful attempt to suppress NPL ratios, the AMC solution is still only a temporary one. The underlying conditions for their build-up in the 1990s and early 2000s – and the risks that these NPLs pose to the financial system – have persisted.

This problem has been extensively researched by economic analyst Karlo Kauko, a financial stability and statistics adviser working at the Bank of Finland's Institute for Economies in Transition. In a 2020 paper, Kauko notes that all else being equal, the interest income of a bank diminishes if claims on its customers turn into NPLs. This is true regardless of whether the bank reports the NPLs or not. To estimate the extent to which Chinese banks may have "hidden NPLs", Kauko uses stochastic frontier analysis to calculate the expected rates of return on 100% healthy loans across various Chinese banks, and so represent "a hypothetical profit-maximising Chinese bank with no credit quality problems". He then compares these perfect rates of return to the actual interest income from Chinese banks' financial statements. The difference in these figures, he suggests, represents the lost interest income from underperforming loans.

Essentially, then, the gap between potential interest income and actual interest income is used as a proxy for loan quality – the larger the gap, the more underperforming loans there are present on the loan book.

Kauko's research reveals significant gaps between the potential interest income and the actual interest income of the 113 Chinese banks analysed, including the five largest state-owned banks, based on financial report data between 2013 and 2018. The paper concludes that the average rate of return on assets – interest income divided by loans – across the sample of banks was 6.4% for the period, while the average rate of return at the efficient frontier was 13.3%. This gap, Kauko suggests, is potentially the result of "hidden NPLs" – and he believes that there could be at least double the amount of NPLs in the Chinese banking system than officially reported. Remarkably, this is a conservative estimate. Other research, conducted as recently as 2021 and published by the World Bank, suggests that NPLs in the Chinese banking system may be up to four times higher than officially reported.

Expanding his analysis further, Kauko found that banks that were highly dependent on interbank funding, as opposed to customer deposits, were more likely to have more hidden NPLs than banks not heavily dependent on interbank funding. This insight is particularly striking given that in the US it was the highly leveraged financial institutions which were dependent on interbank funding that faced failure during the Global Financial Crisis. Both Bear Stearns and Lehman Brothers relied heavily on the interbank market: the latter required $200 billion worth of overnight funding each day, representing roughly a third of its total assets at the time of its bankruptcy.

Performing this calculation for every financial year between 2015 and 2018, Kauko's analysis also revealed that the gap between potential interest income and actual interest income across the Chinese banks analysed is steadily getting bigger, suggesting that the quality of these banks' loan books is deteriorating, on average, and that many NPLs are not being disclosed. Exacerbating the problem is the fact that the Chinese economy has been decelerating for the last ten years, and particularly so since 2016. Kauko notes that the gap between the actual rate of return and the potential return of a perfectly healthy loan book remained relatively constant between 2013 and 2015 but widened significantly in 2016, coinciding with the sharper slowdown of China's economic growth rate around that time. This observation suggests that if economic conditions worsen, NPLs will invariably rise as a result, putting even more pressure on Chinese banks. Although the Chinese banking system may have effectively suppressed reported NPL ratios in the last two decades, the system has not demonstrated that it has rid itself of these bad debts in the only real way possible: the write-down of losses, which would ultimately have to be absorbed by equity holders – in the case of China, primarily the government.

At year-end 2020, total banking assets in China stood at $49 trillion. With an official NPL ratio of 1.98%, this implies a total of $970 billion worth of NPLs. At an absolute minimum, this means that NPLs present in the Chinese banking system are roughly equivalent to 7% of GDP in 2020, a figure that does not include the NPLs held by the AMCs; that is, NPLs not accounted for on banks' balance sheets. If almost half of all NPLs are not being immediately recognised by the banks, as Kauko's analysis conservatively suggests, and NPLs are being moved to AMCs every year, then there is a very real possibility that NPLs in China are easily more than 14% of the nation's entire GDP. If these losses were to be immediately written down, the Chinese government, as the primary holder of Chinese banking equity, would be liable for losses in the region of $2 trillion.

In summary, while China's reported NPL levels have remained relatively subdued in recent years and nowhere close to the double-digit highs of the 1990s and early 2000s, it is unlikely that this reflects an actual significant decrease in NPLs. Rather, the introduction of the AMCs, which have bought NPLs from Chinese banks at an accelerating rate, has allowed Chinese banks to instantly disregard bad loans from their NPL equations. In addition, the rapid accumulation of assets in the Chinese banking system since the turn of the century, mostly in the form of new loans – as well as through the creation of new loans by rolling over loans that have not been repaid – has resulted in a larger denominator in the NPL ratio equation, which, in turn, produces a smaller NPL ratio than would be credibly expected.

Another factor affecting the size of China's reported NPLs is perhaps less obvious: it relates to the way in which Chinese banks classify their assets in general and, specifically, to how they recognise NPLs.

In China, banks must use a "five-bucket" rating system to classify their loans in terms of credit risk. These classifications or "buckets" are, in order of least risky to most risky, Pass Loans, Special Mention Loans, Substandard Loans, Doubtful Loans and Loss Loans. According to the China Banking and Insurance Regulatory Commission (CBIRC), Substandard Loans, Doubtful Loans and Loss Loans should be classified as NPLs. Special Mention Loans, however, do not necessarily have to be classified as non-performing. According to the regulator, banks are permitted to use "good quality collateral" to support the categorisation of loans that are more than 90 days past due as Special Mention. Thus, although the loans have displayed non-performing characteristics, because the bank does not expect to make a loss due to the existence of good quality collateral, it is not required to classify the loans as NPLs. This allows the bank to avoid labelling these loans as NPLs almost indefinitely – a practice that is in direct opposition to the rules set out by the Basel Committee on Banking Supervision (BCBS).

Published in 2006, the BCBS's "International Convergence of Capital Measurement and Capital Standards: A Revised Framework" aims to harmonise the existing accounting and regulatory framework for asset categorisation across banking regions, and is designed to be uniformly applied to *all* jurisdictions. In the framework, the BCBS provides very clear criteria for classifying non-performing loans. The first and most important criterion relates to the definition of default. A default occurs when either the bank considers the lender unlikely to pay its credit obligations in full – irrespective of any recourse that the bank may achieve through actions such as recovering collateral – or if the lender is past due by more than 90 days on any material credit obligation, including interest, capital payments or fees. The second measure of a non-performing exposure is when a loan is not 90 days past due, but it is deemed credit-impaired. The third measure is if there is any evidence that full repayment based on the contractual term is unlikely without recourse to collateral or the use of other risk mitigants.

In essence, the BCBS considers a loan to be non-performing if it is restructured or treated in a manner that would suggest it may be potentially non-performing, or if a payment has not been made 90 days past the due date. Notably, the BCBS also clearly states that "collateralisation or received guarantees should have no direct influence on the categorisation of an exposure as non-performing".

The rules set by the Chinese banking regulator differ from those of the BCBS in three significant ways. First, not all loans 90 days past due are classified as being in default. Second, Chinese banks allow for the consideration of collateral when classifying loans – in direct contrast to the BCBS's classification process. And third, Chinese banks are permitted to restructure loans in certain circumstances without the need to classify those loans as non-performing.

Each of these deviations from the BCBS's rules regarding NPL classification could drastically change the calculation of regulatory capital for the bank. According to the Basel II definition of default – upon which all subsequent Basel accords are based – once a loan is in default, the normal provision calculations for estimated portfolio losses cannot be used. Instead, the best estimated expected loss (BEEL) equation must be used, which commonly results in the realisation of much higher capital charges. The greater the capital charge that a bank faces per unit of asset value, the lower the leverage and, therefore, the lower the return on equity and, subsequently, the less attractive the bank becomes as an investment.

Given these divergences, it is surprising that so little action has been taken against Chinese banks, especially considering that various regulatory discrepancies have been identified and made public by important international organisations, including the IMF. In December 2017, the IMF released a report in which it concluded that Chinese banking authorities should review the current loan classification requirement "which permits banks to use good quality collateral to support categorising loans more than 90 days past due as Special Mention, and the lack of clarity in what constitutes good quality collateral for this purpose". The IMF noted that the practice of classifying loans in this way makes it difficult to properly assess an increase in credit risk at an individual bank level and at a system-wide level, adding that this could potentially result in lower provisions being held by Chinese banks. The IMF also recommended that the CBIRC should review "the requirement permitting loans granted to small enterprises to be classified as non-performing loans (NPLs) only when they are more than 180 dpd [days past due]" as this practice results in a slower recognition of problem loans and delays the detection of an increase in credit risk.

For long-term observers of the Chinese state, it may not come as a shock that China does not follow the same banking rules and regulations as the other nations that are members of the Basel Committee on Banking Supervision. After all, China is a one-party communist state that has in the recent past, among other things, purposely devalued its currency to gain a strategic trade advantage over its competitors, effectively censored free speech and the independent media within the mainland, and enforced stringent laws in Hong Kong to suppress pro-democratic entities. It has also been accused of human rights violations in its treatment of its Uyghur population, utilising a network of "re-education camps" to detain over a million members of the Muslim minority in what the BBC has described as "an oppressive system of mass surveillance, detention, indoctrination, and even forced sterilisation". Other global media outlets have openly called it an act of genocide.

By comparison, deviating from international best practice on loan classification may seem trivial. It is nonetheless distressing that other members of the BCBS have not brought more attention to the fact that such a divergence in regulatory adherence is taking place within the member state that is home to the largest banking system in the world. The lack of action is especially surprising when considering that, in the past, significant divergence from agreed-upon banking regulations has been met with a strong response from the international community.

Although the BCBS does not explicitly hold a mandate to enforce its rules and regulations, it still has significant power in the global banking landscape. Founded in 1974 by the Group of 10 nations in the aftermath of serious disturbances in international currency and banking markets, the BCBS wields a power that ultimately resides in its status. Comprising central bankers from the most powerful economic nations in the world, the BCBS should essentially be thought of as an exclusive banking club. Upon the promulgation of regulations, it can exclude nations or individual institutions from the co-operative network of banks included in its membership if they do not comply with the regulations agreed upon by the representatives on the Committee. As a result, to remain part of the banking fraternity globally, individual countries tend to adopt the BCBS's rules into national law far more quickly and with far less resistance than they have adopted proposals for international environmental regulations, such as the Paris Agreement, for example. Thus, while the regulations of the BCBS are not locally enforceable by the Committee itself, the reason national regulators do enforce these rules is simple: there is *usually* an immediate and extreme penalty – never explicitly stated, but very much implied – for defying the rules. Should a country not comply with BCBS rules, it will become an outcast in the international banking system and may, for example, be excluded as a counterparty in cross-border transactions.

The power of the global banking fraternity is not just theoretical but has been wielded in the past, most notably in the case of Gazprombank. Gazprombank is a privately owned Russian bank set up as a subsidiary of its parent company Gazprom, a partially state-owned natural gas company and the largest company in Russia by revenue in 2020. In this case, owing to the ongoing funding of rebels that aimed to destabilise eastern Ukraine, Gazprombank was sanctioned by the US Department of the Treasury in 2014 under the presidency of Barack Obama, and all US banks were prohibited from participating in any capital market transactions with Gazprombank. The US was joined by 28 EU nations, which also imposed sanctions on the Russian bank. As a result, Gazprombank suffered severe shortages in funding and ultimately required liquidity support from the Russian government.

Given China's significant divergence in classifying NPLs – which in turn significantly impacts the extent to which capital is set aside for these loans – the BCBS should have been compelled to take a harder line in enforcing its regulations across all member states' jurisdictions. Instead, as evidenced in a 2017 paper published by the BCBS's Financial Stability Institute, the Committee has deliberately avoided the issue. In the paper, the BCBS states that "notwithstanding the benefits of regulatory asset classification systems, it is difficult to compare the level of 'problem assets' across jurisdictions due to various differences in the definitions that underlie regulatory classification frameworks and how they are implemented". The BCBS also conducts a Regulatory Consistency Assessment Programme to periodically review the extent to which domestic regulations in each member jurisdiction are aligned with the minimum regulatory standards agreed by the Committee. In 2013, in a report focused specifically on China's implementation of risk-based capital standards as outlined in the updated Basel III framework, the BCBS provided Chinese banks with a "LC" (Largely Compliant) rating. The Committee determined in the report that while several divergences from the regulatory standards had been identified, these discrepancies were "not material". An update of the report was published in 2019, which showed that no measures had been taken to address these discrepancies.

Such a judgment by the BCBS stands in direct opposition to its most central objective – that of international convergence and harmonisation of international banking regulations. Bear in mind that in 2006, when the BCBS completed its revised version of the Basel II framework, its primary aim was to "secure international convergence on revisions to supervisory regulations governing the capital adequacy of internationally active banks". On the very first page of the revised framework, the BCBS states that the document serves as the formal agreement by all member nations for measuring capital adequacy standards, and that it has been "endorsed by the Central Bank Governors and Heads of Banking Supervision", which constituted the members of the Committee at the time.

Given the explicit statement of these global ideals, it is disconcerting that the BCBS would nullify its own primary objective of international convergence on the regulation of capital adequacy by allowing such significant divergence from these standards by one of its members. And not just any member, but the member with the largest banking system in the world. Such inaction not only undermines the project of adequately regulating international banking practices, but also weakens attempts at multilateralism in many other areas, from climate change to human rights. Critically for the global financial system, it also allows significant risk to build up unhindered in much the same way as it did two decades ago in the years before the Global Financial Crisis.

7

BROWNIAN MOTION, STRING THEORY AND THE PROLIFERATION OF MATHEMATICS IN BANKING

During the Cold War, the competing ideologies of communism and democracy spawned a period not only of great fear and conflict, but also of profound technological innovation. Powered by the competition for intellectual and scientific superiority between the US and the USSR, advances in military technology in the 1960s and '70s made their way into civil society in the decades to come – most notably, the personal computer and the internet. These tools have revolutionised almost every aspect of human life and driven huge growth in e-commerce, creating a global online marketplace in which a multitude of transactions takes place between buyers and sellers from around the world, at rates that were previously inconceivable.

Economic growth in the US was spurred on by the policy decisions made under President Bill Clinton, who took office in 1993 as the country emerged from another recession. Clinton's fiscal policies increased income tax rates for top-earning individuals and raised corporate tax while curbing certain corporate subsidies. The signing of the North American Free Trade Agreement, which eliminated tariffs between the US, Canada and Mexico, also helped boost the economy, as did the significant reduction in government spending that was achieved by reforming the country's welfare programme. In tandem with Clinton's fiscal regime, which reflected a mix of free market and socialist ideas, the Federal Reserve, led by Alan Greenspan, kept interest rates low. The combined effect was a positive one: the US economy entered a prolonged period of growth. Productivity increased, unemployment decreased, inflation fell, poverty was reduced, and a \$203-billion budget deficit in 1994 was transformed into a budget surplus of \$128 billion by 2001.

Banks were also granted an opportunity to boost their profitability during this period, and in turn fuel further economic growth, through a combination of low interest rates and regulatory flexibility. Under the administration of President George HW Bush, the Financial Institutions Reform, Recovery and Enforcement Act of 1989 had imposed a capital requirement on banks, primarily to guard against the risk of bank failure, but also to protect banks against the risk of a decrease in the value of underlying assets. This meant there was, essentially, a capital requirement for long-term government bonds, which can lose value when interest rates rise. In the 1990s, however, with interest rates predicted to stay low, the Fed allowed banks to disregard the capital requirement for long-term government bonds, which boosted bank profitability in the short term owing to the relatively high return on long-term bonds compared to Treasury bills.

As the US economy began to grow, so did the capitalist aspirations of much of the nation – ultimately to breaking point. The excesses of the financial industry at this time have been famously depicted in film, notably by Oliver Stone in *Wall Street* at the time (1987) and Martin Scorsese in *The Wolf of Wall Street* a quarter of a century later (2013). These excesses were also documented in 2003 by Nobel Prize-winning economist Joseph Stiglitz – who served as chairman of Bill Clinton's Council of Economic Advisers and subsequently as the chief economist of the World Bank – in his book *The Roaring Nineties*. Investment in information technology firms and dotcom start-ups drove huge growth in the stock market. Many investors took on increasingly high risks in the belief that these companies would soon generate significant profits, caught in a frenzy of what Alan Greenspan would later dub "irrational exuberance".

With an abundance of capital in the market, competition between these companies grew rapidly even as actual business focus was lost, with larger and larger portions of start-up capital being spent on marketing rather than on the development of products. The memorable story of the pets supply company Pets.com was typical of the era. Founded in November 1998, Pets.com became a household name thanks to its high-profile marketing campaign and signature sock puppet mascot, which appeared on *Good Morning America* and was interviewed by *People* magazine. In January 2000, Pets.com paid a reported $1.2 million to air a commercial during the Super Bowl. By November of that year, within two years of its establishment, it had been liquidated owing to mismanagement – and this was not an unusual case. Beneath the glossy veneer of success of many companies loomed serious financial vulnerabilities.

As businesses scrambled to disguise just how precarious the situation was, a tacit acceptance emerged of the practice of adopting complex financial and accounting techniques to boost the appearance of companies' performance to attract more investment. Many of these were not technically illegal, but they were nonetheless misleading to shareholders. In addition, tax incentives led many companies to alter their rewards structures so that executives received stock options rather than more tangible financial benefits better aligned to recent performance. This in turn incentivised an increasing number of executives to engage in misleading accounting practices. Overall, there was a distinct shift in focus from a company's business performance to its stock price – and the use of any and all accounting and financial structuring techniques to boost it. These practices were, to some extent, aided and abetted by the global accounting firms that provided both consulting and auditing services to these banks and other financial institutions – generating fees and themselves growing significantly in size, and in some cases implicitly condoning the behaviour of what came to be known as regulatory arbitrage. The pursuit of free-market ideals was being significantly overextended, producing a kind of hyper-capitalism where the pursuit of profits was justified by virtually any means. As *Wall Street*'s Gordon Gekko famously explained it: "Greed, for lack of a better word, is good."

Misleading and illegal activity in the financial sector was further incited by the broader move towards deregulation in America, which manifested itself most significantly in the passing of the Gramm-Leach-Bliley Act in 1999. This removed some of the fundamental barriers between commercial banking and investment banking that had been in place for almost seventy years. It would prove to be a significant contributor to the growing level of risk in the financial system. The high-leverage, big risk-taking ethos of investment banks quickly overshadowed the conservative approach that commercial banks are trusted to take in managing people's money. In addition, it introduced dangerous conflicts of interest, as investment banks were now hypothetically able to extend loans to the same companies whose stock they were pushing. This pattern of behaviour was strongly associated with the breakdown of barriers between investment banking and commercial banking, and mirrored closely the behaviour that had led to the Wall Street Crash of 1929.

It was under these circumstances that there emerged several cases of fraud and misconduct, the consequences of which sometimes extended beyond the financial or reputational ruin of individual bad actors, to the failure of entire corporations. Famous examples include the collapse of Barings Bank in 1995 thanks to "rogue trader" Nick Leeson, the Procter & Gamble vs Bankers Trust case in 1996, and the Enron accounting scandal in 2001. While companies accused of wrongdoing were often quick to point out that crimes had been committed by only a few individuals and that their behaviour was not a reflection of the ethics of the business, they were undeniably a reflection of the larger cultural forces dominating the Western world at the time. It was a period in US history driven by the blind pursuit of profits and the celebration of wealth, and it was against this backdrop that ethics became somewhat pliable.

Rather than self-regulating – as Milton Friedman had argued they always would be – the free markets of the 1980s and '90s had created an environment in which bad actors thrived, manipulating the idea of personal freedoms in the process, and mangling it into something cold and self-serving.

———

At the centre of the growth in the financial industry during the 1990s were complex financial instruments known as derivatives, which had experienced a surge in popularity since the 1970s. Derivatives were nothing new. They had been used since ancient times, with the first recorded example of a derivatives transaction occurring in Greece in 600 BCE, when olive oil trader Thales of Miletus negotiated what were effectively call options on olive oil that would be delivered after harvest. But derivatives remained largely unstandardised and unregulated until the founding of the Chicago Board of Trade in 1848, which brought a degree of order to the practice of negotiating derivatives contracts, at that time usually based on grain yields. The size of these markets began to balloon as other commodities were traded and more exchanges were established around the US, including the Kansas City Board of Trade, the New York Cotton Exchange, the Minneapolis Grain Exchange, and the Butter and Cheese Exchange of New York, predecessor of the New York Mercantile Exchange. In the 1920s and '30s, legislation was drafted to regulate these exchanges, most notably the Grain Futures Act in 1922, which aimed to increase transparency in grain futures trading to prevent market manipulation, and its successor, the Commodity Exchange Act in 1936, which stipulated several requirements related to a list of certain commodities in a bid to strengthen the markets.

As the scope of derivatives trades expanded, the Commodity Exchange Act was amended, and in 1974 it was replaced by the Commodity Futures Trading Commission Act, which established the Commodity Futures Trading Commission, a government agency charged with the regulation of US derivatives markets, including futures, swaps and certain kinds of options. By this time, derivatives trading had grown significantly more complex owing to two main factors. First, the failure of the Bretton Woods System had introduced significant commodity price volatility; and second, there had been a significant rise of interest in speculation as individual traders tried to profit through the prediction of fluctuations in the prices of the assets underlying derivatives transactions. This practice was rapidly becoming more attractive and more sophisticated owing to the major advances in technology taking place during the 1960s and '70s, with computers enabling counterparties to run ever more complex pricing models on which to base their trade decisions.

Uncannily, it was in 1973 – in the same year that such high levels of economic volatility were being experienced because of the failure of the Bretton Woods System and the onset of the OPEC Oil Crisis – that arguably one of the most important developments in financial mathematics was made by the economists Fischer Black and Myron Scholes. In their seminal paper "The Pricing of Options and Corporate Liabilities", they introduced the Nobel Prize-winning Black-Scholes formula for the pricing of options, which transformed speculation in derivatives markets forever by providing a seemingly reliable mathematical basis upon which trading decisions could be based.

Advances in financial mathematics had driven significant interest in the development of a model for option pricing since the 19th century. The first notable achievement was not made until 1900, when a Frenchman named Louis Jean-Baptiste

Alphonse Bachelier submitted his PhD thesis, entitled *Théorie de la spéculation,* or *The Theory of Speculation,* while studying mathematics at the Sorbonne in Paris. Bachelier had undertaken an analysis of an exchange-traded futures contract, where the underlying asset was French government *rentes* – perpetual coupon-paying bonds – listed on the Paris Bourse. At the time, *rentes* were considered relatively secure investments with a nominal value that generally hovered around 100 francs and fixed returns, typically between 3% and 5%. In his thesis, Bachelier noted that there was so much new information influencing the price of the bonds at any given moment that the movement of the bond prices could not be predicted. "The determination of these fluctuations depends on an infinite number of factors," he wrote. "It is, therefore, impossible to aspire to mathematical prediction of it. Contradictory opinions concerning these changes diverge so much that at the same instant buyers believe in a price increase and sellers in a price decrease." Bachelier was particularly interested in how investors make decisions in a world of such uncertainty.

Something very similar to the random movement in bond prices that Bachelier described had already been observed in the world of science in 1827 by British botanist Robert Brown. He had noticed that, when viewed under a microscope, pollen particles suspended in water appeared to move randomly, though there did not appear to be any external force moving them and they had no way of propelling themselves. Brown was unable to explain the movement of the particles – which became known as Brownian motion – but in 1905, no less an authority than Albert Einstein proved that the movement of the particles was the result of their collision with tiny molecules that were moving in the water. Thus he had confirmed the existence of atoms. Einstein's *Investigations on the Theory of the Brownian Movement* described how the constant random collision of atoms with the pollen particle from all sides created the spontaneous movement of the particle that Brown had observed. Although the trajectory of the particle was random, Einstein reasoned that it would be possible to calculate the probability of the particle moving a particular distance and found that – like many other random phenomena in the world – the frequency distribution of the particle's probabilistic movement was normal. This made it possible to determine statistically the most likely paths that the particle would follow. Around the same time, Bachelier achieved a similar insight regarding bond prices, enabling him to mathematically model fluctuations in bond prices based on the probability distribution of future bond prices rather than on the predictability of returns.

Bachelier's ideas were well received in the mathematics community. The work presented in *Théorie de la spéculation* set the course for developments in stochastic analysis and probability theory over the next century, laying the academic groundwork for several pivotal concepts, including the Markov property, the theory of Martingales, the Chapman-Kolmogorov equation, and the connection between Brownian motion and the heat equation. Bachelier remained unknown in the world of finance until 1955, when his work on options pricing was uncovered by the academic community, leading to a wave of intense development in financial modelling. It was during this period that the collaboration between Fischer Black, Myron Scholes and Robert Merton resulted in the publication of the hugely influential Black-Scholes formula.

In the late 1960s, Robert Merton was completing his PhD at the Massachusetts Institute of Technology (MIT), in which he linked the price of a warrant to the price of the underlying stock in much the same way that Bachelier had demonstrated a relationship between the *rentes* and the option contract. After receiving his PhD, Merton joined the MIT Sloan School of Management, working alongside Scholes, who had received his PhD from the University of Chicago in 1969, and Merton Miller. Through Sloan, the two men were introduced to Fischer Black, who was working at a consultancy firm, having obtained his PhD from Harvard in 1964. Black was well known among the academic community, having published several important papers during his career, including one detailing the development of the capital asset pricing model.

In 1973, Black and Scholes described a partial differential equation known as the Black-Scholes equation, which could be used to calculate the value of options and other derivatives. Resting on Bachelier's assertion that stock price movements are probabilistically normally distributed, the model essentially implies that very large movements in stock prices are unlikely. And empirical tests performed by the economists proved it to be remarkably accurate for pricing options – at least when the markets behaved rationally. Merton proposed certain important modifications to the formula in the year of its initial publication, and the result was a more widely applicable version that was quickly adopted in the early 1970s, seeming as it did to bring scientific order to a highly volatile financial environment.

With investors emboldened by the mathematical support that the Black-Scholes formula provided for decision-making – despite the fact that it was based on academic theory and subject to some important limitations – options trading quickly swelled into a market worth billions of dollars. Derivatives exchanges grew to accommodate all kinds of contracts, including currency, debt and index derivatives, and there was a marked rise in over-the-counter transactions (as opposed to those through formal exchanges) as well, which led to the creation of new financial instruments called swaps. In 1973, the Chicago Board of Trade also became the first exchange to list standardised, exchange-traded stock options when it opened the Chicago Board Options Exchange (CBOE), which became the official exchange for options trading in the US. When the CBOE started, it was restricted to listed call options, but by 1975 it had introduced computerised trading and by 1977 it had grown to include put options.

In time, the CBOE further expanded to accommodate a wide range of financial products, with annual exchange volumes reaching 100 million option contracts in 1984 and over one billion option contracts by 2008. This growth was assisted in no small part by the fact that at this time the derivatives market also remained largely unregulated and opaque, with only the counterparties involved in the transaction having full knowledge of the size of the deal and the risks involved. Importantly, the identities of the counterparties themselves were also often unknown, hidden behind a complex series of offshore trusts and companies. At this time, there existed no regulatory requirement for the legal entities that were the ultimate beneficiaries of a trade to be identified in any explicit way.

Adding further risk was the fact that these trades were being conducted with the assistance of financial models that were being applied almost universally, despite being essentially based on a set of simple assumptions made by Bachelier many years previously on a very limited market of French bonds. Indeed, while Bachelier's thesis is still recognised as providing one of the most critical theoretical breakthroughs in mathematics, his theory had not been developed for application across all financial markets. Nonetheless, the underlying assumption that the apparently random change of value in financial assets could be predicted using the mathematically convenient and elegant Gaussian (normal) distribution was transformed into hardened theory by the financial statisticians who formed part of the Chicago School in the 1970s, and taught in Western universities for decades.

The danger of using mathematical models without a clear understanding of their shortcomings is not a risk specific to the financial sphere; it is embedded in the application of any mathematical model or grand academic theory to real-world phenomena. One particularly pertinent example of this is string theory, an area of scientific inquiry that has confounded physicists for decades.

In contemplating string theory, one of the more memorable episodes of the popular television series *The Big Bang Theory* comes to mind. In this episode, the quirky theoretical physicist Sheldon Cooper drunk-dials his hero Stephen Hawking after one too many glasses of wine. Sheldon has just decided to give up on string theory, which has been the subject of his life's work until that point, and is going through what his bubbly neighbour Penny likens to a breakup in a romantic relationship. Sheldon must come to terms with the fact that none of the work he has undertaken in relation to string theory has come to anything, and accept that the time has finally come to end this line of inquiry, in search of a subject of study that will prove more productive. "It's me again," slurs Sheldon on Stephen Hawking's answering machine. "I gave up string theory. You should give up black holes and we can totally solve crimes together!"

At the heart of string theory is an attempt to discover an underlying theory that would connect two of the most significant areas of research in theoretical physics: the theory of general relativity and quantum theory. On the one hand, general relativity, one of Einstein's most revered achievements, is primarily concerned with the force of gravity, and it accurately describes and predicts the universe's largest phenomena, such as stars and galaxies. On the other hand, quantum mechanics focuses on three non-gravitational forces – the strong and weak nuclear forces, and electromagnetism – to explain the smallest phenomena of the universe, such as atoms and subatomic particles. Together, these two theories – which have individually been exhaustively proven – provide a scientific explanation for almost all the physical features of our world. They are, however, fundamentally different, and to date irreconcilable.

For years, scientists have been searching for an underlying theory capable of reconciling the principles of general relativity with those of quantum theory, and in so doing provide a single, comprehensive scientific framework that successfully incorporates the physics underlying both gravity and the other three fundamental forces. The quest for such a theory has garnered intense attention among the scientific community for more than a century. If it were to be developed, it would be known as the theory of everything, capable of providing a cohesive scientific framework that could fully explain all physical aspects of the universe.

String theory has perhaps come closest to providing this unifying master theory. At its most basic level, it deviates from standard physics by suggesting that, rather than being composed of physical particles, all matter in the universe should be conceptualised as one-dimensional vibrating strings of energy. The vibration is the result of the four fundamental forces acting upon the strings, which propagate through space into multiple dimensions and interact with one another. The concept of dimensions is particularly important, as, in addition to the four we encounter in daily existence – time plus the three standard spatial dimensions of length, width and height – the mathematics underlying string theory assumes there are at least six other spatial dimensions occupied by these strings.

Rather than offering a neat set of mathematical equations that can reliably predict real-life phenomena, string theory comprises many complex calculations that frequently have several solutions, owing to the multiplicity of dimensions assumed by the theory. Collectively, these equations offer a guiding framework, but they do not offer a concrete, provable formula for predicting or explaining the physical features of the universe. After all, while an equation may fail to accurately predict a phenomenon of *this* world, it may accurately reflect a phenomenon in an alternative dimension. And it is here that the crux of the fascination with string theory lies – for, as it stands, it can be neither proved nor disproved.

The ideas on which string theory is built emerged during the 1980s, but while it is regarded as one of the most mathematically sophisticated areas of theoretical scientific research, there is – at least to date – no experimental or observational evidence to support it, making it something of a rabbit hole, down which many real-life Sheldon Coopers have plunged. Indeed, for almost forty years, string theory has dominated research in theoretical particle physics, with more scientific research papers produced on the subject than any other. The theory has also won a degree of renown among the scientific community, and it has become something of a rite of passage for PhD candidates in particle physics to contribute something on string theory.

For the layperson, what has been potentially more interesting than the theory itself is the steadfast refusal of its proponents to abandon it, despite the dearth of empirical evidence to support its validity. Fascinated and wholly convinced by the mathematics that underlies it, many researchers have dedicated much of their life's work to something that exists only in a theoretical realm with seemingly little connection to the real world. There is perhaps no better example than string theory to demonstrate the desperate human need to impose a structure or framework on the world so that it may be understood, explained and predicted – and no better example of the limitations of these tools in a world that does not always neatly conform to equations and models.

The tension that exists between the desire to exert some degree of control on real-world phenomena and the challenges of doing so has also played out in the financial sphere, where mathematical models have become embedded as essential, though somewhat uninterrogated, tools for understanding and predicting movements in markets. While these tools are undoubtedly useful, no matter how elegant the mathematics underlying them may be, they are always limited in their ability to perfectly capture real-world events and provide sound projections. The reason for this is that all models are based on certain assumptions, and while these assumptions may be accurate most of the time, there are certain circumstances in which they do not apply. The Black-Scholes-Merton model, as an example, is based on the assumption of a normal distribution in the changes in value of the underlying equity positions, which is useful in a rational market but proves inadequate in the case of exceptionally large movements, especially negative movements. The crux of the problem is that while these kinds of movements are probabilistically unlikely, historical empirical data demonstrates that they do happen, and not infrequently.

There is an innate desire in Western culture, particularly prevalent during the 20th century, to create a theoretical framework that can comprehensively explain all worldly phenomena. This has expressed itself not only in science through the pursuit of string theory, and in finance through the proliferation of mathematical models, but also in economics through, for example, the theory of monetarism, and more generally in culture, most recently through the social scientific theories of intersectionality. Although these theories and models may be useful devices for gaining insight into complex phenomena, they are almost always limited in their ability to fully encapsulate the true nature of what they are trying to measure or explain. Thus one of the fundamental problems underlying the extreme volatility and market hysteria that entered the Western banking system in the 1970s and persisted into the 1980s was the excessive reliance on mathematical models proposed only theoretically by a relatively small number of mathematical economists, but adopted widely in practice, to the exclusion of any other form of insight or inquiry into risk or pricing. This is the risk that arises when scientific theories are advocated as incontrovertible facts and deemed the *only* reliable way of interpreting how the world operates.

Fischer Black himself was well aware of the limits of financial mathematics. "In the end, a theory is accepted not because it is confirmed by conventional empirical tests, but because researchers persuade one another that the theory is correct and relevant," he noted in a 1986 article for *The Journal of Finance*. Indeed, the paradox of mathematical models too often forgotten is that an over-reliance on these tools limits an understanding of the world rather than enhances it – leading invariably, in the case of economics, to financial crises.

8

THE INVESTMENT-LED
GROWTH DILEMMA

Despite the steady decline of the Chinese economic growth rate since the Global Financial Crisis, President Xi Jinping announced in a CCP conference in November 2020 that his government planned to double the size of the Chinese economy by 2035. This declaration came even as the Covid-19 pandemic brought the global economy to its knees, resulting in China's first quarter of negative GDP growth, in Q1 of 2020, since 1992. To achieve Xi's bold ambition, the Chinese economy will have to grow at an annual rate of 4.7% for the fifteen years until 2035. While this may not seem impossible, given that the Chinese economy grew by 6.1% in 2019, the intentions of the Chinese leadership will be challenged by the fact that there has been a prolonged deceleration, particularly over the last decade, in China's economic growth rate. This is in addition to the problem of an ageing population that is putting significant pressure on an already strained workforce.

As many analysts have pointed out, including those even from China's own Bureau of Statistics, the current and future composition of the Chinese population is perhaps the greatest obstacle to achieving the country's fifteen-year growth goal. Largely owing to the one-child policy, which became constitutionally enforced in the early 1980s and was held in place until 2015, the Chinese population has gradually become older, with the fertility rate, as a measure of children per adult female, gradually decreasing. This trend was exacerbated by the tendency of many Chinese families to actively seek out having a boy rather than a girl, driven by traditional notions that male heirs can carry on the family bloodline and go on to earn higher salaries compared to their female counterparts, thereby creating less of a financial burden on the family. Over time, this has resulted in a significant surplus of men without wives, known in China as *guang gun*, or "bare branches" – tens of millions of men of prime marriage age in each generation who remain unmarried, without wives to bear children and sustain a youthful population. In 2021, census data showed China's population was growing at the slowest rate in decades, and that people over 65 now made up 13.5% of the population, compared to 8.9% in 2010. Thus there has been a radical transformation of the population dynamics in the country over the last four decades, to the extent that there may soon be too few adults of working age to support the enormous and ageing population. Indeed, it was the effect of distorted population dynamics on economic productivity that was one of the reasons that the Japanese economy slowed significantly in the 1990s.

The Japanese slowdown provides a second lesson for China observers: the inability of an investment-led growth strategy to sustain high economic growth over the long term. This strategy, as implemented in nations such as Japan and Brazil, often experiences a period of initial success but has historically ended in failure. It can be divided roughly into three phases of development.

In the first phase, there is a focus on financing and building desperately needed infrastructure, which serves as invaluable investment in the country, resulting in rapid but unequal economic growth. In both Japan in the 1960s and Brazil in the 1980s, economic growth averaged over 10%. At this point a small proportion of the population – often politically aligned groups – tends to benefit disproportionately from the increased spending on infrastructure and development projects. Debt and growth rise almost in tandem, so that the total debt burden remains manageable.

In the second phase, there is a move to rebalance growth drivers away from heavy investment and government expenditure towards consumer-led growth. This comes with the expectation of higher wages. As a result, economic growth begins to lose momentum, but debt keeps increasing at the same pace as before. Between 1960 and 1970, Japan began its shift from a low-wage to a high-wage economy, and subsequently, growth collapsed from over 12% in 1960 to just 0.4% by 1970. For the next four decades, Japan's GDP growth averaged under 4%, and in the 2010s it averaged under 1%. Similarly, in Brazil, GDP growth dropped dramatically from over 9% in 1980 to -3.1% by 1990. In the next two decades, it averaged under 2.5%, and in the decade from 2010 it remained under 1%.

In the third and final stage of the investment-led growth cycle, debt levels become unsustainable, as investment becomes increasingly impotent and growth gradually stagnates, ultimately resulting in a rapid correction. Bad debts must be realised to reach equilibrium, otherwise a full-blown financial meltdown may ensue. In the early 1990s, Japan experienced such a crisis, resulting in what has been called the "lost decade". The crisis was triggered by the collapse of asset prices in 1991 – a price bubble that was inflated by banks issuing increasingly risky loans, combined with rapid growth in the real estate market fuelled by wild speculation and low interest rates. In Brazil, a similar collapse took place between 1979 and 1983, when a combination of external factors, including a significant increase in oil prices and a sharp increase in interest rates, caused the country to default on its sovereign debt – and it became ever more indebted owing to its stubborn investment-led, export-driven economic growth strategy.

The similarities between the course of events that took place in Japan and Brazil in the 1980s and '90s and that are playing out presently in China cannot be discounted. The CCP has embarked on a potentially irreversible path of increased government expenditure, with every yuan of expenditure resulting in less GDP growth each year. The increased spending has led to a total debt level – including government, household and corporate debt – that is by most estimates greater than 300% of GDP, as of 2020. This problem is being further compounded by the demographic challenge of an ageing population and significant global macroeconomic headwinds, including a global pandemic and an intensifying trade war with the US, which is dampening already subdued economic growth rates.

For these reasons, China's fiscal position, as it enters what may be considered the third phase of its investment-led growth cycle, should be of great concern to the global financial community in general, and the banking community in particular.

"China's fiscal policy is bewildering," wrote *Bloomberg*'s unnamed "QuickTake" author on 13 March 2020 in an article entitled "Unravelling the Mysteries of China's Multiple Budgets". Each year, the Chinese government releases four different budget reports to cover all levels of state revenue collection and expenditure. But, as the author noted, the reports do little to clarify what is ostensibly an extremely opaque account of the state's annual revenue collection and, more importantly, its spending. A considerable part of government spending is "in the shadows": analysts suggest that the state hides the true size of its spending and, with that, the true extent of the country's growing budget deficit.

According to the official main budget – the "general public budget" – the Chinese government spent approximately 23.5 trillion yuan in 2019, roughly $3.4 trillion at the time, representing 24% of its $14.4 trillion GDP. Comparatively, the US government spent $4.5 trillion in 2019, representing 21% of its $21.4 trillion GDP. China's main budget does not, however, include all government expenditure, as there is also a "government fund" budget and a "special bond" budget – introduced in 2015 – which account for a further $1.4 trillion and $300 billion of spending, respectively, as well as $200 billion of savings from the previous year's budget, which was also spent in 2019.

In total, this means reported government spending in 2019 was in the region of $5.3 trillion, representing 37% of GDP – a significantly higher ratio of government spending to GDP than for the US, at 21%. Furthermore, this spending figure does not include state asset management and social security insurance expenditure, though these expenses are relatively small in relation to the rest of the national budget.

In recent years, the Chinese government has run a budget deficit, meaning that government spending outstrips revenue collection in the timespan of a given year. Many nations across the world run budget deficits, which are most often funded by the sale of government debt to investors in the form of government securities, such as bonds. In 2019, as reported by China's Ministry of Finance, the government collected $4.5 trillion in revenue from various sources, including taxes, tariffs and the sale of government land – a revenue channel that is unique to the Chinese state, as the communist government legally owns all land in China and collects land sales revenue for transferable land-use rights sold to individual homeowners or developers.

The difference between revenue and expenditure – the budget deficit – was thus in the region of $800 billion when including all reported forms of government spending in 2019; this represents 5.6% of GDP. In comparison, the US ran a federal budget deficit of $984 billion, representing 4.6% of GDP that year. In the UK, the budget deficit to GDP ratio was much smaller, at $53 billion at the time, equivalent to just 1.9% of its $2.8-trillion GDP. Further comparisons, as of 2019, to nations such as France, with a budget deficit to GDP of 3%, India at 4.6%, and South Africa at 6.7%, also seem to indicate that China's deficit is comparatively high. Meanwhile, certain large economies, such as Germany, actually ran a budget surplus that year.

There is, of course, an important caveat to consider when comparing various countries' expenditure to revenue: the assumption that reported revenue and GDP figures are accurate, or at least within a reasonable margin of error. In the case of China, however, this is a very large assumption to make when considering the opacity of its reporting.

While even the officially reported figures suggest that China seems to be running a substantial budget deficit, particularly considering its nominal size compared to that of other nations, perhaps more concerning is the steadily widening gap between revenue and expenditure. In the last decade, China's budget deficit as a proportion of GDP has more than doubled, from under 2% in 2010 to over 5% in 2019. And this trend appears to be continuing into the next decade, with government expenditure expected to grow significantly – while GDP growth decelerates – owing in some part to significant amounts spent to support and stimulate economic activity during the Covid-19 pandemic.

While, as noted above, most nations have run a budget deficit in the last decade – and, in most nations, government expenditure increases each year – the case of China is exceptional in its aggressive year-on-year expansion of the government budget. Based on figures from the "general public budget" – which does not include spending from the "government fund" and "special bond" budgets – spending has increased from $1.14 trillion in 2009 to $3.46 trillion in 2019. This represents a compound annual growth rate (CAGR) of 11.7% across the period. Comparatively, federal government spending in the US increased from $3.5 trillion to $4.4 trillion in the same period, representing a CAGR of 2.3%. In the UK, government spending has increased even less, from \$1.07 trillion to \$1.09 trillion, representing a CAGR of just 0.15%.

In contrast to the slower increases in government spending in the US and the UK during the 2010s, China has more than tripled its government expenditure in the same timeframe, while simultaneously experiencing a significant slowdown in its GDP growth. The divergence of these two numbers has been of great concern for the Chinese government, which has desperately attempted to counteract gradually decelerating economic growth by rapidly increasing government expenditure year-on-year to boost productivity. In 2018, it implemented significant tax cuts in the hopes of stimulating economic activity. Despite these efforts to reverse the downward trend in annual GDP growth, by the end of 2019 the Chinese economy had slowed to its lowest growth rate in 28 years – just *before* the devastating global economic effects of the Covid-19 pandemic were beginning to be realised.

———————

"What's happening to the Chinese economy is pretty obvious, I think, to all people in China," says Anne Stevenson-Yang, the director and co-founder of J Capital Research, a financial research firm specialising in providing institutional investors with primary research on China's macroeconomics. "Investment-driven growth reaches a peak and then doesn't work any more."

Yang is an American citizen who lived in China for over 25 years, working as an industry analyst and trade advocate, heading up the US Information Technology Office and running the China operations of the US-China Business Council between 1993 and 1997. She went on to found J Capital in the US in early 2007. Taking into account China's last decade of decelerating economic growth, despite an increase in government expenditure, Yang says, "You end up spending so much money simply keeping afloat the old investments that you can't actually increase the activity of the economy. But it's actually worse than that. The economy has become so completely dependent on these investment streams that if you take them away you are left with no growth."

Another major concern for many analysts such as Yang is the target-driven nature of China's economic reporting. There is a deeply entrenched culture in communist China of hitting growth targets, which pervades the economy at every level, from the largest state-owned enterprises and banks to much smaller government-funded operations. Leaders in these organisations are compelled by the state to meet growth targets year-on-year, motivated by the fear of punitive action by the CCP. Indeed, the worth of every state-owned enterprise and government organisation in China is measured by the extent to which it contributes to GDP – and it is these vast and sprawling state-owned enterprises that directly constitute more than 40% of China's GDP. That's not to forget the tens of thousands of companies and many millions of employees that are in turn reliant on business from these organisations.

"Every man, woman and child in China is trying to make sure that the Chinese economy rises in value, that prices rise, and that assets stay high and rise, and that there is enough stimulus to create growth," says Yang. "That is the maniacal focus of basically every human being in China right now. Not on value, not on creating something new, but on making sure asset prices stay high." This single-minded obsession with growth is an apt example of what has become known as Goodhart's law.

In a 1975 article, British economist Charles Goodhart noted, "Any observed statistical regularity will tend to collapse once pressure is placed upon it for control purposes." This idea was further refined and broadened beyond economics and statistics by anthropologist Marilyn Strathern, who generalised the concept in the succinct and powerful phrase, "When a measure becomes a target, it ceases to be a good measure." This appears to be exactly the case in China's all-consuming focus on driving up GDP growth.

To meet these often-unrealistic growth targets – and for citizens to continue to buy goods and services that are becoming more expensive within China, even as they remain inexpensive outside the country – companies and individuals have taken on enormous debt, as evidenced by the massive increase in banking assets in China in the past decade, as well as the pronounced increase in household and corporate debt. The inevitable result of this will be a continual deceleration of the Chinese economy until a major correction or crunch occurs, revealing the weakness that underlies what has been the constant government funding of massive state-backed projects and state-owned enterprises.

9

DERIVATIVES AND DEREGULATION

The power the CCP holds over China's banking system, and the government's current use of the banking system to further specific ideological goals, are sharply reminiscent of the political interference that occurred in the American financial system during the 1990s. One of the most prominent channels through which this occurred was the President's Working Group on Financial Markets.

On the 19th of October 1987, some of the largest markets in the world collapsed. The crash was both unexpected and severe, with the S&P 500 losing over a fifth of its value in a single day of trading, and the Dow Jones Industrial Average dropping by 22.6% in what was at the time the largest one-day stock market decline in history. In the wake of what became known as the Black Monday crash, President Ronald Reagan established the President's Working Group on Financial Markets, comprising an elite collection of high-ranking government officials and market experts.

The express purpose of the President's Group was to investigate the causes of the dramatic decline in the markets and to recommend ways in which the government, under its presiding laws and regulations, could prevent a similar market crash in the future. Reagan was a staunch believer in the power of the free market and minimal government intervention, so it was somewhat ironic that the Group's scope and mandate steadily expanded over the years. In the decade following its inception, it gained significant power and influence, stepping in to intervene directly at key moments to stabilise markets at times of extreme volatility.

By the mid-1990s, the President's Group – or the "Plunge Protection Team" as *The Washington Post* later dubbed it – consisted of around twenty members, the most important of whom were arguably Arthur Levitt, the chairman of the Securities and Exchange Commission; Alan Greenspan, the chairman of the Federal Reserve; Robert Rubin, the secretary of the Treasury between 1995 and 1999; and later Lawrence "Larry" Summers, who succeeded Rubin in 1999 until 2001. Some way behind these powerful individuals in terms of clout was the chair of the Commodity Futures Trading Commission (CFTC), Brooksley Born.

"I was told about Brooksley Born," said Levitt in an interview with PBS's *Frontline* in 2009. "I was told that she was irascible, difficult, stubborn, unreasonable." The *Frontline* interviewer was questioning Levitt about his relationships with each of the other members of the President's Group, and though Levitt followed this statement with a more complimentary account of Born, his opening line was telling. Born was appointed to the position of chair of the CFTC by Bill Clinton in 1994 and officially took up office in 1996. She was an obvious candidate for the position, being one of the foremost experts in financial law in the US at the time. Laws and regulations concerning complex financial instruments were her speciality – particularly those governing the trade of derivatives.

Upon taking up her new position, Born immediately set out to tackle an issue related to a controversial incident concerning complex derivatives contracts. It was a case between multinational Procter & Gamble (P&G) and investment bank Bankers Trust, and she believed it should be a significant turning point in the regulation of the derivatives market in America and, indeed, across the globe.

At the centre of the case in question were two complex interest rate swaps. The first, agreed in November 1993, involved a principal amount of $200 million and a five-year swap. According to the agreement, for the first six months of the trade, P&G would pay a floating rate on the principal amount that was 75 basis points below commercial paper rates. From May 1994, for the remaining four and a half years of the deal, the company would pay a floating rate determined by a complex formula developed by Bankers Trust, which was based on five-year and thirty-year Treasury rates. In the best-case scenario, if interest rates remained low and within a fairly narrow range, P&G would save a total of $1.5 million annually on its interest bill. Assured that it was unlikely that interest rates would change substantially, P&G entered into a second highly leveraged interest rate swap contract with Bankers Trust in February 1994. With a principal amount of $93 million and a term of four and three-quarter years, in the best-case scenario the swap would yield a total saving of $940,000 for P&G. Just two weeks later, however, the company found itself in serious trouble when interest rates began to rise significantly.

In the subsequent court case, P&G argued that Bankers Trust had purposely distorted key aspects of the deals to encourage the firm to take a high-risk position, which it had been misled to believe was relatively safe. Specifically, P&G asserted that a lock-in provision had been agreed with Bankers Trust, which allowed the multinational to lock in the interest rate on which payments would be based at any time within six months of making the first deal, to protect it from an unexpected rise in interest rates and to limit its losses. When interest rates started climbing in March 1994 – just four months after the initial deal was made – P&G saw it as the ideal moment to exercise the lock-in provision. But it claimed that it was cautioned against doing so by Bankers Trust, which argued at the time that this would be a costly move. Owing to the highly leveraged nature of the swaps, if P&G exercised the lock-in it would lose far more money than it had initially expected – $157 million to be exact – as it would be paying an interest rate that was more than 14% above the commercial paper rate. P&G would be better off waiting and seeing if interest rates fell within the next two months, Bankers Trust advised, and use the lock-in then.

Interest rates continued to rise in the following weeks. With no reprieve in sight by April 1994, P&G decided to exercise the lock-in, which resulted in the firm having to pay an interest rate that was 16.4% above the commercial paper rate. P&G refused, and instead filed a lawsuit against Bankers Trust, claiming that the latter had purposely obfuscated the degree of risk associated with the trades and encouraged a false sense of safety with the lock-in clauses. Bankers Trust filed a counter-suit, demanding that the money be paid, and arguing that P&G's misfortune had merely been the result of unpredictable and uncontrollable market forces. Bankers Trust maintained that all its dealings had been "legal, proper and appropriate", and insisted that P&G had understood all the risks of the deal before agreeing to it. And, as many commentators pointed out, surely the end-users of derivatives should be responsible for the products they willingly buy.

The US District Court judge overseeing the case, Judge John Feikens, appeared to agree with this and ruled against P&G on several points, highlighting the fact that because the trades in question were derivatives and not more highly regulated securities, Bankers Trust did not have a fiduciary obligation to protect P&G's interests. Despite this, and somewhat surprisingly at the time, Bankers Trust decided to settle the case before Judge Feikens could make his final ruling, with P&G only paying $35 million of their losses. Although Bankers Trust had just about won the case, there was, it turns out, one piece of evidence it seemingly wanted to suppress, even if it meant forgoing more than $100 million owed by P&G.

This evidence came in the form of recorded phone calls originating from within the company – the result of the common practice of recording the details of trades in case of later disputes. On some of these recordings, leaked to *Business Week* in 1995, Bankers Trust traders could be heard boasting about how much profit they were making off the trades with P&G and laughing about how little their client seemed to understand the degree of risk that it had willingly opened itself up to. "They would never know. They would never be able to know how much money was taken out of that," said one Bankers Trust employee, referring to the profits earned by the bank in the deals that had proved so catastrophic for P&G. "That's the beauty of Bankers Trust."

By 1996, having analysed the case between Bankers Trust and P&G, and becoming ever more concerned about the lack of transparency in America's rapidly expanding over-the-counter (OTC) derivatives market in general, Brooksley Born and her team at the CFTC initiated investigations into the regulations governing the derivatives market at the time. This was the first step in a larger process that would lead to the proposal of new regulations to supplement the existing ones created by the Federal Reserve System, the Options Clearing Corporation and the National Association of Insurance Commissioners, for example. Specifically, the CFTC's research culminated in a "concept release", which determined "how best to maintain adequate regulatory safeguards without impairing the ability of the OTC derivatives market to grow and the ability of US entities to remain competitive in the global financial marketplace".

Born was particularly concerned about the regulations that governed the handling of swaps – transactions between banks, insurers and other entities in which counterparties essentially take opposite views on the future of interest rates by betting against each other in an interest rate swap contract. In these contracts, banks often take on interest rate risk on behalf of their counterparty, who would be offered a fixed rate of interest, "swapping" it for a floating rate of interest. Critically, swaps were almost always conducted between counterparties over-the-counter rather than through formal exchanges, where transactions are by law recorded and reported to regulators. This made swaps notoriously opaque, with little to no information being provided to any third parties, including regulators, regarding the nature of these transactions or the legal entities that were the ultimate beneficiaries of swap contracts.

The OTC derivatives market was essentially a black box, and this complete lack of transparency was what most concerned Born, as only those entities taking part in the transactions had any knowledge of the terms of the deals and, most importantly, the risks accompanying them. Given that these were often multi-billion-dollar transactions, and that by the end of 1998 the OTC derivatives market had a gross market value of over $3.2 trillion and a nominal face value of about $80 trillion, they were risks not merely to the parties involved in the transaction, but to the financial system as a whole.

———

When Brooksley Born first met Alan Greenspan in 1996 to discuss her plans regarding the regulation of the OTC derivatives market, she had only recently been named head of the CFTC, then a relatively small and obscure institution. Greenspan, on the other hand, had been a senior Washington official for decades, first as co-ordinator on domestic policy under Richard Nixon in 1968, then as chairman of the Council of Economic Advisers under Gerald Ford from 1974 to 1977, and thereafter as chairman of the Federal Reserve under various presidents since 1987, when he took over the reins from Paul Volcker. Before his long and illustrious career in Washington began, Greenspan had made his fortune on Wall Street, where he was, among other things, chairman and president of Townsend-Greenspan & Co, an economics consulting firm in New York. Simply put, Greenspan was a celebrity in the world of finance at the time. And his reputation had been bolstered by the relentless economic growth and financial success throughout America, and especially on Wall Street, in the 1990s, thanks in no small part to his easy money policies.

It was no secret that Greenspan was a champion of free-market economics and a fervent believer in the Objectivist economic philosophy of Ayn Rand. Indeed, Greenspan was a member of Rand's inner circle, known as the Ayn Rand Collective, having read *Atlas Shrugged*, her magnum opus, while it was still being written in the 1950s, and contributing several essays to her book *Capitalism: The Unknown Ideal*, published in 1966. Rand's Objectivism adopted an oppositional stance to government regulation for the purpose of protecting the average citizen. "America's abundance was not created by public sacrifices to 'the common good', but by the productive genius of free men who pursued their own personal interests and the making of their own private fortunes," she wrote. "They did not starve the people to pay for America's industrialisation. They gave the people better jobs, higher wages, and cheaper goods with every new machine they invented, with every scientific discovery or technological advance – and thus the whole country was moving forward and profiting, not suffering, every step of the way." Rand's philosophy championed a purist form of capitalism based on an unfettered laissez-faire economic system in which, she argued, if the state allowed individuals to excel without hinderances and restraints imposed by the government, they would ultimately pull the rest of their countrymen and women up with them.

From the start, Born would have been aware that her view on government regulation of financial markets was in direct opposition to that of Greenspan's. What she perhaps did not know, however, was just how far the Fed chair would go to impose his own beliefs on the system. By early 1998, Born's team was preparing to publish a report on its findings on the current state of regulation in the derivatives market. Before even coming close to releasing the document to stakeholders, it encountered strong opposition from senior government officials in Washington, including Greenspan, Summers and Rubin. It is worth remembering that this was the late 1990s – the heyday of capitalism. The dotcom bubble was rapidly inflating and some newly listed internet companies were experiencing their valuation double almost on a weekly basis. The markets were a runaway train, powered by speculation, low interest rates and favourable financial regulations. What Born was attempting to do, in a metaphorical sense, was to step in front of this train and slow it down – and there seemed no way to do so without getting seriously hurt.

The first phone call to Born regarding the CFTC's concept release came from Summers, who reportedly warned her that if she continued to pursue regulatory changes to the OTC derivatives market, important people in Washington would turn their back on her, especially those in the Federal Reserve and Treasury. Instead of frightening Born off, however, Summers's strong reaction to her investigation sparked intrigue. "What was it that was in this market that had to be hidden?" Born asked reporters in 2009, years after the fact when she was provided an opportunity to publicly recount her version of events. America was only just beginning to emerge from the Global Financial Crisis and Born's story was the subject of great public interest as those critical of the financial sector reflected on the failure of policy-makers to rein in the OTC derivatives market almost a decade before. "Why did it have to be a completely dark market?" she asked. "It made me very suspicious and troubled."

Legally, the CFTC was independent from any other agency, including Treasury and the Federal Reserve, reporting directly, and only, to the president. This was something of a problem for Greenspan, Summers and Rubin, who wanted to put an immediate stop to Born's crusade. But they knew there was another way they could derail her plans – through the President's Working Group. Not only were all three men part of the Group, but Rubin steered the committee at the time. They also had another important ally in Arthur Levitt. When Born circulated a draft of the concept release for review by various stakeholders before publication, Rubin therefore called an emergency meeting of the Group to address the release and to convince Born to take the matter no further. According to Michael Greenberger, director of the Division of Trading and Markets at the CFTC at the time and a member of the Group, Greenspan was furious during the meeting. He warned Born in no uncertain terms that what she was about to do would be a grave mistake. If she were to implement these regulations in the OTC derivatives market, he said, the entire financial system could potentially be destabilised. Rubin, Summers and Levitt rallied behind Greenspan, and by the end of the meeting Born, outnumbered and caught off-guard, appeared to have been silenced. Just two weeks later, however, the concept release was published.

The response by the President's Group was swift and decisive. On the day of the report's publication, a joint statement by Greenspan, Rubin and Levitt was published, under the authority of the Department of the Treasury, declaring that the proposed regulatory changes would be detrimental to the stability of financial markets. "We have grave concerns about this action and its possible consequences," the statement read. "The OTC derivatives market is a large and important global market. We seriously question the scope of the CFTC's jurisdiction in this area, and we are very concerned about reports that the CFTC's action may increase the legal uncertainty concerning certain types of OTC derivatives." Owing to the independence of the CFTC, however, the only way the President's Group could stop Born was by convincing Congress to block her regulatory proposals.

In the months that followed, Born appeared four times before Congress to plead her case, in front of the House and the Senate. "The size and nature of this market create a potential for systemic risk to the nation's financial markets that requires vigilance by federal regulatory authorities," she stated. When asked directly by congressional members what her agency was trying to protect against by implementing these regulations, she replied, "We are trying to protect the money of the American public, which is at risk in these markets." But Born's passionate plea seemed to fall on deaf ears.

As was evidenced in the various congressional hearings, many congressmen and congresswomen simply did not see the need, or perhaps did not understand the necessity, for regulation in an industry that had in the last decade been so successful. With the economy booming and the stock market growing at an incredible rate, it seemed almost counterintuitive to begin tampering with what was apparently a winning formula. This view was only reinforced by the statements made by Greenspan, Rubin and Levitt, which argued that the new regulations Born was proposing would create great uncertainty in the market, that the motivations for new regulations were largely unfounded as there was little to no evidence of fraud or unethical behaviour among participants in the OTC market, and that the CFTC was acting beyond its mandate. "Regulation of derivatives transactions that are privately negotiated by professionals is unnecessary," stated Greenspan during one hearing, "Regulation that serves no useful purpose hinders the efficiency of markets to enlarge standards of living." Summers concurred, stating that "the parties to these kinds of contracts are largely sophisticated financial institutions that would appear to be eminently capable of protecting themselves from fraud and counterparty insolvencies."

One politician who openly opposed Born's proposed regulations was Republican senator Phil Gramm. "I see no evidence whatsoever to suggest that this is a troubled market," he stated during a Senate meeting. "It also seems important to me that we recognise that we set up a Working Group following the 1987 market decline, and I think that is the proper venue to work in this area and to make recommendations to the [sic] Congress. I feel very strongly that we should not have one agency innovate in this area and create some real or supposed jurisdictional dispute or jurisdictional expansion and, in doing so, create very substantial financial problems." This was the same senator who would a year later become the co-sponsor of the industry-shaping Gramm-Leach-Bliley Act, a critical piece of legislation that accelerated the general trend of financial deregulation by essentially allowing the previously separated activities of investment banking and commercial banking to be rejoined.

Gramm's opinion was echoed by many other politicians. With Congress due to go into the summer recess for the month of August, it seemed unlikely that a decision on Born's legislation would be made anytime soon. But then, less than three weeks after Born's last congressional hearing in late July, and in the middle of the recess, trouble hit thousands of miles away, in Moscow. On the 17th of August 1998, Russia devalued its currency, defaulted on its domestic debt, and declared a moratorium on repayment of its foreign debt. The Russian default immediately and radically impacted global financial markets – especially the derivatives market, a fact that could not be ignored thanks to the near-failure of Long Term Capital Management.

————————

From 1994 until 1998, Long Term Capital Management (LTCM) was undoubtedly the most exciting hedge fund in the world. In less than three years, LTCM amassed over $100 billion in assets under management, with annual returns of 40%. It was founded by former Salomon Brothers trader John Meriwether, and its board of directors included the former vice-chairman of the Board of Governors of the US Federal Reserve, David Mullins, and famed economists Myron Scholes and Robert Merton – the originators, alongside Fischer Black, of the Black-Scholes-Merton model for pricing options, and winners of the Nobel Prize in Economics in 1997. Investors clamoured to get into the fund, certain that the pedigree of its management would make it impervious to failure.

LTCM, in a sense, embodied the unfettered capitalist ideology that dominated America during the 1990s. The firm employed the brightest minds in finance and deployed the most cutting-edge technology, combining this with extremely complex mathematical models, sanctified by Nobel Prize-winners, to make millions of dollars in the financial markets for already very wealthy clients. LTCM was also essentially operating in a legal grey area, dealing primarily in complex securities that were notoriously under-regulated, including billions of dollars in exposures to completely opaque OTC derivatives deals.

Specifically, LTCM specialised in fixed-income arbitrage, a strategy pioneered by Meriwether. This exploits the pricing differences in fixed-income securities, such as bonds, and is executed by buying a security in one market for immediate resale at a higher price in another market. In hedge fund management, the strategy usually involves identifying a pair of similar securities, where one security is priced below what is perceived by the market to be the normal price and the other is priced above it. The under-priced security is purchased by the trader while the over-priced security is sold short. When the prices revert to the perceived normal price, the trade is liquidated for a profit. Opportunities for executing this trading strategy are difficult to detect and must usually be acted on immediately. To facilitate this, great interest began to emerge in the development of complex mathematical models capable of predicting market prices and identifying outliers.

Leading the way in model development was LTCM's dream team of financial experts. The firm was notoriously secretive about its strategies and the quantitative models that were driving them, and it scattered trades between banks to prevent any one of them gaining enough information to track its movements.

On the back of its early successes, LTCM began to expand its scope, venturing further into the complex realm of fixed-income arbitrage across several different jurisdictions and currencies, with significant exposure to emerging markets. LTCM's investment strategy was based on detecting and exploiting opportunities in markets that were often overlooked by others – but these were generally small and required large-sized investments to make a profit. The firm therefore became increasingly leveraged. At the beginning of 1998, it held $129 billion in assets with an equity figure of $4.72 billion – a leverage ratio of 27:1. Almost a decade later, Lehman Brothers would have a similar ratio when it failed, heralding the Global Financial Crisis.

The first signs of trouble for LTCM came in July 1997, when Thailand defaulted on its foreign debt and the Thai baht collapsed, causing a domino effect across the economies of East Asia. International stocks plummeted as volatility in the US market began to increase and investors turned to Treasury bonds for security. Then came the Russian default in August the following year. By the end of the month, the Dow Jones Industrial Average had dropped by 13% and the flight to Treasury bonds escalated, causing long-term interest rates to fall. LTCM lost $553 million in one day. Within a month it was down almost $2 billion.

For many, the sudden end of LTCM's winning streak came as a shock. But despite its early successes, there were some who had always been critical about the degree to which LTCM's strategy was reliant on the idea of completely rational markets. The firm's approach assumed a predictable level of volatility in bonds – but the reality is that bond prices had displayed unpredictable volatility in the past decade and that changes in prices are also

THE END OF MONEY

driven by behavioural factors. The devaluation of the rouble and Russia's subsequent default were beyond the limits of what LTCM had assumed possible. Indeed, many considered this something of a one-off event, portraying LTCM as a victim of highly unusual movements in the market that nobody could have predicted. But there was also fault to be found in the firm's overall business approach, which relied almost exclusively on mathematical models and which did not take sufficient cognisance of extreme historical scenarios. This would have shown that the impact of the Russian default on bond yields and arbitrage spreads was not unprecedented, as similar movements had occurred several times since the US's departure from the Gold Standard in 1971. An objective view of Russia's political and economic circumstances – including factors such as its high debt levels and widening bond spreads, the pegging of its currency to the US dollar, and declining global oil prices – should have alerted market participants to the risk of a default, which had been mounting for three years.

LTCM's losses were compounded by a further failure of its models: they did not take into account the fact that these events were not independent of one another, which had the effect of magnifying risk, rather than diversifying it. Believing that the Russian default would not occur, and that market volatility would decline during the year, LTCM had made bold moves in the early part of 1998. By later that year, the firm was in significant trouble – it had lost $4.8 billion and held $400 million in equity with assets totalling about $100 billion, now implying a leverage ratio of roughly 250:1. Banks began to worry that if LTCM were to default, all fifty of its counterparties would also find themselves in a dire position. If LTCM fell, the knock-on effect could bring down the global financial system. The fund was essentially too big to fail – and, thus, the US Federal Reserve, under Greenspan's guidance, brokered a deal with some of the largest Wall Street banks, including Bear Stearns, JPMorgan, Lehman Brothers, Merrill Lynch, Morgan Stanley and Goldman Sachs, to save LTCM with a $3.65 billion bailout.

The near-failure of LTCM highlighted just how fragile and interconnected the financial markets were at the time – to such a degree that failure in one institution could mean failure for many. It also revealed just how dangerous and opaque the OTC derivatives market had become. This was demonstrated by the fact that of the $4.8 billion that LTCM lost by late 1998, the largest portion of this loss, some $1.6 billion, was related to swaps – the very instrument Brooksley Born was most concerned about regulating. In the build-up to LTCM's failure, no regulatory authorities had any idea of the level of risk that the firm was taking on, nor did they know that the firm was putting at risk the stability of many other counterparties and perhaps even the entire financial system in the process – because LTCM had no legal obligation to share its financial transaction and counterparty information with third parties.

After LTCM's collapse, sentiment around the regulation of financial markets began to change, though Greenspan showed no sign of giving up the fight to keep the markets deregulated. "How many more failures do you think we'd have to have before some

regulation in this area might be appropriate?" US representative
Maurice Hinchey asked Greenspan in a congressional hearing in
October 1998, referring to the failure of LTCM. Greenspan was
defiant in reply: "I know of no set of supervisory actions we can
take that will prevent people from making dumb mistakes." True
to his beliefs, Greenspan made the argument to Congress that
the failure of LTCM was an anomaly and not an indication of the
market as a whole. Following the hearing, not only did Congress
vote not to impose any new regulations on the OTC derivatives
market but, under pressure from the powerful chairman of the
Federal Reserve, who was supported by the force of the financial
lobby behind him, Congress passed legislation that actively
prohibited the CFTC from regulating the derivatives market in
any shape or form. Not long after this ruling, in January 1999,
Born wrote to President Clinton saying that she would not seek
another term as chairperson of the CFTC and that she would be
returning to private practice as a lawyer.

In the two years that immediately followed her resignation,
there was significant further deregulation of financial markets
under the Clinton administration, most notably through
the passing of the Gramm-Leach-Bliley Act in 1999, which
effectively repealed the Glass-Steagall Act of 1933. As previously
mentioned, the Glass-Steagall Act was passed in the wake of the
Wall Street Crash of 1929 and the subsequent Great Depression.
During this period, Congress had grown increasingly concerned
about the degree to which commercial banking operations had
become vulnerable to losses from volatile equity markets, and
therefore sought to insulate commercial banks from the much
riskier activities of investment banks. The former simply took
deposits and made loans, while the latter were involved in

security sales and trading. Together, US Senator Carter Glass and fellow Democrat Henry Steagall sponsored a piece of legislation that advocated the separation of commercial and investment banking to protect depositors from these riskier activities. The provisions covered by their Act – which was signed into law by President Franklin D Roosevelt as part of the Banking Act of 1933 – prohibited investment banks from taking deposits and prevented commercial banks from dealing in non-government securities for customers. Crucially, it also counteracted the conflicts of interest that arose when banks used deposits to underwrite securities and then sell them to their own customers. It had been this very activity – in which banks provided leverage to their customers – that had led to the stock market bubble and the Crash of 1929.

The Glass-Steagall Act essentially insulated commercial banks from the risks associated with financial speculation to guard against their collapse. There was, however, a downside to this strict regulation. By the 1970s, banks had begun to object strongly to the Act on the grounds that it was making them uncompetitive in international markets. If commercial banks could also participate in investment banking activities, they argued, they could improve the return for their shareholders while reducing risk by diversifying their products. By having the freedom to involve themselves in both investment banking and commercial banking activities, banks could ensure that their businesses remained intact during both good and bad economic periods. It was the most idealistic argument that could be expected of free-market thinking, and it quickly gained traction.

During the 1980s and '90s, banks increasingly started to look for loopholes in the Glass-Steagall Act that would allow them to once again bring together commercial and investment banking. They were aided in this endeavour by the Federal Reserve's strong desire to expand banking powers, leading it to favour broad interpretations of the Act. In 1999, the Gramm-Leach-Bliley Act (GLBA) was approved by Senate and subsequently signed into law by Bill Clinton. Named after its sponsors, Senator Phil Gramm and Representatives Jim Leach and Thomas Bliley, the GLBA removed the market barriers that the Glass-Steagall Act had instituted, effectively rejoining investment banking and commercial banking activities.

Spearheading the implementation of the GLBA was the renowned economist and then secretary of the Treasury Larry Summers, who claimed that the Act showed that the US was ready to move on from outdated laws and embrace "a system for the 21st century". Summers was also central in driving the Commodity Futures Modernization Act, passed in 2000, which effectively deregulated the OTC derivatives market, while simultaneously ensuring that OTC contracts themselves were legally enforceable. In other words, the Act ensured investment banks had access to the legal apparatus associated with trading through a formal exchange – most notably by ensuring their protection in the case of defaulting counterparties – while also maintaining the opacity of OTC derivatives trading. Essentially, investment banks were able to have their cake and eat it. By the early 2000s, they had manoeuvred themselves into a position where they were free to go about their business unchecked, with the full backing of the law should their counterparties fail to uphold their side of the deal.

For many people, the passing of the GLBA was nothing more than a formality, given that by the late 1990s commercial banks were already increasingly engaging in activities associated with investment banking. As one infamous example, Lehman Brothers was raising deposits by selling what became known as "Lehman Minibonds" through commercial banks in other parts of the world, such as Hong Kong. These banks were selling the minibonds to customers, many of them retired, who had little to no understanding of the risks involved, and who lost everything when Lehman failed in 2008. The Hong Kong Monetary Authority subsequently ordered its local banks to repay 60% of the principal amount invested to customers under the age of 65, and 70% to those over 65.

For people like Brooksley Born, the passing of the GLBA was a watershed moment in which the government had failed to safeguard the economy and the financial system. Those who saw the threat warned that the deregulation of the financial system would produce the same conflicts of interest that had caused the Wall Street Crash of 1929 and precipitated the Great Depression. As quoted in *The New York Times*, Senator Byron L Dorgan was particularly prescient. "I think we will look back in 10 years' time and say we should not have done this, but we did because we forgot the lessons of the past and that that which is true in the 1930s is true in 2010," he said. The prescience of his words would prove uncanny, given that history would soon repeat itself, first in the stock market crash of 2000 and then, far more severely, in the 2007/2008 Global Financial Crisis. For advocates of stricter regulation in the financial system, there was no better proof of the need for some form of state intervention and a regulatory apparatus that would govern the rules that represent the boundaries of the free market, ensuring that it operated in a manner that was both fairer and more stable.

―――――――

Most people over the age of 30 can recall what they were doing on the 11th of September 2001, when their otherwise normal Tuesday was interrupted as they were drawn to a nearby television to watch in disbelief the footage of two hijacked aeroplanes – one a United Airlines flight and the other an American Airlines carrier – crashing into the Twin Towers of the World Trade Center in New York. Within two hours, both the North and South towers had collapsed. Still reeling, the world was informed that a third plane had crashed into the Pentagon, and a fourth into a field in Pennsylvania. Nearly 3,000 people were killed on the day, and a further 6,000 injured.

The 9/11 attacks remain one of the most shocking events in modern history – in mere moments, the entire population of the world's most powerful country had been reduced to a state of panic, fear and confusion, seemingly without warning. Research conducted in the following years would reveal, however, that this should never have been the case. In 2004, the US National Commission on Terrorist Attacks upon the United States, better known as the 9/11 Commission, released a report detailing how in the years leading up to the events of that day, several studies conducted by government commissions and private think-tanks had indicated the growing threat of terrorism to America and urged government intelligence agencies to strengthen their capabilities in the detection and prevention of terrorist activities. In particular, the Commission highlighted repeated recommendations that the issue of poor co-ordination between America's various intelligence agencies – of which there were seventeen – be urgently addressed to improve the sharing of critical information that would enable the country to pre-empt any attacks. These recommendations had largely gone unheeded, with one study concluding just nine months before 9/11 that America's institutional weaknesses had rendered it highly vulnerable to a terrorist attack.

In her 2009 book *Spying Blind: The CIA, the FBI, and the Origins of 9/11*, Amy Zegart, a director at the Center for International Security and Cooperation at Stanford University, reveals the extent of the dysfunctionality of the system. She notes at least 23 separate occasions on which the CIA and FBI could have intervened directly to prevent the 9/11 attacks, if only the two agencies had shared the information they had independently been gathering. The CIA knew, for example, that two of the hijackers had been in the US long before the attacks took place, using their real names on official documents such as passports and in the telephone directory. It had also identified several of these individuals' contacts – many of whom, unbeknown to the CIA, were the targets of past and ongoing FBI counterterrorism investigations. Unfortunately, the information gathered by the two agencies remained isolated within their relative departments, and it was only after the fact that the agencies realised their combined intelligence would have been enough to raise the alarm about the impending attacks.

Crucially, the hijackers had also used their real names to open US bank accounts, into which funds were transferred from facilitators in Germany and the United Arab Emirates, as well as from Khalid Sheikh Mohammed, "the principal architect of the 9/11 attacks", according to the 9/11 Commission's report. In total, it is estimated that the attacks cost Al-Qaeda roughly

$500,000, $300,000 of which passed directly through the hijackers' bank accounts, to pay for flight training and living expenses in America. "Neither the hijackers nor their financial facilitators were experts in the use of the international financial system," the Commission explicitly states in its report. "They created a paper trail linking them to each other and their facilitators. Still, they were easily adept enough to blend into the vast international financial system without doing anything to reveal themselves as criminals, let alone terrorists bent on mass murder."

The reason for this was because banks were not required at this time to monitor and report on suspicious transactions in a manner that would have connected the financial activities of the hijackers to the intelligence that had been gathered by the CIA. If they had, they might have also noticed, in the days before the 9/11 attacks, that trading in derivatives on both United Airlines and American Airlines stock had been unusually erratic, with the put-to-call ratio for American Airlines reaching 6:1 and for United Airlines reaching 25:1. Ordinarily, this ratio should be about 1:1. Although in the Commission's 2004 report this was deemed not to be the result of insider trading, subsequent research conducted after the release of the report by several independent academics and financial experts suggests that it is possible that the purchase of put options in the airlines' stocks was consistent with informed investors having prior knowledge of the attack, and having traded their positions before the attack.

Achieving a definitive conclusion on the issue is complicated significantly by the fact that these transactions were often performed through shell companies based in offshore domiciles, which ensured that those who benefited from them were hidden behind an opaque screen that protected their anonymity and concealed their involvement in the financing of terrorism. It was exactly this lack of transparency that had concerned Brooksley Born and prompted her efforts to regulate the OTC derivatives market just a few years before the attacks took place.

Tragically, it was only after 9/11 that the danger of deregulating the derivatives market was acknowledged by policy-makers, and it was a danger that extended far beyond simply threatening the stability of the financial system. The physical safety of society as a whole had been jeopardised and the risk of allowing the market to remain opaque had become authentically personal. This was demonstrated in the case of financial services firm Cantor Fitzgerald, which was situated on the 101st to 105th floors of the North Tower of the World Trade Center. Every person who reported for work on the day of the attacks perished – a total of 658 of 960 employees. It is not unreasonable to point out that a solid line can be drawn directly from derivatives market deregulation to intermittent violent attacks on Western civilisation and the loss of lives.

In the wake of 9/11, it began to dawn on policy-makers that if stricter market conduct regulations were in place, the financial system could become a powerful extension of the state security apparatus, performing a pivotal function in monitoring illegal and terrorist activities. This realisation ushered in a new era of banking, in which the responsibilities of financial institutions have been significantly extended through, for example, anti-money laundering (AML) and combating the financing of terrorism (CFT) regulations. Through these regulations, banks have now been made responsible for investigating the origins of the funds that are transferred through their systems and for flagging suspicious transactions, providing critical information to intelligence agencies in support of larger state efforts to detect and prevent criminal and terrorist activities.

While there may be arguments that can be made against the imposition of market conduct regulations on banks as private enterprises, these arguments are superseded by the fact that a particularly effective way to rein in terrorism and to slow down organised crime is to make the financial intermediation process that supports these activities more difficult. To achieve this, either private enterprise must be required to co-operate with the state to identify transactions that may be connected to money laundering and terrorism financing, as is generally the case in the West, or all financial intermediation must be directly overseen by the state, as is the case in China. Without financial institutions performing this crucial function there is a significant risk of greater amplification of criminal and terrorist activities around the world.

Since 9/11, there have been a number of terrorist attacks in Western cities, including the 2004 Madrid train bombings, the 2005 London bombings, the 2015 Paris attacks, the 2016 Nice truck attack and the Orlando nightclub shooting in the same year. Collectively, more than 500 people were killed in these attacks, but had banks and other financial institutions not been co-opted to continuously monitor transactions and report suspicious activities, this horror may potentially have been far worse. In countries such as Afghanistan, Iraq, Nigeria, Syria and Somalia, by contrast, terrorists kill thousands of people every year, according to the Global Terrorism Index. It is precisely because of the clear benefits to society of AML and CFT regulations that the growing anti-establishment ethos among the general public, which actively seeks to operate outside the bounds of the formal financial system, is of notable concern. This is most obviously manifest in the rise of cryptocurrencies – a subject to return to.

In sum, the distrust of Western culture in its own institutions and its underestimation of the importance of the formal banking system has now morphed into an active, broad and persistent notion that the system itself, not only its bad actors, should be discarded and replaced.

10

CHINA'S MINSKY MOMENT

In May 2020, as the Covid-19 pandemic swept the world, S&P Global Market Intelligence reported that China's mid-sized, locally focused lenders were experiencing a growing risk of bank failure due to an accelerating increase in borrowers not repaying their loan instalments in a timely manner. In its analysis, S&P found that city commercial banks had experienced the sharpest uptick in non-payment in the first few months of 2020 and that large rural banks on average had the highest rate of officially reported non-performing loans, at over 4%. This research suggests that even officially reported non-performing loan (NPL) numbers in China are steadily rising across all levels of the banking system. And if asset quality continues to deteriorate, "rural banks would face pressure to book higher provisions, which would weigh on profits, as well as capital levels".

Six months after the release of the S&P report, Baoshang Bank, a regional commercial bank based in the Chinese autonomous region of Inner Mongolia, filed for bankruptcy and began the process of liquidating its assets. This marked the first time in twenty years that the Chinese government had allowed a bank on the mainland to collapse entirely, resulting in shareholders' and unprotected creditors' rights being liquidated. A year and a half earlier, in May 2019, the national financial regulator had taken control of Baoshang Bank, citing "severe credit risk" as its reasoning. This was largely brought on by gross misappropriation by the bank's controlling stakeholder, Tomorrow Holdings. Upon taking over Baoshang Bank, the central bank stated that the majority shareholder had chipped away at the risk controls and corporate governance to such an extent that Tomorrow Holdings was able to extract loans from the bank at will, with little consideration given to commercial viability. Between 2005 and 2019, the bank had extended 347 loans to 209 shell companies related to Tomorrow Holdings, totalling over $22 billion – all of which became delinquent.

In the wake of Baoshang Bank's collapse, Reuters reported that the shock government-led takeover of the regional commercial bank had "revived concerns about the health of hundreds of small lenders as the slowing economy results in more sour loans, testing their capital buffers and draining their reserves". In the week following the local lender's collapse – before excess liquidity was provided by government authorities – the Chinese banking system experienced a sharp liquidity squeeze. Alarmed by the government's decision to allow a commercial bank to fail for the first time in twenty years, larger banking institutions became unwilling to lend to smaller institutions, fearing that their counterparties had now become a greater credit risk.

Just months before Baoshang Bank's collapse, the government had stepped in to rescue Hong Kong-listed Bank of Gansu, which had suffered a liquidity crisis after one of its majority shareholders was unable to repay its debts. In July 2020, the state announced a plan to raise the stakes of state-backed equity holders in the bank, to replace embattled private shareholders and to inject a considerable, yet undisclosed, amount of liquidity into the bank to keep it afloat. In 2019, the bank, which employs more than four thousand people, reported that its NPL ratio of personal business loans had skyrocketed to 14.1%, from 4.7% the year before. Bank of Gansu also reported publicly that its profits had dropped 85%, from 3.44 billion yuan in 2018 to 509 million yuan in 2019. Upon the release of the reports of the drastic decline in the lender's financials, depositors panicked and rushed to withdraw their funds from the bank's branches.

This response from depositors was not unprecedented, as bank runs in China have increased generally over the last few years. In 2020 alone, there were at least four other cases of bank runs at small and medium-sized banks, including Yangquan Commercial Bank, Bank of Baoding, Bank of Hengshui and Bank of Huludao. In each case, the government stepped in to assure depositors that their money was safe. Individuals who were accused of "causing panic" and "spreading rumours" were arrested.

The potential for runs on Chinese banks is compounded by the country's growing problem of over-indebted households and corporations. This has in recent years drawn the attention of Chinese authorities, prompting a response by the People's Bank of China (PBOC) in its annual financial stability report in 2019. PBOC noted that "the debt risks of the household sector and some low-income households in some regions are relatively prominent", and encouraged banking regulatory authorities to enforce tougher policies to guard against an undue increase in household and corporate debt. In 2019, Fitch Ratings reported that 117 corporate bonds had been defaulted on by Chinese companies – a record number of defaults in one year. The vast majority of defaults, over 80%, were at non-state-owned organisations, mostly in the construction and engineering sectors. Simultaneously, new bond issuance was also at a record high.

To sustain its growing debt, the Chinese economy is obliged to grow, and yet the fundamental assumption of growth cannot be taken for granted. The Federal Reserve of San Francisco, for example, has concluded through its own research that China's official growth has been "implausibly smooth since 2013". Similarly, Capital Economics, an independent economic research firm operating out of London, has observed that the Chinese government's GDP estimates, and subsequent reporting, have been "too perfect" since 2012, with final reports almost never deviating from estimates. Prior to 2012 deviations regularly occurred, both above and below expectations, as was to be expected. Capital Economics also pointed to anomalies in Chinese GDP data that have been a cause for concern. One such anomaly is found in the construction industry. For years, construction's component of GDP moved in tandem with cement production, but from 2014, if charted alongside one another, construction growth has raced ahead of growth in cement production.

It is these kinds of anomalies that make certain economic analysts question the veracity of official GDP figures, though most of them do not openly make the claim that the government is doctoring its statistics. Anne Stevenson-Yang, of J Capital Research, is not one of those analysts. Her scepticism about China's official GDP figures is based on over a decade of research conducted by her firm into Chinese companies and the nation's economy as a whole, as well as her own experiences working in government positions for the US in China. Yang notes that while China was still reporting growth figures of over 6% in late 2019 and early 2020, her company's research indicates that real growth was closer to 2% – though she herself admits it is near-impossible to come to an exact figure concerning China's GDP.

Stevenson-Yang's scepticism has been echoed by others as well, even within China. In 2007, for example, Chinese premier Li Keqiang, at the time party secretary of Liaoning Province, referred to China's GDP figures as "man-made and therefore unreliable". He proposed that more reliable proxies such as electricity consumption and rail cargo volumes should be used as a measure of economic activity. And the need to consider such an alternative was made obvious in 2015 when, after a damning report released by the National Audit Office in China, several local governments admitted that they had artificially inflated their GDP numbers for years. These findings came to light after local governments reported sharp declines in GDP growth in 2015, under closer scrutiny by national auditing bodies. "If the past data had not been inflated," said one unnamed government official to the local Chinese publication *China Daily* in 2015, "the current growth figures would not show such a precipitous fall."

In 2019, the Brookings Institution, a non-profit public policy organisation based in Washington DC, released a

54-page report entitled "A Forensic Examination of China's National Accounts". The authors begin the paper by noting, "China's national accounts are based on data collected by local governments. However, since local governments are rewarded for meeting growth and investment targets, they have an incentive to skew local statistics. China's National Bureau of Statistics adjusts the data provided by local governments to calculate GDP at the national level." Using publicly available data relating to industrial output, construction metrics and value-added tax receipts, as well as several other local economic indicators which they believe are "less likely to be manipulated by local governments", the authors then calculated revised estimates of local and national GDP numbers. The authors concluded that the official GDP growth figures reported by the Chinese government were at least 1.7% higher on average between 2008 and 2016 than their own estimates, and that the officially reported investment and savings rate was at least 7% higher over the same period. This suggests that the Chinese economy may well already be in a far more precarious position than officially recognised.

Greatly exacerbating the GDP issue is the fact that *all* investments contribute to the GDP calculation, and not just productive ones. This is particularly pertinent to China because so much of the investment in the economy is driven by the government. Because of this, local and national governments were, in the past, incentivised to spend lavishly on public development projects, no matter their economic feasibility, as all investment contributes to boosting official GDP figures, even when completely unproductive. In turn, when these GDP targets were met, even if only as a result of wasteful spending on unproductive projects, local governments were rewarded by the national government with more budget the following year.

Post-2017, however, there has been a sea-change in Chinese policy, in which Xi Jinping for the first time demanded growth without excessive lending. At the five-yearly National Financial Work Conference, the Chinese premier stated that deleveraging at state-owned entities is of the utmost importance. This has been a particularly difficult task for local government officials and SOEs to fulfil, accustomed as they are to what was previously an unlimited supply of debt.

China's construction industry is a critical cog in the GDP growth machine, though many analysts have called into question the sustainability and economic viability of China's ceaseless proliferation of mega construction projects – often state-backed. A prominent example of an excessive and unsustainable project is Tianducheng, or "the Sky City", constructed as a replica of Paris near Hangzhou in Zhejiang Province, and opened in 2007. Miles outside the city centre, surrounded by farmland, is an entire imitation city, complete with a 108-metre-tall imitation of the Eiffel Tower, hundreds of apartment blocks in classic Parisian-style architecture, replica Parisian streetlamps, cafes and walkways, and even certain famous landmarks from the French capital, including the Fontaine de l'Observatoire, the Bassin d'Apollon and the Trocadéro. While the replica town was meant to host over 10,000 residents, there were only around 2,000 occupants in Tianducheng by 2013.

Throughout China, there are dozens of replica cities and towns like this, including replicas of Florence, Hallstatt, Portofino, Jackson Hole, Dubai and, of course, Las Vegas – which ironically has its own replica Eiffel Tower, mimicking the replica Eiffel Tower that stands outside the (real) Paris Las Vegas Resort & Casino in downtown Las Vegas. Most of these projects are built using government funding or debt raised by local banks. But this is not where it ends. Beyond these extravagant replica towns and cities are thousands more state-endorsed construction projects that have been completed or are being planned. Many of these may not seem so obviously absurd to the impartial observer as a replica of Paris erected on an obscure piece of rural farmland in a lesser-known Chinese province, yet they are often just as costly and wasteful.

The most ambitious of these projects sometimes take the form of largely uninhabited cities, which have over the years been dubbed "ghost cities" by the Western media. One of the most well-known is the new district of Kangbashi, where a prefecture of Ordos City in Inner Mongolia was erected 25 kilometres from the city's centre in 2003. An ambitious government project, the ultra-modern city within a city includes state-of-the-art architecture, large stadiums and extravagant public spaces adorned with massive statues and monuments celebrating the Mongolian heritage of the region. Appearing as if from nowhere in the middle of the inhospitable Mongolian desert, Ordos Kangbashi is strongly reminiscent of Las Vegas, but on an even larger scale. Built from the ground up, it was designed to attract more than a million residents to its hundreds of new high-rise apartment buildings and lavish public facilities. Once construction was complete, it took more than a decade for

100,000 residents to move into the new district. For more than ten years, apartment buildings stood largely empty, malls were without tenants, the grand soccer stadiums were never filled, the museums had no visitors, and the new library gathered dust.

For a long time, a large proportion of the residents were the construction workers themselves, who lived in the new district as they kept working on more projects to improve the city's appeal. Many real estate investors from across China and abroad bought into the vision of the project and purchased more than 90% of the apartments by the time construction was completed – but very few of the apartments were occupied with residents over the next decade. Rental prices were far too high for those living in the rural surrounds or those already settled in Ordos City just 25 kilometres away. In response, the Chinese government relocated the Ordos City municipality to the new district and forced government officials to take up residence there. The government also closed and demolished several schools in the towns surrounding Kangbashi, effectively leaving parents with no choice but to send their children to school in the new district. Today, a significant proportion of Kangbashi's industry is centred on tourism, as locals and foreigners come from far and wide to view what has become known as the largest ghost city in the world.

Ordos Kangbashi is just one of the dozens of ghost cities and hundreds of failed city-planning projects littered across China. Local governments and businesses of all sizes are compelled to keep building, to keep producing and to keep growing, if for no other reason than to fulfil GDP targets set by the state, irrespective of demand for the products being made or for the buildings being built. This is the weakness of the Chinese command economy: because it is not driven by demand, it results in over-capacity in certain sectors and under-capacity in others. Despite the economic realities that determine demand for companies' products, businesses must simply continue to fulfil their government-mandated quotas, at all costs. If companies cannot sustain themselves financially by selling enough goods or services to cover costs, as is the case with a large proportion of state-owned enterprises, then they must seek external assistance, most often in the form of bank loans from state-owned banks.

Ultimately, struggling, economically unfeasible businesses – dubbed "zombie enterprises" by media outlets such as Reuters – must therefore take on an ever-increasing amount of debt to reach their production targets, but they do so at an ever-decreasing rate of efficiency. The result is that these businesses fall into an inescapable debt trap – a debt trap that has, perhaps ironically, helped to turn China's banking system into the largest in the world.

———

Defying logic to some extent, given the proliferation of ghost cities with minimal occupancy, property prices have skyrocketed in China in the last decade. This is especially true in financial centres such as Shanghai, where demand is so intense that investors are required by developers to enter a lottery to buy a new apartment. As *The Wall Street Journal* suggested in a 2020 article entitled "The $52 Trillion Bubble: China Grapples with Epic Property Boom", the similarities with the US property boom before the Global Financial Crisis are telling. At the peak of the US property boom in the 2000s, approximately $900 billion a year was being invested in residential real estate; in China, in the twelve months before June 2020, roughly 9.66 trillion yuan ($1.4 trillion) was invested in residential real estate. And it seems the impact of the coronavirus pandemic – which resulted in millions of job losses in China and the most severe economic impact on the global financial system since 2008 – has not slowed down the incredible rise in property prices and investment in the property industry. In fact, more funds flowed into residential real estate in June 2020 than in any month prior.

A major force driving this frantic housing investment rush is the fear that the yuan may depreciate in the coming years. This would cause inflation as the nation's economy gradually returns to smaller and smaller quarterly growth figures. As a result, many Chinese families today own more than one home, opting to invest heavily in housing rather than stocks and bonds. This decision is primarily motivated by the belief that the government will not allow asset prices to depreciate, regardless of the health of the broader economy. Research conducted by the Southwestern University of Finance and Economics in Chengdu, China, has estimated that on average 78% of Chinese families' wealth is tied up in residential property, compared to 35% in the US. Additionally, 96% of urban Chinese households owned at least one property in 2019, compared to only 65% of urban American households. Owing to this massive surge in property investment, residential home prices in many Chinese cities, relative to income, have reached levels comparable to some of the world's most expensive urban real estate. Average home prices across China reached 9.3 times average income in 2018, compared with 8.4 in San Francisco, for example.

Real estate investment in China contributed an estimated 13% of the nation's GDP in 2018 – an important consideration. Furthermore, up to a fifth of the entire Chinese economy is linked to residential real estate through industries such as construction, cement manufacturing or furniture making. Despite this already concentrated risk, however, China Evergrande Group, the country's biggest home builder, raised its sales target for 2020 by a full 23% from its January estimate, after strong sales in March of that year. Six months later, in October, Fitch Ratings reported that Evergrande held 835.5 billion yuan ($121 billion) of interest-bearing debt – up from $4.7 billion in 2010, which represents a 38.4% compound annual growth rate of debt over the ten-year period. This made it the most indebted real estate company in the world, the debt burden of this single property company now exceeding the total government debts of many nation states, including Denmark, Hungary and Romania. And yet Fitch chose not to change its credit rating for the company in October 2020, granting Evergrande a B+ with a stable outlook (a "B" rating suggests that a material default risk is present with a limited margin of safety remaining).

In November 2020, it was reported that Evergrande had been denied a long-awaited backdoor listing plan in Shenzhen, through a reorganisation plan with Shenzhen Special Economic Zone Real Estate & Properties Group. The denial of the listing, which the company was relying on for new equity funding, raised concerns that Evergrande may face a severe cash crunch in the near future, as debts come due to major stakeholders. Eventually, Fitch downgraded Evergrande's credit rating from

B+ to B in June 2021 – the first rating change in five years – citing "ongoing pressure for Evergrande to downsize its business and reduce total debt". In the days that followed, Evergrande's share price immediately declined 4%, contributing to a total decline in the price from January to September 2021 of more than 80%. In August 2021, the People's Bank of China and the China Banking and Insurance Regulatory Commission jointly released a statement in which Evergrande was publicly instructed to "actively diffuse debt risk and maintain real estate and financial market stability". Just over a week later, in an interim earnings statement, the company warned that it risked defaulting on its debt if it could not raise sufficient cash, adding that it would be seeking to increase asset sales, reduce costs and attract new investors in an effort to prevent a liquidity crisis.

At the time of going to print, the financial position of Evergrande had significantly worsened and its situation was being described as the potential catalyst of financial contagion.

In 2017, Chinese central bank governor Zhou Xiaochuan issued an ominous warning: given the country's disproportionate indebtedness, slowing growth and inflated asset prices, he believed China could be headed for a "Minsky moment".

Hyman Minsky, active in the second half of the 20th century, was an American economist and distinguished scholar at the Levy Economics Institute of Bard College. Famed for what has been dubbed the "Minsky moment" in economic circles, Minsky described how periods of financial excess, excessive borrowing and increased speculation inevitably result in significant market corrections, and often market crashes. According to Zhou's observation, China has had many of those criteria in place for several years now: a rapidly growing budget deficit; government, household and corporate debts that are, in combination, in excess of 300% of GDP as of 2020; and intensifying macroeconomic headwinds that are suppressing already slowing economic growth. The manner in which China's enormous state-run banks are potentially contravening some of the most important rules and regulations set out by international banking regulatory bodies, specifically developed to prevent massive economic crises, may be amplifying the size and severity of the significant deleveraging that must at some point occur.

Of further concern, as has been shown, China has experienced highly inflated real estate prices for the last decade, fuelled by easy credit, low interest rates, investor speculation and government policy, with state-led investment providing an elevated base for the country's property market. This was the case both in the US before the Global Financial Crisis and in Japan before the Japanese banking crisis in the 1990s.

In the case of Japan, many of the loans taken on by developers in the build-up to the asset price collapse in the early 1990s – loans for ambitious and expensive projects such as the building of golf courses, theme parks and resort hotels – were supported by the government in the name of economic growth and employment creation. Similarly, in the US, in the build-up to the collapse of the real estate market in 2007 and 2008, the US government, under both Republican and Democratic presidents, had promoted the idea of every American owning a home, resulting in regulations that forced banks to issue a certain quota of subprime mortgages to households that would otherwise not have qualified for these loans.

When the price bubbles burst in Japan and in the US, the consequences for financial markets were devastating. In Japan, in 1997, several of the nation's largest banks and insurance firms failed. It had taken more than five years from the time the bubble burst in 1992 for these large financial institutions to collapse, but when the seriousness of the situation was finally recognised, the contagion effect between the banks and other financial institutions was rapid and severe. When Nissan Life Insurance failed in April 1997, the interbank lending market experienced a sharp contraction, as other institutions, locally and abroad, feared their Japanese assets were now in danger of default. This resulted in a drastic increase in the price of interbank funding for Japanese banks, known at the time as the "Japan premium". As it was a significant source of funding for the under-capitalised Japanese banks, the sharp increase in the cost of interbank funding put enormous pressure on these institutions, in combination with a rapid sell-off of bank stocks, resulting in several more banks and insurance firms failing in the following months. Since 1998, the Japanese economy has never really recovered to pre-crisis levels; except for a rare spike in 2010, no form of government stimulus has managed to boost GDP growth above 3%.

In a manner that foreshadows the evolution of the Chinese economy, the Japanese macroeconomic environment was characterised by high economic growth and near-zero inflation in the second half of the 1980s, leading to a significant decline in the country's risk premium and a marked upward adjustment in its growth expectations. This in turn drew significant foreign direct investment, and boosted local spending and credit extension, resulting in rising asset prices, especially on the stock exchange and in real estate markets. The balance sheets of Japanese banks grew at a record pace and credit extension reached an all-time high, aided in no small part by the relaxation of banking regulations and capital controls.

An IMF working paper, published in 2000, described how weak Japanese regulations relating to loan classification led to the country's banks being slow to recognise and then write off loans that had little to no probability of recovery. Not unlike Chinese banks today, these institutions maximised loopholes in local regulations that allowed banks to delay provisioning for bad loans until formal bankruptcy procedures were under way. Japanese banks were also reluctant to let their borrowers default, opting rather to restructure large proportions of bad loans, recapitalise outstanding interest, extend the duration of the loan, or even issue new loans to enable their clients to pay off their existing interest – in effect, lending them money so they could continue to lend them money. This was all in a desperate attempt to stave off accounting for loan losses and to reduce the amount that needed to be provided for non-performing loans (NPLs). As the IMF paper states, the suppression of recognised NPLs was made possible only by the fact that "the loan classification and provisioning requirements (and their enforcement) were weak, and banks were able to classify non-performing loans as performing immediately upon the restructuring of loans".

In 1993, the Japanese government created the Cooperative Credit Purchasing Company (CCPC) for the sole purpose of buying NPLs from banks and undertaking recoveries on these loans – a strategy that once again foreshadowed what was to come in China, which established its asset management corporations (AMCs) in the early 2000s for the same purpose. When selling these loans to the CCPC, Japanese banks were permitted to recognise the difference between the book value and sale price of these loans as a tax-deductible expense, which bolstered the banks' income statements in the short term. However, as the IMF paper noted, "while the CCPC provides the banks with some tax relief for their non-performing loans, it does little, if anything, to facilitate the asset recovery process".

Thus there exists in China today several of the same warning signs that heralded the Japanese banking crisis in the 1990s and even the Global Financial Crisis in the following decade: a highly leveraged banking system that is not aligned with international best practices of risk management, a rampant property market where speculation is rife and in which huge amounts of debt are fuelling skyrocketing prices, and a growing sovereign-level budget deficit problem being compounded by a decelerating economy.

11

ARCHEGOS AND LEHMAN: HISTORY REPEATING ITSELF

To those who knew him personally, Bill Hwang was a humble and unassuming man, and above all else a devout Christian. "I try to invest according to the word of God and the power of the holy spirit," said Hwang in a 2019 video made for his charity, the Grace & Mercy Foundation. The foundation has donated millions of dollars to various other charities, mostly Christian organisations such as the Fuller Theological Seminary and Washington's Museum of the Bible. "In a way," Hwang explained, "it's a fearless way to invest. I am not afraid of death or money."

After graduating from the University of California and earning an MBA from Carnegie Mellon University, Hwang joined the esteemed New York hedge fund Tiger Management as an analyst in 1996. There, founder Julian Robertson instilled in his employees a brazen approach to investing, teaching them to "live with losses" and reminding them on occasions when large losses were incurred that "it's only work". Leveraging his experience at Tiger Management, Hwang set up two of his own funds in the early 2000s, Tiger Asia Management and Tiger Asia Partners. Over the next decade, the funds were largely successful, with Tiger Asia Management accumulating $10 billion in assets under management at its peak and earning generous profits for its clients. In 2012, however, Hwang's credibility was seriously undermined when the Securities and Exchange Commission (SEC) charged him and the head trader at his two funds, Raymond Park, with insider trading and market manipulation.

According to the SEC's press release, published on 12 December 2012, Hwang and Park participated in two private placements for stocks of Bank of China and China Construction Bank between 2008 and 2009 – an arrangement where the respective banks offered the sale of shares directly to investors, facilitated by Hwang's funds, without placing those shares on the open market. Because of the private nature of the transaction and the material non-public information involved, Hwang and his funds were required to sign confidentiality agreements regarding the information and were restricted from trading in the shares of the respective companies until the transaction and its details were made public. In violation of the agreement, Hwang apparently ordered his head trader to take short positions in each stock in the days prior to the private placement. In this manner, according to the SEC's filing, "Hwang and his firms illegally profited by $16.2 million by using the discounted private placement shares they received to cover the short sales they had entered into based on inside information about the placements."

In the filing, the SEC further alleged that on at least four occasions Hwang and his firms attempted to manipulate the month-end prices of the two Chinese bank stocks in question, in order to collect inflated management fees from their clients.

With management fees dependent on the scale of assets under management, Hwang instructed his head trader to purposely place losing trades on Bank of China and China Construction Bank shares, both to depress the share price to benefit their short positions, and to increase their assets under management and thereby allow them to collect more management fees. Through this scheme, says the SEC, Tiger Asia Management was able to amass approximately $496,000 of fraudulent management fees in just a few months. Hwang ultimately settled the case. Though he never admitted or denied wrongdoing, he and his firms paid fines and disgorgements to the value of approximately $44 million to the SEC, and he was forced to close his two public hedge funds.

The very next year, in 2013, Hwang opened Archegos Capital Management, a private family office with no outside investors and capitalised with his own money. "Archegos", a word that often appears in the New Testament, is Greek for "one who leads the way". At that point, following the SEC charges and settlement, very few investors would have trusted Hwang with their money, so the entity of a family office made perfect sense. More than that, though, it allowed him to avoid as much regulatory scrutiny as possible, and was thus the ideal legal vehicle for the exorbitant levels of risk he wished to take. In the US, it is illegal for individual investors to buy securities with more than half of the money borrowed on margin, but for hedge funds, and indeed a family office, these restrictions do not apply. Taking advantage of these lax regulations, Hwang had turned the initial $200 million of his own money into more than $10 billion by early 2021, taking on ever larger and ever more leveraged positions in the process.

Initially, Hwang leveraged his positions roughly two times; for example, he would use $1 million of his own capital and borrow another $1 million to buy $2 million worth of securities. But in time, the various investment banks that were providing Archegos with prime brokerage services, including Goldman Sachs, Morgan Stanley, Credit Suisse, UBS, Deutsche Bank, Nomura and others, allowed him to increase his leverage significantly – more than five times in most cases and up to eight times in certain positions. In the case of Goldman, when the investment bank's prime brokerage requested that Hwang be brought on as a client in 2018, the compliance department initially refused, considering him a significant risk to the firm, both financially and reputationally. However, at some stage in the next two years, presumably noticing that other investment banks were doing business with Archegos and realising that the bank was losing out on hundreds of millions of dollars in fees and trading opportunities, Goldman changed its mind about Hwang and decided to take him on as a client. In this way, Hwang managed to bypass the risk management and compliance departments of some of the largest investment banks in the world, only a few years after being charged by the SEC for fraud, insider trading and market manipulation. Not only did he become their client, but they allowed him to borrow billions of dollars of their money to place risky, highly leveraged bets on the stock market. For the investment banks, the commissions were evidently worth the risk.

The risk inherent in Hwang's already highly leveraged trading strategy was compounded by the large concentration of his investments in just a few stocks. In early 2021, Hwang's portfolio was dominated by just a handful of different companies' shares, primarily from America and China, including large positions in US media conglomerates ViacomCBS and Discovery Inc, Chinese technology-driven education company GSX Techedu, Chinese internet services company Baidu, Chinese e-commerce company Vipshop, Chinese music streaming company Tencent Music and the British-Portuguese online luxury fashion retail platform Farfetch.

To maximise his exposure to these stocks while minimising the amount of capital required to secure the assets – as well as to maintain anonymity in the market – most of Hwang's positions were purchased using derivatives contracts called total return swaps. In simple terms, a total return swap involves a contract between two parties, where one party (the receiver) agrees to pay the other party (the payer) a set rate, either fixed or variable, for the duration of the agreement; and the other party (the payer) makes payments based on the performance of the underlying asset, including the income and capital gains that the asset generates over the duration of the agreement. The underlying assets for total return swaps could include stocks, bonds or market indices. In Hwang's case, numerous total return swap agreements were entered into with various investment banks' prime brokerages, which bought and held shares on his behalf, and received an agreed-upon rate over the duration of the contract's period for this service. In return, Hwang received any capital gains or dividends that resulted from the positive performance of the underlying assets.

In such a transaction, while the payer (the prime brokerage) holds the asset in its name, the receiver (Archegos) assumes all performance, or market risk, that is related to the performance of the underlying asset. This means that if the price of the asset moves against him, the receiver is liable to cover the losses. While the payer does not assume performance risk for the fluctuation of the price of the asset, the transaction *does* bear credit risk for the prime brokerage, for if the receiver defaults on his obligations, the investment bank is still in possession of the faltering asset.

For hedge funds – or, in this case, Hwang's family office – total return swaps serve two important functions. First, these financial contracts allow the investor to gain significant exposure to an asset with a minimal cash outlay, as these instruments are often bought on margin – which is to say, they are highly leveraged. Second, they leave the investor with a great deal of anonymity in the market. Because the prime brokerage buys the underlying asset on behalf of its client, there is no public record of which entity has bought and gained exposure to the underlying asset in a total return swap agreement; this is simply recorded in the investment banks' own documentation. Taking advantage of this, Hwang was able to enter into contracts with multiple investment banks' prime brokerages, taking leveraged positions at each and exposing these banks to billions of dollars of risk, without any of them knowing where else he had made similar agreements.

In this way, Archegos managed to accumulate enormous positions; for example, becoming one of the largest investors of all issued ViacomCBS shares. In so doing, it spread its many highly leveraged derivatives across multiple investment banks and across several continents, without these institutions ever having a clear view or understanding of their client's total risk profile.

In the three months between early January and late March 2021, the share price of ViacomCBS increased 180% – from around $36 a share on 4 January to $100 a share on 22 March. In the same timeframe, the share price of Discovery Inc increased roughly 150%, from $30 per share to $75 per share. Upon consideration of these significant increases in the companies' share prices, beyond the reasonable explanation of any fundamental analysis, various industry commentators suspected that a "whale" – an individual investor with enough capital to buy or sell large volumes of a share to manipulate its price – was moving the market. They were right. The whale in question was Bill Hwang, owner of the family office Archegos Capital Management.

On Tuesday the 23rd of March 2021, ViacomCBS announced a $3-billion stock sale to fund the company's expansion into the media streaming market. Upon release of the news, the market reacted swiftly and sharply: the ViacomCBS share price fell 9%, from $100 the day before, to $91 at the close of trading. The next day, Wednesday the 24th, ViacomCBS announced the pricing of the stock sale, setting the price of 20 million shares of its Class B common stock at $85 per share and 10 million shares of its Series A Mandatory Convertible Preferred Stock at $100 per share. The market didn't like the news, and the share price dropped a further 23%, from $91 to $70.

For Archegos, this sudden and significant drop in the share price of one of the firm's largest positions was disastrous. As the share price dropped, the various prime brokerages that had entered into leveraged swap contracts with Archegos prompted Hwang to deposit more funds into the firms' trading accounts to achieve the maintenance margin – a request for capital known as a margin call. If the investor does not, or cannot, deposit the required amount of margin into its trading account in a timely manner, the brokerage has the right to sell assets linked to the account, regardless of the market price, to meet the margin call.

On Thursday the 25th, unable to post the capital required for numerous margin calls, Hwang arranged a conference call with his banks to attempt to persuade them not to sell his positions, arguing that the share price of his exposures would bounce back. During this call, the various investment banks, including Credit Suisse, Nomura, Morgan Stanley and Goldman Sachs, realised, perhaps for the first time, the true extent of Hwang's exposures. Considering the seriousness of the situation, some of the banks decided to hold off for a few days, hoping that the share price would recover. Goldman, however, rejected this strategy.

On Friday the 26th, as the market opened, Goldman Sachs immediately offloaded almost $4 billion worth of derivatives related to Hwang's holdings, effectively becoming the first mover and consequently the least affected by the ensuing share price collapse. Over the course of the day, Goldman would sell in the region of $10 billion worth of shares of ViacomCBS, Baidu and Tencent Music, causing precipitous drops in these companies' share prices. Deutsche Bank and Morgan Stanley soon followed, respectively selling blocks of $8 billion and $4 billion in shares related to Hwang's positions. By the close of business that Friday, the share prices of the companies in Archegos's concentrated portfolio were decimated, with ViacomCBS down 50% for the week.

As the first movers, Goldman Sachs and Deutsche Bank escaped with the least losses – if any – of all Archegos's prime brokerages when liquidating their positions. For Nomura and Credit Suisse, and to a lesser extent Morgan Stanley, the decision not to sell their exposures immediately was extremely costly. In the weeks after Hwang defaulted on his margin calls, Credit Suisse and Nomura announced respective losses of $4.8 billion and $2 billion related to their Archegos exposures. Morgan Stanley reported a less severe $911 million loss. Other prime brokerages of banks, including MUFG, Mizuho, UBS and Wells Fargo, also announced that they had suffered losses of varying degrees. For Credit Suisse, the loss was larger than the annual profits the banking group had recorded in preceding years, with net income equating to roughly $3.5 billion in 2019 and $2.9 billion in 2020. The Archegos disaster resulted in the investment bank losing $960 million in the first quarter of the 2021 financial year and forced it to suspend its dividends. The response by the banking group was to slash bonuses and fire seven high-ranking executives involved in the incident, including the group's chief risk and compliance officer, Lara Warner, and the head of the investment bank, Brian Chin, as well as several traders and lower-ranked risk managers.

———————

In the aftermath of the collapse of Archegos Capital Management, the chair of the US Senate Banking Committee, Sherrod Brown, wrote letters to several of the investment banks involved, seeking answers about the implosion of the family office and how these enormous multinational financial institutions could allow a single client to cause such significant damage to their financial stability. In his letter to Credit Suisse, Brown wrote, "I am troubled, but not surprised, by the news reports that Archegos entered into risky derivatives transactions facilitated by major investment banks, resulting in panicked selling of stocks worth tens of billions of dollars and those banks collectively losing nearly $10bn."

Other lawmakers, including Democratic senator from Massachusetts Elizabeth Warren, also voiced their concerns. Archegos had "all the makings of a dangerous situation – largely unregulated hedge funds, opaque derivatives, trading in private dark pools, high leverage, and a trader who wriggled out of the SEC's enforcement," Warren said in a statement to CNBC. "Regulators need to rely on more than luck to fend off risks to the financial system: we need transparency and strong oversight to ensure that the next hedge fund blow-up doesn't take the economy down with it."

In a similar statement, Lael Brainard, the head of the Federal Reserve's Financial Stability Committee, said, "The potential for material distress at hedge funds to affect broader financial conditions underscores the importance of more granular, higher-frequency disclosures." In what is essentially an echo of Brooksley Born's concerns about the opacity of derivatives markets in the 1990s, Brainard went on to say, "The Archegos event illustrates the limited visibility into hedge-fund exposures and serves as a reminder that available measures of hedge-fund leverage may not be capturing important risks."

The implosion of Bill Hwang's Archegos Capital Management and the resultant losses incurred by some of the largest investment banks in the world are, in many ways, reminiscent of the systemic risks created by the extreme leverage and lack of transparency of the derivatives positions of investment banks in the years leading up to the 2007/2008 Global Financial Crisis. In particular, the incident exhibits striking similarities to the series of events that preceded the failure of Lehman Brothers in September 2008. Like Archegos's collapse – the result of extreme leverage and risk being hidden by the opaque nature of the derivatives contracts being utilised – Lehman made use of derivatives to build up dangerously leveraged positions. Even more strikingly, Lehman also made use of an infamous financial instrument called the Repo 105 which, in much the same manner as the techniques used by Archegos, enabled the investment firm to conceal the extent of its true risk profile from regulators and the public, thereby prolonging the firm's collapse and intensifying the systemic shock waves that rippled through the global financial system as a result.

For the Wall Street investment bank Lehman Brothers, 1969 proved to be a landmark year. It was the year that senior partner Robert Lehman died, and the year that a young Richard Severin Fuld Jr joined the firm as an intern. Starting out trading commercial paper, Dick Fuld progressed well and earned a reputation as a competent fixed-income trader. Having began right at the bottom and steadily climbed the ranks, Fuld eventually went on to work at Lehman Brothers for 39 years, commanding the firm as chief executive for the last fourteen of those – making him the longest-serving Wall Street CEO at the time. "As long as I am alive this firm will never be sold," Dick Fuld was known to say, so proud was he to be a "Lehman-lifer". "And if it is sold after I die, I will reach back from the grave and prevent it."

The year before Fuld took over as CEO, in 1993, Lehman Brothers made an annual loss of $102 million. In 1994, it was spun off from its parent company American Express – which had acquired what was known as Lehman Brothers, Kuhn, Loeb Inc in 1984 for $360 million – to list independently on the New York Stock Exchange as Lehman Brothers Holdings Inc, and from that point its fortunes started to change. For the next fourteen years, under the guidance of its new chief executive, Lehman Brothers Holdings performed extrremely well, with its biggest year of revenue and earnings – $60 billion and $4 billion respectively – coming in the fiscal year ending November 2007. This was reported at the end of January 2008. During his tenure as CEO, Fuld not only successfully guided the firm through numerous crises but also aggressively grew what was the oldest investment bank in the United States at the time into one of the biggest financial firms in the world.

Having taken a substantial knock in the Asian Financial Crisis in the late 1990s, Lehman Brothers looked to recover its diminished revenues and embattled share price in the coming years. In line with all the major investment banks at the time, Lehman pursued a high-leverage model that relied heavily on the interbank market, and thereby on the confidence of their banking counterparties, to fund its daily activities. To understand the extent of this leverage, by 2008 Lehman Brothers had amassed $680 billion in assets, while holding just $22 billion in capital – a ratio of 31:1, which was on par with investment banks such as Bear Stearns, Merrill Lynch and Morgan Stanley at the time. By the early 2000s, Lehman was also significantly increasing its exposure to the property market in the US, then growing at a rapid pace. This was due in large part to an extremely low interest rate environment, as well as the easily accessible mortgage loans provided by banks at the time.

As described in the official bankruptcy documentation, which became known as the Valukas Report, Lehman Brothers had by the mid-2000s gained significant exposure to the real estate and mortgage market through a variety of complex financial instruments. These included commercial real estate, residential home loans, residential mortgage-backed securities and collateralised debt obligations. Ultimately, it was this concentrated exposure to the housing and mortgage market, and not necessarily Lehman's highly leveraged position in and of itself, that would prove to be the undoing of the firm.

While many associate Lehman with the securitisation of real estate-related assets in the form of mortgage-backed securities and collateralised debt obligations, it was also one of the first Wall Street investment banks to gain direct exposure to the mortgage origination business. In 2003 Lehman bought Aurora Loan Services, and in 2006 it acquired a second home loans business, the West Coast subprime mortgage lender BNC Mortgage LLC. By late 2007, these two subsidiaries were in combination signing new loans at a rate of nearly $4 billion every month, further increasing Lehman's already heavily exposed balance sheet to the US housing market bubble.

In the Valukas Report – which was compiled over eighteen months by government analysts, Lehman staff and their external auditors, Ernst & Young – it was found that the valuation of Lehman Brothers' real estate-related assets was significantly overstated. "As the level of market activity declined in late 2007 and 2008, resulting in valuation inputs becoming less observable, and certain of Lehman's assets became increasingly less liquid, Lehman progressively relied on its judgment to determine the fair value of such assets," notes the report. "Fair value" is the method of determining the value of the asset through its orderly hypothetical sale in the market, as prescribed by the financial accounting standards at the time.

These "self-priced" assets, as the Valukas Report called them, would come under increasing scrutiny by market participants, particularly following Lehman's first two quarterly reports of 2008. In April, a well-known short-seller, David Einhorn of Greenlight Capital, made it publicly known that he believed there was good reason to question Lehman's fair value calculations, since it had significant exposure to a battered commercial real estate market and should have taken billions more in write-downs than it did in early 2008. "Lehman does not provide enough transparency for us to even hazard a guess as to how they have accounted for these items", Einhorn noted, contributing to the scepticism. He suspected that "greater transparency on these valuations would not inspire market confidence".

When several statements of a similar nature began circulating in the press, market sentiment slowly started to turn against the firm. For Lehman Brothers – as had been the case for Bear Stearns just months prior – confidence in the integrity of the firm was vital, as the slightest crack in its credibility would be detrimental to the continued funding of its highly leveraged operating model by its banking counterparties in the interbank market. Without this continued short-term funding, Lehman would go out of business overnight, and for this reason it would do everything in its power to maintain its image as a reliable banking entity within the interbank market – even if this meant manipulating its balance sheet to make the firm appear to the public eye more liquid than it really was.

———————

In the extensive Valukas Report, an entire chapter is dedicated to the Repo 105 tactic, an accounting ploy used extensively by the faltering investment bank to maintain a facade of liquidity in the period leading up to September 2008. These repurchase agreements were used "to temporarily remove securities inventory from its balance sheet, usually for a period of seven to ten days, and to create a materially misleading picture of the firm's financial condition in late 2007 and 2008." A Repo 105 transaction was nearly identical to a typical repurchase agreement, but with one critical difference: instead of being accounted for as a loan that needed to be paid back to the temporary holder of the securities, it was recorded as a sale of inventory, allowing Lehman to conveniently shift billions of dollars of risky assets off its balance sheet, while simultaneously recording a cash injection equivalent to its self-priced assets.

In common repurchase agreements, an obligor, or borrower (such as an investment bank), will borrow funds from an obligee, or lender (another bank), on a short-term basis, in exchange for securities to be used as collateral for the loan, which the obligor has agreed to repurchase on a specified date and at a specified price that includes an interest payment to the obligee. Ordinarily, repurchase agreements are recorded as short-term funding by the obligor, but in the case of Lehman, the bank "did not disclose the known obligation to repay the debt", according to the Valukas Report. To do this, Lehman exploited an accounting standard loophole where it agreed to a higher price of 105% for the securities, hence the name Repo 105, allowing the firm to record this as a "sale" of securities, and so move the securities off its balance sheet indefinitely. While this would not have been approved by US authorities, the report describes how Lehman managed to obtain a legal opinion from the British law firm Linklaters affirming that the technique was, in fact, legal, thanks to the less stringent financial regulations that applied to its European broker-dealer in London, Lehman Brothers International, governed under English law.

This short-term transaction was used increasingly by Lehman Brothers in the last few quarters before its collapse, allowing the investment bank to use the funds from the numerous Repo 105 transactions to pay down other liabilities, thereby reducing both the total liabilities and the total assets reported on its balance sheet and lowering its leverage ratios. And, as would later be divulged by former Lehman global financial controller Martin Kelly, the timing of these Repo 105 transactions was explicitly co-ordinated with the end of each financial quarter, with the express aim of artificially bolstering the firm's financial reports. In testimony to the examiner after Lehman's collapse, Kelly claimed that he expressed concerns to two consecutive Lehman CFOs, Erin Callan and Ian Lowitt, advising them that "the lack of economic substance to the Repo 105 transactions meant reputational risk to Lehman if the firm's use of the transactions became known to the public". It was later discovered that in the second quarter of 2008 Lehman had used the Repo 105 technique to move $50 billion off its balance sheet.

Despite every effort to hide its true financial position, on the 9th of June 2008 Lehman Brothers recorded its first quarterly loss since its independent listing on the New York Stock Exchange, ending a run of 55 consecutive quarters of profitability. In a desperate effort to disguise the bad news, CEO Dick Fuld announced on the same day that the firm would raise $6 billion in capital from investors through the sale of shares – but the announcement only spooked the market further. Upon posting the $2.8 billion loss, the market reacted swiftly and dramatically, punishing Lehman's share price and sending it to its lowest point in more than ten years. While disappointed by the loss, Fuld told reporters that he still believed Lehman was well positioned for a recovery.

Later that year, however, Lehman's position had become a concern for the US government, and on 13 September 2008 the president of the Federal Reserve of New York, Timothy Geithner, called a meeting to discuss the investment bank's future. Facing imminent bankruptcy, Fuld assured government regulators that he had initiated discussions with both Barclays and Bank of America for the sale of Lehman Brothers, to avoid a calamitous collapse of the firm. Ultimately, neither Bank of America nor Barclays would agree to the terms of a sale, with the latter ostensibly only interested in scooping out the good assets of the failing investment bank – which it eventually did, just days after Lehman's bankruptcy.

Having failed to secure a sale, Lehman Brothers filed for Chapter 11 bankruptcy protection just before 1am Eastern

Standard Time on 15 September 2008, reporting bank debt of $613 billion, bond debt of $155 billion, and assets worth $639 billion. That same day, Lehman shares dropped by over 90% in value and the Dow Jones index lost more than 500 points – one of the biggest single-day drops since the 9/11 attacks in 2001. Lehman's collapse was the largest investment bank failure since the collapse of New York-based Drexel Burnham Lambert in 1990, and the bankruptcy marked a turning point in the financial crisis. It also triggered, in the same week, the dramatic collapse of the American International Group (AIG), which subsequently received a government bailout of $182 billion.

Like Lehman Brothers, other large investment banks also suffered from bloated positions in the subprime mortgage securities market, including Bear Stearns and Merrill Lynch, which would ultimately be sold to JPMorgan and Bank of America respectively. But the fact that Lehman Brothers was left to fail makes it a unique case – a decision that many believe was a grave mistake, in retrospect, including former Merrill Lynch CEO John Thain. In an interview with the BBC, Thain noted that the amount of money it would have taken to save Lehman – $20 or $30 billion – would have been marginal "compared to the destruction in value that followed the Lehman bankruptcy, the complete shutdown of the credit markets, [and] the billions and billions and billions of losses that were experienced in the markets subsequently".

The day after Lehman went into bankruptcy, the secretary of the Treasury, Hank Paulson, told the press, "I never once considered it appropriate to put taxpayer money on the line in resolving Lehman Brothers." But with the benefit of hindsight, in 2010, he said, "I ought to have been more careful with my words. Some interpreted them to mean that we were drawing a strict line in the sand... and that we didn't care about a Lehman collapse or its consequences. Nothing could have been further from the truth. I had worked hard for months to ward off the nightmare we foresaw with Lehman. But few understood what we did – that the government had no authority to put in capital, and a Fed loan by itself wouldn't have prevented a bankruptcy."

Today, the argument is still made that it was an oversight by government to let such a systemically important institution completely collapse – especially since Bear Stearns had already been rescued in March of that year and that many other firms in a similar position would be bailed out in the weeks and months to come. The retrospective justification given by the US Treasury for not saving Lehman Brothers was that, at the time of the firm's collapse in September 2008, it was not yet within Treasury's mandate to put money into a private firm to cover its obligations, unless that institution could directly influence the stability of the US dollar. It would not be until the introduction of the Troubled Asset Relief Program on 3 October 2008 – making available $700 billion in government funds to purchase toxic assets and equity from financial institutions – that the US Treasury could more readily bail out private institutions through the purchase of troubled assets.

In the wake of the collapse of Lehman Brothers, Dick Fuld came under immense scrutiny from authorities, who wanted to know how the giant investment bank had found itself in such a disastrous position in 2008. In the congressional hearings that followed, Fuld blamed politicians for not recognising the overly lax mortgage lending regulations in the build-up to the crisis. He also argued that the collapse of the investment bank was caused by the unregulated naked short-selling of Lehman shares, accompanied by false rumours about the firm's financial health.

In November 2008, Fuld sold his $13 million seaside mansion in Florida to his wife for $100 to avoid repossession in case of legal action against him. But despite receiving a grand jury subpoena in connection with three criminal investigations led by the United States Attorney, Fuld was not convicted on any charges. Ultimately, the court could not convincingly argue that Fuld, or any Lehman Brothers executive for that matter, had knowingly misrepresented facts that would result in a charge of fraud, even though the examiner's report stated that Fuld's conduct "ranged from serious but non-culpable errors of business judgment to actionable balance sheet manipulation".

In 2018 – ten years after the collapse of Lehman Brothers – Fuld emerged from a long sabbatical and decided to make a return to Wall Street. His new firm, Matrix Wealth Partners, caters to wealthy family funds seeking corporate finance advice. In a statement about his new venture, the former Lehman CEO says that the modern economic environment provides "clear opportunities in a flawed and highly fragmented financial services market".

In the lobby of Fuld's newly rebranded financial advisory firm, visitors and potential investors are greeted by a large artwork proclaiming, THAT WAS THEN THIS IS NOW. The irony could not be more profound when considering Lehman Brothers' collapse alongside that of Archegos. Though the failures are separated by over a decade, the unadulterated greed and reckless behaviour in these cases are chillingly similar – two tales of hubris and unashamed manipulation of a system that remains open to abuse. And it is for this reason that public trust in financial institutions has only eroded further, rather than improved, in the years since the Global Financial Crisis, as the financial industry continues to suffer the consequences of bad actors and inadequate correction, while inexplicably ignoring the lessons of the past.

12

PLUNDERING THE
DEVELOPING WORLD

"I know you're not following what I'm saying anyway, right?" says Leonardo DiCaprio straight into the camera. "That's okay, it doesn't matter. The real question is this: Was all this legal?"

DiCaprio is playing the part of Jordan Belfort in Martin Scorsese's loosely biographical film *The Wolf of Wall Street*, released in 2013. After losing his job in the market crash of 1987, Belfort takes up a position at a boiler room brokerage firm on Long Island that specialises in selling worthless penny stocks to unsuspecting investors. What follows is a tale of drugs, alcohol, sex and all manner of excess, as Belfort hones his talents as a master salesman with no moral compass, defrauding investors of millions of dollars along the way. While telling the story of one man's perversion by the temptations of Wall Street, the film also represents, in a wider sense, the greed and amorality that exist within the free-market capitalist system in general, and specifically how such elements thrived in the wild and unregulated environment of the financial services industry in the 1990s.

On the 12th of January 2014, DiCaprio won the Golden Globe for Best Actor in a Motion Picture, Musical or Comedy. In his acceptance speech, he first thanked Scorsese before joking about how a film about financial fraud, debauchery and the excesses of Wall Street had been placed in the category of musical or comedy. Finally, near the end of his speech, DiCaprio specifically name-checked three men. "Joey, Riz and Jho, thank you for not only being collaborators, but taking a risk on the movie," he said. The three men DiCaprio was referring to were, in order, Joey McFarland, an American film producer and the co-founder of Red Granite Pictures, the film production and distribution company that produced the movie; Riza Aziz, the other co-founder of Red Granite Pictures and the stepson of the Malaysian prime minister at the time, Najib Razak; and Jho Low, the apparent mastermind behind the looting of billions of dollars from a state-sanctioned Malaysian development fund called 1MDB.

1Malaysia Development Berhad was created in 2009, when the prime minister of Malaysia at the time, Najib Razak, entered into a joint $2.5-billion partnership with the private Saudi oil services company PetroSaudi International to set up a sovereign development fund. Led by Prime Minister Razak, as the chairman of the fund, 1MDB purportedly set out to use the sale of government-guaranteed bonds to enter strategic economic deals, especially within the transport and energy sectors, that would modernise and revitalise the economy of Malaysia. Its first proposed undertaking, in 2010, was to develop the old airport at Sungai Besi, Kuala Lumpur into a modernised transit hub, connecting various high-speed rail networks to the airport site to turn it into a new centre for business and trade. Dubbed Bandar Malaysia, the project was estimated to cost in the region of $500 million.

1MDB's next two significant undertakings were the purchase of Tanjong Energy Holdings from Sri Lankan oil tycoon Ananda Krishnan for $2 billion and the announcement of the Tun Razak Exchange, both in 2012. The Tun Razak Exchange, named after Prime Minister Razak, was an ambitious fifteen-year, multi-billion-dollar development project covering seventy acres in the heart of Kuala Lumpur, aimed at transforming the site into a world-leading financial centre. It was to be crowned by the Exchange 106 skyscraper, which at 445 metres would make it the third-tallest building in Malaysia, comparable in the minds of the developers to landmark buildings in other global financial centres, such as the Shard in London, One World Trade Center in New York (also known as the Freedom Tower) and the Shanghai International Finance Centre.

It was at this stage, in 2012, with the sovereign wealth fund gathering momentum and credibility, that Najib Razak and the fund's special adviser, Jho Low, decided to ramp up its funding programme even further. What followed was a massive cash injection into 1MDB in the form of three rounds of bond issuances, between 2012 and 2013, to the value of $6.5 billion, facilitated by Goldman Sachs as the underwriter. It was a decision for which the investment bank would, years later, come under severe scrutiny by international regulatory bodies, including the US Securities and Exchange Commission (SEC).

In its first few years of existence, 1MDB existed largely without controversy, albeit demonstrating little evidence of material progress in terms of infrastructure development to the benefit of the Malaysian economy in its initial ventures. In the five years following the announcement of the redevelopment of the Sungai Besi airport, for example, no ground was broken at the site, and a number of the proposed transport connection plans, including the high-speed railway links to the area, were discontinued. And it would not be long before 1MDB's previously unquestioned operations were put under severe scrutiny.

In January 2015, after many months of deliberation, retired Swiss financial services professional Xavier Andre Justo handed Malaysian-born British reporter Clare Rewcastle Brown a hard drive with 90 gigabytes worth of data stolen from the servers of his ex-employer, PetroSaudi. On the hard drive were thousands of emails detailing the early communications between PetroSaudi's founders – Tarek Obaid and Prince Turki bin Abdullah, the seventh son of King Abdullah bin Abdulaziz, the monarch of Saudi Arabia at the time – and the politically connected individuals who conceived the idea of, and set in motion, the 1MDB sovereign fund, including Najib Razak, his stepson Riza Aziz, and their accomplice Jho Low.

While not directly involved in the deal between PetroSaudi and 1MDB, Xavier Justo had accessed information about the deal during the time he was employed at the company, from 2009 to 2011. In September 2013, having left PetroSaudi, Justo reached out to Rewcastle Brown for the first time, informing her that he possessed critical information regarding the individuals involved in 1MDB. Rewcastle Brown was a veteran reporter who had once worked for the BBC but had gone on to start her own publication, the *Sarawak Report*, which focused on exposing corruption in her country of birth, Malaysia. In early 2014, she travelled from London to Thailand to meet her Swiss source in the lobby of the Plaza Athénée hotel in Bangkok. Having been shown snippets of emails and bank transfer confirmations during their meeting, Rewcastle Brown knew the information Justo possessed would be vital in uncovering the true story behind 1MDB. There was a hurdle to overcome, though: Justo wanted $2 million for the purchase of the data.

By late 2014, political and public anger towards 1MDB had started to increase significantly. Rumours had begun to circulate that the fund was losing money at an alarming rate, and that it soon would not be able to cover the interest payments on the billions of dollars it had borrowed in bond issuances and other forms of debt instruments. By November, it was publicly known that 1MDB had taken on almost $11 billion in debt from various sources, including the $6.5 billion worth of government-guaranteed bonds underwritten by Goldman Sachs – but it was not publicly known at the time that a significant portion of the borrowed billions were never going to realise a return on investment, because they had been spent by Najib Razak and his co-conspirators on jewellery, jets, yachts, precious artwork and luxury apartments, none of which would ever benefit the people of Malaysia.

Rewcastle Brown did not have immediate access to $2 million to purchase the information from Justo outright, but she was aware that *The Edge*, a Malaysian business publication run by a former banker-turned-media tycoon, Tong Kooi Ong, had been covering the progress and shortfalls of 1MDB extensively since its inception in 2009. In late 2014, Rewcastle Brown reached out to Ong and informed him that she had found information that could expose the politically connected individuals at the very heart of the sovereign development fund, including the Malaysian prime minister himself.

Ong agreed to meet with Rewcastle Brown and Justo in Singapore, along with the editor-in-chief of *The Edge* and a number of IT experts to verify the authenticity of the data. It was at this meeting, in January 2015, in a conference room in the five-star Fullerton Hotel, that Justo divulged the incriminating links between PetroSaudi, 1MDB, Najib Razak and the man who supposedly worked behind the scenes to make it all happen, the mysterious Malaysian businessman Jho Low. Upon hearing the revelations, Ong agreed to purchase the data from Justo for the asking price of $2 million, and on the 28th of February 2015 Rewcastle Brown published an article on her website that claimed she had evidence that $700 million had disappeared from the 1MDB fund and had been distributed to various private Swiss bank accounts and offshore shell companies linked to the founders of the sovereign fund, specifically naming Najib Razak. The headline in the *Sarawak Report* read, in capital letters, HEIST OF THE CENTURY.

––––––––––

"I got a friend, he got some money," says Jamie Foxx with a big smile on his face in 2013 when asked on *The Jonathan Ross Show* what he did on New Year's Eve in 2012. "He flew me, Leonardo DiCaprio, Jonah Hill and some other cats, and we flew to

Australia, right, and we did the countdown in Australia... then jumped back on the plane and then did the countdown in Vegas. That's crazy, right!" Amused and impressed by the story, the live audience applauds loudly as Foxx recounts the tale of how he and his fellow A-listers flew around the world in two Boeing 747s turned into flying casinos, racing against time to experience two New Year's countdown parties in a single night. The friend with "some money" was Jho Low.

Low Taek Jho, known by his friends and business associates as Jho Low, was born to a wealthy Malaysian family and educated at Harrow, the elite boarding school in the UK also attended by the likes of Winston Churchill and the former prime minister of India Jawaharlal Nehru. At Harrow, Low rubbed shoulders with the children of wealthy and powerful families, becoming close friends with Riza Aziz, the stepson of Najib Razak. After school, Low attended the University of Pennsylvania's Wharton Business School, where he continued to network with the wealthy and the influential, including many politically connected Malaysians, and made friends with oil-rich families from Kuwait and Jordan.

Low was known as a smart and capable individual, with an elite Ivy League education, who could speak five languages. Winning the confidence of his friends and their families, Low began managing the money of various wealthy acquaintances after university, using his wide network to gain access to exclusive investment opportunities for his friends' capital. One friendship in particular that would pay off was with Riza Aziz.

In April 2009, Mohammad Najib bin Tun Haji Abdul Razak, better known as Najib Razak, was sworn in as the sixth prime minister of Malaysia. By this time, Jho Low had become a confidant of the new prime minister through his relationship with his stepson, Riza Aziz. There was a Malaysian sovereign fund already in existence when Razak came into power, but it was relatively small and specialised, specifically for the use of the development of one province, Terengganu state, from which it derived its name – Terengganu Investment Authority (TIA). Four months after Razak's inauguration, the management authority of TIA was transferred to the Minister of Finance Incorporated and the fund set out to raise five billion Malaysian ringgits (about $1.2 billion) by means of the issuance of special bonds called Islamic medium-term notes through the Malaysian-based AmInvestment Bank. The issuance of the bonds was arranged by TIA's new special adviser, Jho Low, appointed by the prime minister of Malaysia himself.

Upon the transfer of power of the sovereign fund, its name was changed to 1Malaysia Development Berhad – *berhad* being a Malay term designating a public limited company – and Prime Minister Razak became the chairman of the 1MDB board, with the power to hire and fire any other member of management. To justify the change of authority and the expansion of the sovereign fund, Razak announced that 1MDB would provide benefits to a wider spectrum of the Malaysian population if the sovereign fund were to be a national entity rather than a provincial one that served only the residents of one particular province.

Following the special bond issuance and name change in 2009, 1MDB began a journey of rapid expansion, starting with its first strategic partnership with PetroSaudi, facilitated, once again, by Jho Low. Over the next few years, billions of dollars would flow into the 1MDB fund, mainly through the issuance of more bonds, such as those underwritten by Goldman Sachs –

and Razak, Low and various other associates would have direct access to this money, unhindered by any checks and balances, to spend how they wished. And they did so in extravagant and elaborate ways. It took a number of international investigations by various federal investigative bodies, including the US Department of Justice (DOJ), to finally expose the 1MDB scandal, and when they did, the details of how approximately $4.5 billion of the sovereign fund's money was looted and squandered were gradually divulged to the public.

Upon conclusion of the DOJ's investigation in 2016, US Attorney General Loretta Lynch stated that it was "the largest kleptocracy case" ever prosecuted in America and described how "a number of corrupt 1MDB officials treated this public trust as a personal bank account". In the DOJ filings, it is alleged that money from the sovereign fund was used by Razak, Aziz, Low and others to buy, among other things, a mansion in Los Angeles, a penthouse in Manhattan and more than $200 million worth of original artworks by Van Gogh, Monet and Picasso. It also bankrolled the production of two Hollywood films, Scorsese's *The Wolf of Wall Street* and the somewhat easier-to-follow *Dumb and Dumber To*, funded by Red Granite Pictures, the production company co-founded in 2010 by Joey McFarland and Riza Aziz. This, however, was just the tip of the iceberg when it came to the accused's spending sprees, especially if one considers the lavish, indulgent and celebrity-filled lifestyle that Jho Low lived between 2009 and 2015.

———

On the 2nd of November 2012, the day of Jho Low's 31st birthday, guests started to arrive at the Palazzo hotel in Las Vegas, where Low awaited them in one of the Chairman Suites looking out over the city skyline – a suite that set back occupants in the region of $25,000 a night. The guest list included Hollywood celebrities and world-renowned entertainers such as Swizz Beatz and his wife Alicia Keys, the former Fugees member Pras Michel, and actors Benicio del Toro and Leonardo DiCaprio. From the Palazzo, the party was transported in limousines to what looked like an empty aircraft hangar in the Nevada desert, where a carnival scene had been created complete with a full-sized Ferris wheel, a circus trampoline, a trapeze and a dozen professional acrobats flying through the air above the heads of Jho Low's guests. Soon more guests arrived, including actors Bradley Cooper and Zach Galifianakis, rap superstar Kanye West, and reality TV celebrities Paris Hilton and Kim Kardashian. Low had reportedly bought Kardashian a white Ferrari as a wedding gift in 2011; she and Kris Humphries evidently squabbled over it in their divorce proceedings. There were also a number of financiers and investment bankers present at the party, including Goldman Sachs's Tim Leissner, who was involved in securing and facilitating the various multi-billion-dollar bond sales for 1MDB between 2012 and 2013. Leissner's wife, model and TV personality Kimora Lee Simmons, was there with him.

Throughout the evening, various artists performed on the stage that had been erected for the occasion, including rappers Busta Rhymes and Ludacris, and R&B stars Usher, Pharrell Williams and Chris Brown. But the highlight of the night was a special performance by Britney Spears, who burst out of a giant faux birthday cake to serenade Jho Low with a Marilyn Monroeesque version of "Happy Birthday". After the performances, Low was presented with a Bugatti Veyron wrapped in a giant ribbon – a gift from his brother Szen. Finally, the night was capped with a firework display that lit up the desert sky.

Two years after the party, the gross misappropriation of Malaysia's sovereign development fund, 1MDB, would be exposed, with Jho Low at the centre of the fraud. And none of it would have been possible without facilitation by the global financial system and its complicit institutions. In 2020, after extensive investigations by regulators, Goldman Sachs's Malaysian unit pleaded guilty to violating anti-bribery laws, and the investment banking group agreed to pay $2.9 billion in a settlement with the SEC, to halt further international investigations against the institution at a group level. This came after a prior settlement with the Malaysian government in which Goldman pleaded guilty to a charge of misleading investors, in respect to its role in facilitating the sale of 1MDB bonds.

In documents made public after the various settlements, it was revealed that Goldman earned more than $600 million in fees from the underwriting of the sovereign fund's bonds in 2012 and 2013, an unusually high amount for the services rendered, according to the filings by the SEC. To be clear, $600 million in fees for the underwriting of $6.5 billion represents 923 basis points of the total amount – three or four times the average percentage charged for the underwriting of a large international bond issuance for a sovereign wealth fund.

On conclusion of the DOJ's investigation, the acting head of the criminal division, Brian Rabbitt, emphasised that Goldman Sachs played a "central role" in the looting of the 1MDB fund, since "the bank allowed this scheme to proceed by overlooking or ignoring a number of clear red flags". The SEC details specifically how senior decision-makers at Goldman ignored multiple warnings from their compliance officers about the bank's dealings with individuals from 1MDB – warnings issued well before the investment bank facilitated the bond sales in 2012 and 2013. In 2010 and 2011, for example, the compliance team at Goldman raised concerns specifically about Jho Low, who had applied to become a private wealth client at the investment bank. "I do not believe we will ever be able to get comfortable with this matter," a senior compliance officer noted in an email to his colleagues in 2010. He believed the bank should "shut this down once and for all". In 2011, a managing director in the compliance division said of Low that "we have pretty much zero appetite for a relationship with this individual... This is a name to be avoided." Despite these warnings, Goldman Sachs *did* enter into a relationship with Jho Low and underwrote $6.5 billion worth of bonds for 1MDB, of which a significant proportion was misappropriated.

Before the DOJ's investigation was finalised, Goldman Sachs denied any wrongdoing and repeatedly claimed that it was not dealing with Jho Low. The Goldman executive who was in charge of managing the 1MDB bond sales, Tim Leissner, also initially denied claims that he was in contact with Low, saying, "There definitely was no intermediary on any of the trades. The blogs in Malaysia always try to link a young Chinese [sic] businessman, Jho Low, to 1MDB." Once Goldman reached a settlement with regulators in 2020, however, evidence emerged that at least one of its employees – Leissner – and likely others, had met with Low multiple times. One of those meetings, according to the DOJ's filings, was on a private yacht in the south of France in

2013. Leissner subsequently pleaded guilty to charges of money laundering and bribery put forward by the SEC – bribes used to secure 1MDB's business with Goldman. Leissner was fined $43 million for the illicit payments he received for his role in facilitating the scheme and was barred from ever working in the financial services industry again. He did not, however, face any jail time.

On the 3rd of July 2018, the former prime minister of Malaysia Najib Razak was arrested by the Malaysian Anti-Corruption Commission (MACC), and charged with abuse of power, multiple counts of fraud, money laundering and bribery, and tampering with the 1MDB audit, which was part of a national investigation beginning in 2015. Razak was sentenced to twelve years in prison and fined $50 million for his involvement in the scandal. As of September 2021, he had not served any of his jail time as he appealed against his charges. In July 2019, Razak's stepson, Riza Aziz, was arrested in connection with the scandal by the MACC, but was released shortly afterwards on bail. He was subsequently sued by the current 1MDB administration for his involvement in the looting of the fund, but charges were dropped in May 2020 after he agreed to return $107 million of stolen assets.

As for Jho Low, he is, at the time of writing, still a free man. The US has sought an indictment and continues a criminal case against Low, as does the Malaysian government, but it is reported that he still travels freely between major Chinese cities, while residing in a villa in Macau. Malaysian authorities have stated that they have been unsuccessful in their attempts to extradite Low from China and that the Chinese authorities' co-operation in the matter has "appeared insincere". The Chinese government has vehemently denied these claims.

Low's movement has in some part been aided by Deutsche Bank, which in 2015 – a few months after evidence of Low's involvement in the 1MDB scandal emerged and he was already under investigation by various regulatory bodies – acted as the correspondent bank for the cross-border transfer of $6 million from Low's Swiss bank account to a regional bank in Cyprus. Low then used this money, cleared by Deutsche, to purchase a home in Cyprus and gain a passport to the Mediterranean nation under their "golden visa" investment scheme.

While unable to bring Low before any court, various legal authorities from around the world, including the American DOJ, the Monetary Authority of Singapore, the Office of the Attorney General of Switzerland and others, have managed to locate and seize billions of dollars' worth of assets related to the young Malaysian businessman. Items include high-end real estate in Beverly Hills, Manhattan, Los Angeles and London, the super-yacht *Equanimity* (which has subsequently been renamed *Tranquility* by its new owners), a private jet, original artworks by Picasso and Basquiat, jewellery to the value of $8 million gifted to Australian supermodel Miranda Kerr, rare vintage movie posters and luxury watches gifted to Joey McFarland, and the best actor Oscar trophy won by the late Marlon Brando for his performance in *On the Waterfront* in 1954, which was gifted to Leonardo DiCaprio.

On Monday the 10th of May 2021, the Malaysian government, which has inherited $23 billion in losses from the misappropriation of the 1MDB sovereign fund, stated that it would be suing Deutsche Bank, JPMorgan and Coutts – the private bank that famously serves the royal family – as well as twenty other entities and individuals that the government claims "have been unjustly enriched by wrongfully receiving monies from 1MDB". The claims against them include negligence, breach of contract, conspiracy to defraud, and dishonest assistance. In March 2021, Deloitte reached a settlement with the Malaysian government to the value of $80 million for its role as 1MDB's auditors.

———————

While the Chinese command-economy style of economic growth is driven by an enormous and opaque state-owned banking system that quite possibly veils the true extent of its non-performing loans and distorts accounts and financials, the US free-market system is far from a pure and spotless alternative: it has consistently produced, and to some extent facilitated, criminal behaviour over several decades. To answer the question posed by Leonardo DiCaprio as Jordan Belfort: no, it is not all legal (and Belfort served time for his crimes). This element of criminality has been very publicly persistent since the early 1990s, when Bankers Trust knowingly sold P&G highly questionable derivatives, and it reappears regularly in the form of significant financial disasters such as the collapse of Lehman Brothers in 2008, the remarkably similar collapse of Archegos Capital Management in 2021, and the exploitation of a developing country's sovereign wealth fund through the Western financial system in the 2010s, a financial catastrophe that has yet to be fully resolved.

This criminality – in opposition to the state-driven nature of China's banking system – is usually the work of rogue actors, though it is crucial to note that their misdeeds would not be possible without the assistance and co-ordination of the wider financial system, including global investment banking firms, lawyers, policy-makers, lobbyists, accountants and auditors, all of whom ultimately play their own role. Even after decades of this recurring criminality – evoking a kind of financially malfeasant *Groundhog Day* – there is still debate as to whether there is excessive regulatory oversight and intervention in the financial system. Currently, the capitalist free-market system continues to portray itself as more efficient and innovative than the communist financial system, as existing in China, but ultimately it is severely hamstrung by its own inadequacies. The free-market system has, without question, experienced an identity crisis – posing as a morally superior ideology to the communist system, but repeatedly being revealed to be severely flawed in its own way.

13

THE SUM OF ALL CHINA'S DEBT

When international news agencies, such as CNN, Bloomberg or CNBC, report on a specific nation's debt, they are often citing an official government debt figure, also known as sovereign or public debt, comprising outstanding bonds issued by that nation's government. In the United States, for example, this would be all outstanding US Treasuries – essentially borrowed money, in the form of bonds, to supplement government spending initiatives.

As of 2020, US government debt stood at approximately $27 trillion, representing 130% of GDP. In simple terms, debt-to-GDP signals how comfortably a nation will be able to service the obligations related to its sovereign debts. By comparison, the official government debt reported in China in 2020 stood at roughly $10 trillion, or 66% of GDP. It was also lower than that of Germany (70%), the United Kingdom (97%), France (98%) and – by an enormous margin – Japan (266%), which has the highest government debt-to-GDP level in the world.

Another common metric that is used to assess a country's indebtedness is total bank assets-to-GDP. This is a measure of all outstanding loans that banks headquartered in a specific nation have issued as a percentage of that nation's GDP. Compared to government debt-to-GDP, total bank assets-to-GDP can be a somewhat distorted, or at least a more complex, measure of indebtedness. This is especially the case if a nation's base currency is not considered a reserve currency or "hard currency" – in which case, it is much more difficult, and indeed risky, for a nation to leverage its banking assets-to-GDP without the possibility of a major currency devaluation that could bring down its financial system. Since the collapse of the Bretton Woods System of currency exchange in the early 1970s, a "hard currency" is considered a strong, stable, highly liquid and easily tradable currency. These include the US dollar and the euro, as the most-held foreign reserve currencies, and to a lesser extent the British pound, Swiss franc and Japanese yen.

The most obvious example of the failure of a financial system because it was over-leveraged and based on a non-hard currency came in October 2008, when all three of Iceland's largest banks collapsed. The base currency of Iceland's banks is the krona – not considered a reserve currency by any measure – so it should have been of some concern that the banking system had leveraged itself by up to ten times the nation's GDP by early 2008. Critically, these banks had largely funded their operations on the interbank market by borrowing in foreign currencies, including in euro-, British pound- and US dollar-denominated debt. When Lehman Brothers collapsed in September 2008, sending shock waves throughout the global financial system, the counterparties to Icelandic banks began to panic and started to discontinue their short-term funding. On 7 October 2008, while credit spreads on Icelandic debt continued to widen, the

Icelandic krona collapsed as nervous traders quickly offloaded their remaining Icelandic assets. To make matters worse, on the very next day, major ratings agencies downgraded Iceland's sovereign and bank debt ratings. This ultimately led to a situation where even if the central bank had had the political will to save its banks – to act as the lender of last resort – it did not possess the financial means to do so, since the local currency had lost so much value that it was helpless in persuading foreign lenders to roll over the banks' short-term funding. In the space of a week in late September 2008, Iceland's three largest banks – Kaupthing, Landsbanki and Glitnir – all failed. Sadly, for many local Icelandic families, the banks had encouraged the local population to borrow for their mortgages not in Icelandic krona but in euro. When the local currency tanked, many of these households faced catastrophic financial failure.

In 2020, the three most leveraged banking systems in the world were headquartered, in order, in Hong Kong, the United Kingdom and China. Hong Kong's total banking assets stood at $2.95 trillion, representing in the region of 800% of its relatively small GDP of $365.7 billion. This made it by far the most leveraged nation in the world in terms of banking assets-to-GDP, though its banking assets were far smaller than China's. In the same year, China's total banking assets stood at $49 trillion, making it the largest banking system in the world in dollar terms. As a percentage of the nation's GDP, its banking assets stood at 333%. Sandwiched between the two, the UK

– home to the City of London, long regarded as one of the banking capitals of the world – had total banking assets in the region of $11.5 trillion, representing over 400% of its GDP. A decade earlier, in 2010, its banking assets-to-GDP had been even higher, at over 500%, indicative of the slow deleveraging that took place in the UK after the Global Financial Crisis.

Compared to China and Hong Kong, however, the UK is a highly developed nation, using a hard currency to fund its banking system. In contrast, both Hong Kong and China fund their highly leveraged banking systems with currencies that are not in extremely high demand in the international foreign exchange market – currencies with far less liquidity, stability and clout in the global financial system than the US dollar or British pound, for example. This ultimately makes their financial systems more vulnerable to external economic shocks. Furthermore, in the case of the UK and its highly developed peers – the United States, Germany and France – these nations, unlike China, are liberal democracies with high GDP per capita levels and free-market economies. In China, the GDP per capita in 2020 was in the region of $10,500, compared to $40,300 in the UK, roughly four times greater. Similarly, in the US, Germany, France and Japan, GDP per capita was between four and six times higher than in China in 2020.

In the case of Hong Kong, this small island nation's excessive banking leverage is especially intriguing because the UK's largest bank by assets, HSBC – previously known as the Hongkong and Shanghai Banking Corporation – unsurprisingly does a large portion of its business in Asia. In 2020 HSBC, domiciled in the UK, made more than 90% of its profits in Hong Kong and mainland China. This is not a trivial point. Essentially, the

THE END OF MONEY

three nations most highly leveraged in relation to their banking assets as a percentage of GDP all have one thing in common: a significant proportion of their assets reside in the greater China region.

This reveals that the world's total banking assets are even more concentrated in one region than is immediately evident. Under the "one country, two systems" principle that has been in place since Hong Kong was reclaimed from the British in 1997, the island has been part of the Chinese nation, serving as the Western world's financial plug point to mainland China. In recent years, however, China has been exerting increasing pressure on Hong Kong – theoretically still classified as a democratic territory – to fall in line with the mainland's communist ideology. This has been starkly demonstrated by the imposition of draconian legislation, notably the 2019 Hong Kong extradition bill that allows China to extradite anyone it deems a fugitive in Hong Kong and to put him or her on trial on the mainland. When pro-democratic protests took place in Hong Kong throughout 2019 and 2020, local authorities violently suppressed the demonstrations, arresting pro-democratic leaders and more than ten thousand ordinary citizens. Subsequently, in June 2021, the world witnessed more than five hundred armed police ransacking the offices of one of the last independent pro-democratic media outlets in Hong Kong, *Apple Daily*. This was a clear show of strength by the Chinese government, signalling its agenda to eradicate all pro-democratic elements in Hong Kong. During the raid, *Apple Daily*'s assets were seized, and top editorial staff were arrested and charged with "conspiracy to commit collusion with a foreign country".

THE SUM OF ALL CHINA'S DEBT

Between 2010 and 2020, total banking assets in China more than tripled. Theoretically, if China were to maintain the compound annual growth rate (CAGR) that it experienced in that time, then Chinese banking assets would equate to an astonishing $169 trillion by 2030. Comparatively, if the US maintained the same growth rate that it experienced in the 2010s, it would have $36 trillion in banking assets by 2030. Hypothetically, this would make the banking system of China more than four and a half times larger than that of the US by the end of this decade.

The risk associated with the aggressive growth of China's banking assets is exacerbated by China's already dangerously high corporate debt level as a percentage of GDP. In 2020, the US, the nation with the world's largest economy, recorded outstanding loans to non-financial corporates of $34 trillion, or 160% of GDP. In the same year, China also reported $34 trillion in outstanding loans to non-financial corporations – the same dollar amount as the US (incidentally), but representing roughly 240% of China's GDP. According to a research paper published by the World Bank, China's non-financial corporate debt represented 28% of global corporate debt as of 2018. In terms of emerging economies, China held 70% of total corporate debt. These are numbers that should raise concerns. The World Bank goes on to note that when debt levels are greater than 95% of GDP, this starts to create a significant drag on economic performance. When debt levels become too large, they create what are known as "debt overhangs", which result in companies having to use an ever-higher portion of their revenues to service

THE END OF MONEY

the obligations on their debts. The ultimate consequence of this is an unavoidable debt trap.

Simultaneously, government debt and household debt in China have also grown at a much more rapid pace than in developed nations in recent years. In the US, government debt has increased significantly in the last five years, especially since the advent of the Covid-19 pandemic, recording a CAGR of 7% from 2015 to 2020. But this is a relatively subdued rate compared to the 19% CAGR of China's official government debt recorded over the same period.

Intensifying the problem of China's rapidly increasing debt and banking assets are – as has been shown – the diminishing returns being recorded on these assets, largely caused by issues related to lending practices within the country. The most significant of these is the problem of increasing, and potentially "hidden", non-performing loans within the Chinese banking system, no doubt accelerated by the economic disruption of the Covid-19 pandemic. Asset management corporations (AMCs) in China are taking on an ever-increasing quantity of bad debts every year from their corresponding large state-owned banks while they themselves are under great pressure to eke out any return at all from these toxic assets.

The world really took notice of the trouble building in China's AMCs when, on 29 January 2021, the Chinese government executed Lai Xiaomin, the former head of China's largest AMC, Huarong Asset Management. Three weeks previously, Lai had been found guilty of taking bribes to the value of $280 million over a period of ten years. Apart from corruption, the court also charged him with bigamy. While Huarong was initially set up for the sole purpose of working out distressed debt acquired from its associated government-owned bank, ICBC, the AMC expanded aggressively into new areas during Lai's ten-year reign, including insurance, property development and brokerage services, many of which were never economically feasible pursuits. A similar expansion into ventures beyond the acquisition of distressed debt from their associated banks was also undertaken by the other three large AMCs – Cinda Asset Management, Orient Asset Management and Great Wall Asset Management.

On 31 March 2021, a few weeks after Lai Xiaomin's execution, Huarong announced that its year-end results for 2020 would be delayed because a "relevant transaction" was still being processed, and that its auditors needed time to account for this update in Huarong's finances. The transaction in question was a plan for the central bank of China, PBOC, to buy Huarong's distressed assets through a vehicle called Beijing Chengfang Huida Enterprise Management Co. This is a subsidiary of Cinda Asset Management. The plan was blocked, however, when Chinese banking regulators, in alliance with the Ministry of Finance, rejected the proposed restructuring. Huarong had planned to move over $15 billion of distressed debt assets onto the books of Chengfang Huida, but because the plan was rejected, Huarong was forced to resubmit its annual results. The news of the postponement of Huorong's annual results spooked international investors, sending the price of the AMC's dollar-denominated bonds sharply downward in the week that followed, from 97 cents to 65 cents on the dollar.

After the fact, in mid-April 2021, S&P Global Ratings issued a warning over Huarong's credit profile, citing the hold-up in the release of its results as worrisome, though the ratings agency did not immediately downgrade the AMC's debt. As of June 2020, Huarong had $260 billion in assets under management and had attracted billions of dollars in foreign investment. As of mid-2021, Huarong and its subsidiaries faced $7.4 billion of maturing bonds.

———

Another issue that will likely exacerbate China's debt problem is the fact that it has become the world's biggest lender to developing nations – lending more to these countries than either the World Bank or the International Monetary Fund. In total, the world owes China in the region of $6.5 trillion – largely existing in the form of bonds sold on the open market. But perhaps the most troubling part of this total $6.5 trillion of lending is the $1.5 trillion of direct loans to developing nations, many of which are part of China's ambitious Belt and Road Initiative.

The Belt and Road Initiative was commenced in 2013 by the Chinese government to expand and enhance its trade routes and relations throughout seventy countries, investing heavily in infrastructure such as ports, airports, railways, roads and dams, especially in developing Asian, Middle Eastern and African nations. The problem with these endeavours, however, is that many of the loan agreements made with historically impoverished nations have needed to be continually renegotiated and restructured, as these countries struggle to come up with the large interest payments owing. For China, the strategic advantage of these loans comes in the form of a type of "debt-trap diplomacy", in which not only does China secure access to the raw materials that its borrowers produce, but it also gains an ally at the global negotiating table; for example, at the United Nations. In situations where these nations have a vote in determining the outcome of globally important issues, such as multilateral trade agreements or global environmental policies, China's investment largesse may benefit the greater Chinese cause.

No matter how politically effective they prove to be, the loans to these nations are likely to have poor returns in purely financial terms, which adds to the already heavy debt burden carried by China. This is made evident when considering the economic condition of the countries that owe China the most money: the fifty most indebted nations' stock of debt increased on average from around 1% of their GDPs in 2005 to around 15% by 2017, according to research conducted by the Kiel Institute for the World Economy. Of these nations – often impoverished African states such as Niger, Congo, Ethiopia and Zambia – many owe China more than 20% of their GDP, while some, such as Djibouti, owe as much as 85% in accumulated loans.

––––––––––

The combination of these forces paints a bleak picture for the Chinese financial system in the coming decade. Because of the rapid growth in debt levels each year, the Chinese economy is required to grow at an equal or greater pace to meet its debt obligations. With an ageing population and a declining workforce, maintaining this GDP growth will be made significantly more difficult in the next decade. In an attempt to resuscitate a steadily declining growth rate, the government is increasing its spending each year – aided by banks that have expanded their balance sheets to exceptionally high levels. Despite these efforts, the GDP growth rate continues to trend lower every year.

Hypothetically, the Chinese government could adjust its strategic objectives, slowing down the Belt and Road Initiative, for example, and cease chasing unrealistic growth rates given demographic realities. This would, in theory, decelerate the rapidly increasing debt levels to some extent. The challenge presented by this option is that the Chinese financial system is already overextended to such an extent that it cannot be deleveraged without massive write-downs of bad loans. This would lead to the default of thousands of zombie companies that are only being maintained by the continual extension of new loans or the rollover of existing ones.

It seems inevitable that at some point the cracks will become so wide that there will no longer be a way to paper them over, even with trillions of dollars more of outstanding loans. And it is then that China could experience a major economic slowdown, with global implications, or even a financial collapse – and perhaps even the beginning of its own accompanying era of public distrust in a government that allowed, and actively enabled, this collapse to occur.

14

THE LONDON WHALE
– THE LAST STRAW

Every year since 1991, representatives from Gallup Inc, an American analytics and advisory company based in Washington DC, have conducted telephone interviews with a random sample of more than a thousand adults in the US, asking them to rate their level of confidence in sixteen selected American institutions. The institutions on the list, presented to interviewees in random order, include the military, the medical system, the police, public schools, the criminal system, banks, large technology companies and television news.

In that time, the military has ranked consistently as either the most or second most trusted institution. Other institutions that have generally been listed as those in which respondents have a "great deal" or "quite a lot" of confidence are the church, organised religion and the police, though the police dropped significantly in the rankings in 2020, following the riots after the killing of George Floyd. Conversely, more than 50% of interviewees felt confidence in the medical system for the first time in 2020, in large part due to the positive role it played during the Covid-19 pandemic. On the other end of the scale, Congress has consistently been one of the worst-performing institutions.

Overall, Gallup notes that over the period 1991 to 2020, Americans' trust in the nation's institutions has been on a steady decline, especially from the early 2000s onwards. Certainly, banks have followed this trend. On average, just 36% of respondents in 2020 said that they had either a "great deal" or "quite a lot" of confidence in banks. Back in 2009, following the Global Financial Crisis, and in particular after the failure of Lehman Brothers and the widespread financial chaos and subsequent bailouts that resulted, this dropped to its lowest point since polling began, at just 22%. Its all-time low of 21% was, however, still to come – that was in 2012, the same year that JPMorgan's "London Whale" scandal made headlines across the globe.

In May 2012, JPMorgan announced losses in excess of $2 billion relating to derivatives trading positions. Not long after the initial announcement, the total was revised upwards to losses that could exceed $9 billion under worst-case scenarios. As it happened, the actual loss that JPMorgan incurred was something of an intractable calculation, because certain trading positions held in different units within the bank happened, by pure chance, to cancel out portions of their losses. It was later estimated that the total loss was in the region of $6 billion, resulting exclusively from positions taken in the interest rate market. Although this is a significant sum for any institution to lose, it was neither the sheer size of the losses, nor the notion of losing money through complex derivatives trading positions in and of itself, that was worthy of regulatory attention. Rather, it was the source of the positions that would prove to be the greatest point of contention, resulting in extensive regulatory investigations into JPMorgan's risk management systems and internal controls, as well as a series of gruelling congressional hearings and millions of dollars' worth of fines to be paid by the bank.

At the centre of the case was Bruno Iksil, the trader who had taken the oversized interest rate market positions and who came to be known as "the London Whale". What was most disturbing about Iksil's trades was that they were not made by a Nick Leeson-type rogue trader sitting without oversight in a secluded office in Singapore, for example, as happened with the complete failure of Barings Bank in 1995. Rather, they were extremely large and extremely risky bets taken by a trader reporting directly to the Chief Investment Office (CIO), which in turn reported directly to Jamie Dimon, the CEO of JPMorgan. Ironically, the mandate of the CIO unit included "faithfully executing strategies demanded by the bank's risk management model" – a model intended to identify, evaluate and minimise the risks of the bank.

Iksil had taken an enormous bet that the spread between the London interbank offered rate (LIBOR) and the implied yield of investment-grade corporate debt, based on the price at which listed corporate debt traded on the market, would narrow. To take this bet, he took significant positions in a financial instrument called the Markit CDX North America Investment Grade Series 9 10-Year Index – known to investors as the CDX

IG 9. The index is made up of the yields of 121 investment-grade bonds issued by North American corporations, and is measured as a spread against LIBOR. The higher the value of the index, the greater the spread: this is usually associated with market unease, such as political or economic uncertainty. During periods of market unease, there is usually an associated flight to quality safe-haven assets; subsequently, demand for US corporate debt, as opposed to government debt, should weaken. This would theoretically lead to lower demand for US corporate bonds, lower prices and inversely higher yields for these same bonds. In sum, the index should increase in value during periods of economic uncertainty and decrease in value during periods of relative calm.

By taking enormous short (sell) positions in the CDX IG 9 index, Iksil had essentially made a very large bet that markets would strengthen and that these spreads would narrow – and he had taken the bet unhedged. Had the trading positions been of a nature that corresponded with the idea of carrying out trades to support risk management within JPMorgan as a whole, there would have been corresponding positions in the bank in the opposite direction; that is, positions that assumed market disruption which the CIO unit felt it had to hedge out. Ironically, as it happened, and tellingly in terms of the failure of risk aggregation, other units within the bank *had* taken opposing positions to Iksil. This had occurred unbeknown to him, and certainly not for hedging purposes, but rather because those units felt that the market-moving positions taken by other traders – including their own firm's traders – were incorrect.

As with Nick Leeson of Barings Bank in 1995, it was unexpected market events that blew up Iksil's short positions. In

Leeson's case, his "straddle trade" on the Nikkei 225 – in which fees are earned for selling short positions and long positions at the same strike price on the same index with the view that the market will remain stable – was catastrophically derailed by news of the Kobe earthquake and its ripple effect across the entirety of the Japanese markets. And in Iksil's case, it was the European sovereign debt crisis that moved the markets in unexpected ways.

The global markets in April and May 2012 had become increasingly concerned that the European economic situation was rapidly deteriorating, and that it was now possible to conceive of a Greek sovereign debt default, with the possibility of a domino effect of economic failure throughout Europe. Investors quickly, and in great volumes, withdrew funds from the corporate bond market in a flight to safety. This decreased demand for US corporate bonds and pushed down their prices, increasing their yields and widening their balance-weighted average spread against LIBOR. The result was an increase in the CDX IG 9 index price which – coupled with several large hedge funds deliberately taking the opposite position to JPMorgan's large short positions on the trade – ultimately dealt unprecedented trading losses to JPMorgan's CIO unit, accounting for roughly $6 billion. In general, special departments within banks, such as the CIO unit, are responsible for the measurement and management of the aggregate risk exposure that the bank has to particular risk factors and risk scenarios. On occasion, traders within these divisions have been caught out when they start to take large proprietary positions. In JPMorgan's case, this was a particularly significant position that did not hedge risk but was speculative in nature.

Following the London Whale incident, CEO Jamie Dimon admitted that "egregious mistakes" had been made. Up to that point, Dimon had held a strong position at the negotiating table, respected by both macro-prudential institutions and local regulators. This respect was epitomised when Barack Obama himself – the president of the United States at the time and one of the greatest advocates of reining in greed on Wall Street – came out in Dimon's defence after Whoopi Goldberg, among other commentators from outside the industry, questioned his ethics. In response, Obama said, "First of all, JPMorgan is one of the best-managed banks there is. Jamie Dimon, the head of it, is one of the smartest bankers we've got."

This was not the first time Obama had publicly stood up and made statements in support of Dimon. Commenting on JPMorgan's disastrous decision to acquire Washington Mutual just prior to the Global Financial Crisis, Obama made the following public statement: "You know, keep in mind, though, there are a lot of banks that are actually pretty well managed, JPMorgan being a good example. Jamie Dimon, the CEO there, I don't think should be punished for doing a pretty good job managing an enormous portfolio." Irrespective of the politics embedded in special interests within Wall Street, and of the tight-knit relationship between Wall Street and both the Democratic and Republican parties, the 2012 London Whale event was a significant turning point, following which regulators, investigators, attorneys general and prosecutors seem to have had carte blanche to punish banks.

In the four years from the start of 2012 through to the close of 2015, JPMorgan was fined by the Department of Justice, by the Board of Governors of the Federal Reserve, by the Treasurer of the United States, by the states of California, Delaware, Illinois, Massachusetts and New York, and by many other extensions of government, a total amount in excess of $29.6 billion. Based on the investment bank's financial statements for the four years ending 31 December 2015, this represents 26.4% of after-tax earnings on an annual basis. These fines therefore had a significant impact on shareholder returns over those four years.

JPMorgan was not the only bank to have been affected by the significant shift in attitude by regulators and governments in the US and Europe. Following the Financial Crisis, regulatory authorities adopted an aggressive position against banks in the Western world, particularly from 2012 onwards. As a result, the profits and retained earnings of these banks were significantly reduced, making it even more difficult for them to achieve the increased capital reserve ratios demanded by the regulator.

Between the beginning of 2007 and the end of 2015, more than $138 billion in fines was levied against banks from across the world. In 2007 and 2008, when the Crisis was still under way, regulators at the time were more concerned with saving the banks than fining them. From then on, though, the escalation was astonishing. In the three years from the beginning of 2009 to the end of 2011, for example, banking institutions were fined less than $20 billion, then in the three years from 2012 to 2014 they were fined more than $100 billion − a staggering increase in fines between the consecutive periods. A small selection of the fines levied against Western banks since 2007 include $11.1 billion for UBS in 2008, $7.2 billion for

Deutsche Bank in 2010, $5.3 billion for Wells Fargo in 2012, $13 billion for JPMorgan in 2013, $16.6 billion for Bank of America in 2014, $7.1 billion for Citigroup in 2014, $8.9 billion for BNP Paribas in 2015, $5.1 billion for Goldman Sachs in 2016, $5.5 billion for Royal Bank of Scotland in 2017, and $5.3 billion for Credit Suisse in 2017.

When every bank fine of more than $500 million on public record – of which there are hundreds – is tallied up over an expanded time horizon, from 2007 to 2020, the total for the industry worldwide amounts to more than $300 billion. The vast majority of these were against US and Western European banks. In contrast, there is little on public record of banking fines against banks domiciled in Asia over that period and, most strikingly, there is not a single mention of a bank from China receiving a fine for more than $500 million. The largest bank fine ever handed down by the Chinese banking regulator as of writing was 722 million yuan (about $113 million) against China Guangfa Bank in 2017 for providing illegal guarantees for defaulted corporate bonds sold through an Alibaba-backed online finance platform. The contrast between Western and Chinese banking systems is neatly encapsulated in figures from 2018. In that year alone, Wells Fargo was fined $3.6 billion, Royal Bank of Scotland $4.9 billion, Barclays $2 billion, HSBC $765 million and Société Générale $717 million. Meanwhile, the Chinese banking regulator handed out 190 million yuan ($27 million) of fines – in total – to Chinese banks.

The Western banking system's identity crisis, exacerbated by the London Whale incident in 2012, has led to an era in banking in which there is no longer a fair and equitable relationship between the free-market participants in banking and the regulators of the industry. Before the incident, it could be argued that JPMorgan had commendably navigated the Crisis and come out on the other side as one of the most successful and stable banks in the world, both financially and reputationally – a fact that made Dimon's a significant voice against excessive intervention in the industry. It could even be argued that, at that point in the ongoing ideological conflict between the laissez-faire capitalist agenda and regulators' calls for a more strictly controlled financial system – echoed by an angry public which demanded punishment for the criminality that persisted within the banking system – there was still a perceptible balance of power between the camps.

Once the London Whale had come and gone, however, this balance was upended. The position that Dimon had held as flag-bearer for the independence of banking was wholly undermined when a series of congressional hearings revealed that JPMorgan's CIO unit's "judgment and execution... were poor", that the bank "did not ensure that the controls and oversight of the CIO evolved commensurately with the increased complexity and risks of certain CIO activities", and that "CIO risk management was ineffective in dealing with synthetic credit portfolios". In the mind of the public – manifest in the dismal votes of no-confidence expressed in polls such as those undertaken by Gallup – the credibility of banks, and the public's faith in them, were at an all-time low. It is since this point that the influence of free-market advocates has been even further eroded, and the balance of power dramatically shifted in favour of proponents of stricter controls over banks and the financial system as a whole.

Nowhere can this shift of power, and the subsequent identity crisis, in the Western financial system be seen more clearly than in the meting out of hundreds of billions of dollars' worth of banking fines in the years that have followed the Global Financial Crisis. Simultaneously, following the Crisis, there has also been an unrelenting drive to impose ever more complex and restrictive prudential regulations on the international banking system, reducing leverage, raising capital requirements and imposing counterintuitive liquidity rules that have significantly hindered banks' ability to be profitable.

———————

The Global Financial Crisis and the events that followed, including the London Whale incident of 2012, affected the financial industry in two critical ways. First, they created an enormous erosion of trust in global financial institutions. And second, they introduced a plethora of new and complex banking regulations. These regulations, imposed in some cases nationally and in others internationally, crossing trade and sovereign borders, are the by-product of a deep and angry sentiment within the public sphere. At the core of this sentiment lies the belief that the greed exhibited by banks leading up to the Crisis must be curtailed, necessitating far stricter oversight of the industry. In the wake of the Crisis, the very idea of free-market capitalism – certainly as it took form in the 1990s-style investment banking model – was no longer acceptable to Western governments or to their voters.

For banks across the world, but particularly in the United States, the onslaught of stringent banking regulations represented the end of an era. Before the Crisis, banks had managed to maintain some degree of independence, as private institutions operating in a free market that were theoretically meant to be self-regulating. After the Crisis, this argument no longer held water. Trust and confidence in financial institutions in general, and in banks in particular, had been eroded so dramatically that these institutions – even in America, the champion of the free-market system – had little choice but to co-operate, however reluctantly, with the European mission of global regulation. This mission and its regulations would, its proponents convincingly argued, protect the interests of society as a whole – but they would also directly affect the profitability and competitiveness of the individual banking institutions under their purview.

Beyond this, there are also three significant shortcomings of global banking regulations, as they exist at present, in terms of their ability to gauge and manage risk. The first of these is the extreme complexity of the regulations, which have become overly reliant on mathematical models that are known to be based on flawed assumptions, including the equations for calculating capital for credit risk and market risk. The underlying assumption of these mathematical models is the use of continuous-time finance mathematics on non-continuous data, so that, mathematically, it would be possible to use the normal distribution for all first-difference values. Mathematically, this is elegant, but it is demonstrably not applicable to the financial world in general, and it does not capture the risk of extreme events. The degree to which these mathematical models fail to predict severe risk events is evidenced by the fact that there have been far too many financial crises over the last few decades that these models did not, and could not, predict – perfectly exemplified by the failure of Long Term Capital Management in 1998. Any attempt by the mathematical and regulatory community to adjust for these failures has simply layered further complexity on top of already flawed assumptions. More recently, the introduction of stress scenarios, defined very specifically in the regulations, has attracted capital charges that are added on to existing capital charges and has obfuscated the original intent and meaning of the non-linear mathematical equations that banks have worked so hard to implement. It seems counterintuitive to have linear add-ons to capital charges after complex non-linear equations were used to achieve the required numerical outcomes on which regulators insist.

The second shortcoming of global banking regulations is that they rely on the assumption that all member states will abide by them in a fair and equitable manner. As has been shown, there is strong evidence that this is not the case with China. As the Basel Committee on Banking Supervision (BCBS), as well as other supranational entities such as the IMF, has reluctantly recognised, there are significant differences in the way China classifies its non-performing loans from the clear and detailed manner in which the BCBS articulates the rules for defining them. It is the BCBS's definition of non-performing exposures with which the majority of the world complies, including banks from the US, the UK and countries across Europe. All of these nations' banks comply with the Basel regulations by promulgating the Committee's rules as laws within their respective countries. The BCBS's relatively myopic treatment of China has allowed the largest banking system on earth to become increasingly divergent from international standards.

The third significant shortcoming of the presiding global banking regulations is that they do not sufficiently address critical

21st-century risks that should be of pressing concern for banks, governments and regulatory bodies. One such risk is the rapid proliferation of new technology firms that are not banks but nonetheless offer specific, and often narrow, financial services to the public. These firms, known generally as fintechs, specialise in the intermediation and financialisation process but operate outside the boundaries of the formal, regulated banking system. Another significant risk is the rapid and disturbing increase in inequality worldwide, greatly aggravated by the practices of tax arbitrage and tax evasion, which are facilitated by the continued existence of tax havens across the world. Related to this risk, and further aggravating the problem of inequality, is the radical increase in money supply that has taken place since the Global Financial Crisis and that was particularly accelerated during the Covid-19 pandemic. Finally, perhaps the most overlooked source of risk within the global financial system at present is the advent and proliferation of money that is not controlled by central bankers – cryptocurrency. This risk has grown significantly: Bitcoin reached a market capitalisation of more than a trillion dollars in 2021, and total cryptocurrency assets reached a market capitalisation of more than $2 trillion in the same year – but it has largely been disregarded by international regulatory bodies until very recently.

More so than ever, multilateralism, particularly as it pertains to the institution of banking, has fallen further and further behind what is being celebrated as innovation. To date, these modern risks have been inadequately addressed by regulators, who have done so in a reactive and uncoordinated fashion. They deserve far more attention.

15

FINTECH AND REGULATORY FAILURE

In late 2018, *Financial Times* investigative journalist Dan McCrum gathered his personal possessions together and moved from his usual desk in the newspaper's London offices to a small windowless room next door to the main newsroom. There he pored over pages and pages of classified documents, working on an air-gapped computer to evade any attempts by hackers to access the information he was analysing. The documents were internal records of transactions belonging to German fintech company Wirecard, which McCrum had obtained from whistleblowers among the company's own legal staff at its Singapore headquarters. These documents suggested that Wirecard was engaging in an unethical trading strategy known as round-tripping.

Round-tripping or round-trip trading refers to techniques that are used to create the appearance that a firm is engaging in a higher volume of trades than it actually is. This can be achieved in a variety of ways, most commonly by a company selling securities to another firm under the agreement that it will buy back the same volume of securities at the same price on a future date. This selling and re-buying process produces no actual profits for the firm – but it does, for the purposes of the firm's accounting, make it appear that the company is engaging in a significant number of sales and purchases, projecting an image of corporate growth that is highly attractive for investors. It was a tactic perhaps most famously used by American energy company Enron in the late 1990s to maintain the illusion that the firm was one of the largest and most successful in the US. And Dan McCrum now had evidence in his hands that Wirecard – then the most successful fintech in Europe – was doing something similar.

This was not the first time Wirecard had been suspected of engaging in suspicious financial activity. A decade previously, when the firm was still a little-known payments processor with a primary business of collecting credit card payments from customers on behalf of gambling and porn websites, German shareholders' association SdK had published a report suggesting irregularities in the firm's financial statements. At the time, international audit firm EY (then known as Ernst & Young) was appointed to conduct a special audit, but the report was called into question when it was discovered by German authorities that two of the individuals involved had failed to disclose positions in Wirecard stock. Afterwards, EY nonetheless stayed on as Wirecard's group auditor, and the German firm expanded rapidly over the following six years.

In 2005, Wirecard listed on the Frankfurt Stock Exchange, avoiding the scrutiny that would accompany an initial public offering by acquiring a defunct call centre group already listed on the exchange. The following year, it expanded into the banking space through the purchase of online banking services provider XCOM Bank AG. It was through this deal in particular that Wirecard truly began to establish itself in the fintech market, as XCOM's universal banking licence enabled Wirecard to add a range of banking services to its existing payments processing services through a newly created subsidiary called Wirecard Bank.

Over the next few years, Wirecard grew rapidly. In 2018, the firm reported that it was processing debit and credit card payments for roughly 250,000 merchants. In August of that year, its share price hit a peak of €191 and, with a valuation of around €24 billion, it overtook Deutsche Bank as Germany's most valuable financial services provider. Later that year, it replaced Germany's second-largest bank, Commerzbank, on the Dax 30 index, which comprises the thirty largest German blue-chip companies on the Frankfurt Stock Exchange. It was now an automatic investment for international pension funds.

For Germany, Wirecard's success was something worth celebrating – it was the largest fintech company in Europe, and the only firm of its kind able to compete against American giants such as Plaid and Coinbase. But its success was not unblemished. As the firm gained prominence, the issue of irregularities in its published financial statements re-emerged, becoming a subject of particular interest for Dan McCrum, who had a history of exposing corporate accounting scandals. McCrum was well respected in the world of financial journalism, having previously uncovered accounting scandals at listed law firms Quindell and Slater & Gordon, UK software provider Globo, and Greek fashion retailer Folli Follie, which had fabricated sales on its financial statements for seventeen years. From 2015 onwards,

Wirecard became McCrum's primary curiosity, leading to the publication of the "House of Wirecard" series on the FT's *Alphaville* financial blog.

The concerns raised in early articles by McCrum were lent further support by a separate report published in 2015 by J Capital Research, the US company specialising in the production of research reports on over-valued publicly traded companies, which suggested that Wirecard's Asian operations were significantly smaller than the firm claimed. The allegation was reiterated by a further report, published around the same time, which was compiled by a group of anonymous investors, later to be associated with investigative financial research group Viceroy Research. Following the publication of these reports, Wirecard's share price dropped significantly in 2015, but the firm adamantly denied all wrongdoing, repeatedly dismissing claims made against it as being contrived by short sellers who would profit if the company's stock price dropped. The company even suggested that the *Financial Times* – one of the most highly respected international sources of financial news and analysis – had colluded with these short sellers, purposely timing the publication of negative stories so that those who had taken positions against Wirecard could take advantage of plummeting stock prices.

To intimidate and discredit the newspaper, Wirecard officials even went so far as to attempt to deceive the FT into printing a false story regarding an impending merger between Wirecard and its French rival, Ingenico. Wirecard COO Jan Marsalek personally confirmed to the newspaper that the merger was going ahead when in fact no such deal existed – a truth that was discovered when the FT contacted Ingenico executives to confirm the story and found they knew nothing of the merger. Following the failure of this attempt to prevent the FT from pursuing further stories about Wirecard, McCrum personally became the victim of a social media smear campaign that was later revealed to have been orchestrated by Wirecard representatives. The campaign was based on private correspondence between the journalist and a corporate investigator, which was hacked, doctored and posted online to make it appear as if McCrum was synchronising the publication of Wirecard stories with various hedge funds.

When McCrum received a tip-off from within Wirecard's own Singapore office in 2018, and thereafter obtained evidence of forged invoices and fabricated money flows, his long-held suspicions about the company were confirmed. Among the documents in his possession was a report that revealed evidence of Wirecard's round-trip trading with companies in India. After months of further research, safely hidden in the FT's windowless office to avoid both online and physical surveillance, McCrum was finally ready to publish his story on 30 January 2019. Following due process, the article was first sent to Wirecard to allow the firm an opportunity to comment. No comment came. While McCrum waited, however, his editor took a call from a trader saying he had heard the FT would be publishing a negative story about Wirecard that day – if the company's stock was going to drop, he wanted to know about it beforehand. Nobody outside a select group of individuals within the FT had even known the article was being written, which meant that the leak came from Wirecard itself. The firm had evidently alerted short sellers about the article in a bid to make it appear once again as if McCrum and the FT were engaging in market manipulation.

The FT published the story anyway. Owing to the timing of the publication, to some observers it may have seemed plausible that McCrum was indeed unfairly targeting Wirecard. EY had, after all, signed off on unqualified audits of the firm each year for almost a decade. Even more significantly, following the publication of the story in 2018 suggesting Wirecard was involved in round-trip trading, the German financial regulator BaFin had initiated investigations into market manipulation by Wirecard's detractors. This led to the regulator instituting a two-month ban on short selling to protect the firm from speculators, citing the importance of Wirecard to the German economy. Shortly thereafter, BaFin also filed a criminal complaint against McCrum, as well as several traders and hedge fund managers who had no apparent connection to the journalist or the FT. Wirecard, meanwhile, stated publicly that it would be suing the FT. While its share price did drop briefly on the day the article was published, it quickly recovered, thanks in large part to a $1 billion investment from Japanese conglomerate SoftBank, known for its investment in start-ups, particularly within the technology space. Once again, any suggestions of indiscretion appeared to have been set aside.

Having endured an internal investigation by his employer, in early 2019, McCrum returned to the small windowless FT office to re-examine the documents he had been working on. It was then that he noticed something new: on Wirecard's list of customers for April 2018 were several entities that did not exist at the time of their apparent transactions with the company. Further investigation revealed that not only were the counterparties in its records fictitious, but that large portions of the worldwide revenue and profits reported by Wirecard were completely fabricated.

In October 2019, the FT published another article detailing this fraud, together with the actual spreadsheet that displayed the fake data. KPMG was subsequently appointed to conduct a special audit of Wirecard, and when it published its results in April 2020, it concluded that it could not, in its own words, verify "the lion's share" of Wirecard's reported profits from 2016 to 2018. Just ahead of the release of the report, BaFin filed a criminal complaint against Wirecard for potentially misleading investors. In June 2020, when Wirecard was due to release its 2019 financial results, it instead announced that €1.9 billion allegedly held in two Philippine bank accounts was "missing". A week later, it admitted that the money had never actually existed, and shortly thereafter Wirecard collapsed, filing for insolvency with €3.5 billion owed to creditors. CEO Markus Braun, together with the firm's chief financial officer and chief accounting officer, was subsequently arrested. Wirecard chief operating officer Jan Marsalek – believed to have been the primary orchestrator of the accounting scandal – escaped to Belarus just days before a warrant of arrest was issued and, at the time of writing, remains on Interpol's most-wanted list.

Wirecard was able to get away with deceiving investors for so long in large part because, as a fintech company that offered both banking and non-banking services, it essentially existed between the systems of regulation and oversight that apply to financial services companies. By merging its payments processing services with banking services from the outset, the firm had carved out a highly niche space of operation with no direct competitors; this made it difficult to compare its financial results with any other similar institution. Investors therefore relied on an adjusted set of financial statements that did not comply with International Financial Reporting Standards. While technically legal, it provided an opportunity for the firm to manipulate its earnings and cash flow figures.

In addition to this, Wirecard made use of a roll-up strategy, which involved the aggressive acquisition of smaller firms around the world, but especially in Asia, allowing it to add revenues from these sources to its financial statements, thus obfuscating the lack of organic growth in the company. Wirecard was also able to divert large sums of money by acquiring several of these businesses at a price significantly above market value, as was the case with Indian e-commerce company Hermes Tickets. In October 2015, Wirecard acquired Hermes Tickets when it purchased a package of Indian payments processing businesses for €340 million. Hermes Tickets represented the bulk of the acquisition, yet the firm had been valued at approximately €46 million less than a year earlier. By way of explanation for the radical increase in purchase price, Wirecard claimed that Hermes Tickets' assets had grown substantially in value owing to India's GDP growth and the rapid expansion of e-commerce in the country. However, in acquisitions such as these, large portions of the proceeds of the purchase often did not go to the seller. In the case of Wirecard's acquisition of Hermes Tickets, the location of tens of millions of euros' worth of intangible assets could not be verified.

In addition, Wirecard made use of third parties to process transactions on its behalf for which the German firm did not hold the necessary licence, and then received a commission for doing so. Investigations suggest that as much as half of the global transaction volumes reported by Wirecard were actually processed by these third-party firms, and that half of Wirecard's revenue and almost all of its reported profit were processed through three primary partner companies. Wirecard claimed that this business model was not entirely unusual for payments processing. The problem, however, was that these third-party payments processors were poorly audited, if at all, and the high commissions commanded by Wirecard for these particular transactions suggest that the types of payments being processed were high-risk and potentially illegal in nature. Wirecard made only scant financial disclosures about these firms in its documents, which were not prepared according to international accounting standards.

What was perhaps most striking about the Wirecard scandal, however, was the lengths to which the firm was willing to go to hide what it was doing from the public and to defend itself when any suggestion of misconduct was levelled against it. Wirecard repeatedly insisted that it prioritised regulatory compliance within its operations, stating that it routinely submitted itself to strict internal and external audits and that any concerns raised were always properly investigated. It publicly decried the stories published by the *Financial Times* as "inaccurate, misleading and defamatory", and privately attempted to intimidate and discredit the newspaper and individual journalists. And, most importantly, for years it successfully deflected all scrutiny of its operations by the auditors and the regulators overseeing it.

After the Wirecard story broke, the company that had been auditing it for nearly a decade, EY, attempted to counter criticism for the role it may have played in the scandal, describing Wirecard's deception as "elaborate and sophisticated", and arguing that "even the most robust audit procedures may not uncover this kind of fraud". In its official statement, it claimed that "the EY Germany auditors performed their audit procedures at Wirecard professionally, to the best of their knowledge and in good faith". The argument was also made that, as the auditor, EY was not responsible for investigating potential fraud. Nonetheless it seems perplexing that the auditors should have failed to take notice of any of the warnings about Wirecard that had been reported by the *Financial Times* and other market participants for years before its collapse.

A report compiled by a team of auditors from Rödl & Partner, which was appointed special investigator for the German parliament's inquiry committee, further found that EY had failed to flag fraud risk indicators or sufficiently query certain irregularities in Wirecard's disclosures. In cases where concerns were raised, the auditor also often sought only verbal assurances and clarifications from the company's executives. In addition, the report concluded that much of the data made available by Wirecard to its auditors for the 2018 audit was not detailed enough to verify individual transactions that were reportedly processed by third parties, and was thus not adequately transparent to comply with International Financial Reporting Standards. EY failed to identify this as a concern, and furthermore failed to verify the transactions independently, relying instead on documents and screenshots provided by a third-party trustee and Wirecard itself.

Nonetheless, EY continued to defend itself. In a notable interview with business news network CNBC in September 2020, EY CEO Carmine Di Sibio went to great lengths to even commend his firm for ultimately detecting the fraud, however late it may have been in doing so. "It feels like in a sense you are seeking some credit for having located the fraud eventually," the interviewer responded quite plainly, capturing something of the collective bewilderment of those who had followed the case. "Would you have found it without the amazing work of various journalists, particularly the FT? Is it right to be seeking credit for finding something so late when it's your job to be tracking those things?" Di Sibio was visibly flustered. "We're not taking credit for anything, I'm just explaining some of the facts," he replied.

In the wake of the scandal, EY is facing several lawsuits, including a class action suit involving more than 1,500 Wirecard investors seeking up to €1 billion from the auditor. The firm has also lost several high-profile clients: Deutsche Telekom, Deutsche Bank's asset manager arm DWS, and Frankfurt lenders Commerzbank and KfW all ended their contracts with the auditor in the months following Wirecard's collapse. Perhaps most distressing for EY is the potential loss of Deutsche Bank, which in May 2021 invited firms to compete for its 2022 audit – this only two years after hiring EY to replace KPMG as group auditor.

Meanwhile, the German financial regulator BaFin also became the target of much public contempt for its failure to adequately investigate the allegations brought against Wirecard by the *Financial Times*, and its decision instead to support the firm and target its detractors for market manipulation. Speaking to the press in June 2020, BaFin president Felix Hufeld acknowledged the regulator's failure to act against Wirecard but simultaneously looked to disperse the blame, claiming that there were several parties who ought to be held accountable, from Wirecard's own senior management to the auditors to "a whole range of private and public entities, including my own, who have not been effective enough to prevent something like that happening". BaFin has also stated – rather ironically given the zeal with which it came to Wirecard's defence in 2018 – that, as a technology company, Wirecard is not considered an institution directly under the regulator's supervision. This is a critical point, highlighting the regulatory shortfall that exists for fintech companies. That a financial services company that at one point had a greater market value than any traditional bank in Germany, or any global bank based in Germany, should not be subject to the oversight of the national financial regulatory body in the country is an indictment of the regulatory regime for its failure to address fintech in general. Disturbingly, this is not unusual as far as the regulatory treatment of fintechs is concerned outside Germany and across the world.

In the months after Wirecard's collapse, the German government announced that it would take steps to radically reform the way in which accounting firms are regulated. Most significantly, it initiated the process of transferring the responsibility of monitoring the financial reporting of listed companies from the Financial Reporting Enforcement Panel to BaFin. This is undoubtedly a positive step, as EY's wilful myopia and determined ignorance in the case present, in many respects, an even more profound affront than the fraud committed by the fintech. It is the failure of professional organisations, as well as the regulators themselves, which by virtue of their profession carry a greater degree of social responsibility and are held to much higher ethical standards, that adds most significantly to the relentless chipping away of social trust in the financial industry as a whole. More broadly, there has been too little emphasis placed on the structural failures within the overall financial services system that continue to allow fintech companies to operate outside the laws and regulations governing the banking system.

In contemplating the ascension of fintech in the financial industry, it is worth bearing in mind that the Global Financial Crisis was the direct result of a shadow banking system that ran parallel to the highly regulated official system but was not required to comply with banking regulations. The major investment banks – Goldman Sachs, Morgan Stanley, Lehman Brothers, Bear Stearns and Merrill Lynch – were all highly leveraged, were all counterparties to collateralised debt obligation creation and trading, and were all market makers of unfunded credit default swaps. They were all also responsible for deftly moving mortgage assets off Main Street bank balance sheets, allowing further reckless lending to proliferate. Yet before the Crisis, none of these firms was regulated under the same set of standards that banks were required to comply with. After all, so the thinking went, they were not technically banks.

More than a decade after the Crisis, history is in danger of repeating itself in the case of fintechs. These firms have typically marketed themselves as disruptive alternatives to the established global financial structure, thriving on the threat they pose to formal institutions by being more innovative, providing better services, and improving accessibility to financial services for the unbanked. Initially, this threat was innocuous as most fintech start-ups were focused on one particular service offering, essentially unbundling the package of services offered by traditional financial institutions into individual, highly specialised best-of-breed software offerings. However, as the popularity of fintechs has grown – together with the aspirations of these companies – many have begun to expand their offerings, creating a significant blurring of the line between formal financial institutions and fintechs.

Accompanying the expansion in the burgeoning scope of fintech has been a general sense of naivety regarding the circumstances out of which financial regulation, albeit overly rigorous in certain respects, has emerged. Critically, while fintechs appear to offer many banking-like services, they do not generally operate under full banking licences; instead, they are subject to the lighter rules and regulations associated with, for example, money service business licences in the US or e-money licences in the UK. Under these licences, they are not subject to the same degree of scrutiny as traditional banks and insurers, which ultimately makes them riskier operations than regulated financial institutions. It is only in the wake of several fintech failures – most notably the collapse of Wirecard – that regulators around the world have begun to acknowledge the need to prioritise oversight of these firms. If fintechs wish to be active participants in the greater financial system, it is rational to expect that at the very least they become subject to the same market conduct rules that apply to banks to ensure the protection of society from money laundering, terrorist activities and other criminal endeavours.

16

GLOBAL TAX ARBITRAGE AND THE RISE OF INEQUALITY

"If you can't trust a Swiss banker, what's the world come to?"

So says Pierce Brosnan as James Bond in the 1999 film *The World Is Not Enough*. Indeed, for much of the 20th century, banking secrecy was a point of pride for the Swiss nation, much in the same way that client confidentiality is a point of pride for a doctor or a priest, who are entrusted with the secrets of their patients and parish. In the world of modern finance, however, at least from the early 21st century onwards, the idea of Swiss bank secrecy has essentially been annihilated, largely triggered by the actions of one man, an outspoken American working at one of Switzerland's most prestigious banks.

In 2015, the US Internal Revenue Service (IRS) paid Bradley Birkenfeld a total of $104 million as part of their whistleblower reward programme – this was the highest-ever reward for a whistleblower at the time. "It was vindication," said Birkenfeld on CNBC's *Nightly Business Report* that same year. "And what made me even more happy was it vindicated me against the Department of Justice." In the interview, Birkenfeld explained his journey as a whistleblower against the Swiss bank UBS and his tumultuous relationship with the Department of Justice (DOJ).

Back in 2007, when he was a private banker at UBS, Birkenfeld had approached the DOJ with damning evidence against his company, including thousands of confidential documents, proving beyond doubt that the Swiss bank was knowingly taking on US clients who wished to evade taxes in the United States. Indeed, as Birkenfeld testified, his primary role as a wealth manager at UBS was to approach and convince wealthy Americans to move their money to UBS, taking advantage of the banking secrecy laws in Switzerland at the time to avoid being taxed in the US. But upon turning over this evidence to the DOJ, Birkenfeld was not rewarded as a whistleblower as he had hoped; rather, he was charged in 2009 with "conspiracy to defraud the United States". He was sentenced to forty months in prison and handed a $30,000 dollar fine for not fully disclosing evidence to the state.

Following his revelations, though, the FBI opened an investigation into UBS based on the "Birkenfeld disclosure". The probe found that more than 52,000 US clients held accounts with UBS, with tens of thousands more at other Swiss banks, and that the US was losing out on billions of dollars in taxes annually because of these accounts. Birkenfeld was vindicated, and having served his time he received the enormous payout from the IRS – an agreed-upon 26% cut of the $400 million in tax revenue recovered directly because of his evidence against fellow UBS bankers and their customers. In spite of this, Birkenfeld spoke openly about his contempt for the DOJ in the CNBC interview. Standing in front of a new Porsche purchased with his windfall – complete with a customised number plate that read YOU&US, the slogan of his former employer, UBS – he was asked whether he thought the IRS was happy to write him the cheque. "Oh no," he replied, with a bold smirk on his face. "They were pissed!" A year later, in 2016, Birkenfeld released an exposé of his experiences, provocatively titled *Lucifer's Banker Uncensored: The Untold Story of How I Destroyed Swiss Bank Secrecy*. While Birkenfeld may evoke general distaste, there is at least some truth in the statement that he "destroyed Swiss bank secrecy".

In February 2009, UBS agreed to settle the case against it, paying the US government $780 million in fines for charges of "conspiring to defraud the United States", but the bank refused to disclose information about its customers who were US citizens. The day after the settlement, the US government filed another lawsuit against the bank, urging it to reveal the names of its American clients. Within a few months, the Swiss Financial Market Supervisory Authority, supported by the Swiss government, brokered a deal with the IRS in which UBS was required to hand over 4,450 of the 52,000 names, managing to preserve the anonymity of about 85% of its US customers. Despite this small victory for Swiss bank secrecy, this was just the beginning of the US government's war against tax evasion in general, and against long-standing bank secrecy in Switzerland in particular.

In the years to come, UBS and other Swiss banks were put under increasing pressure, not only by investigations undertaken by US agencies, but also by those conducted by Belgian, German, French and Israeli authorities. There followed a series of high-profile arrests of individual bankers that shook the Swiss financial system to its core. The first of these arrests came in 2010, when Renzo Gadola was apprehended in Miami, Florida, on the charge of helping US citizens avoid paying tax in their home nation by hiding their money in Swiss bank accounts. Gadola, who had been named in the original Birkenfeld disclosure, was also an employee of UBS. Upon his arrest, Gadola co-operated with the government, providing information on his US clients.

Using the information Gadola provided, the US government went on to arrest several other Swiss bankers, including Christos Bagios and Martin Lack, both ex-UBS employees who were charged with conspiracy to abet tax evasion. Raoul Weil, the ex-CEO of UBS's Global Wealth Management and Business Banking division, was indicted, but when he failed to turn up for his court proceeding, the US government issued an international arrest warrant. He was eventually apprehended while on holiday in Italy, and thereafter extradited to the US to stand trial.

In an interview about the various arrests of Swiss bankers between 2007 and 2009, Scott Michel, an expert in tax enforcement law at the law firm Caplin & Drysdale, based in Washington DC, declared, "I think this is the beginning of the erosion of bank secrecy. Not just in Switzerland, but I think in other countries that hope to maintain an economic position in a global economy." Michel's comments were eerily accurate. In 2010, the US ramped up its pressure on foreign financial institutions to unprecedented levels, most pertinently in the form of a powerful internationally applicable tax regulation that would ultimately break the back of Swiss bank secrecy.

Introduced in Congress in 2009 and signed into law in 2010 by President Barack Obama, the Hiring Incentives to Restore Employment (HIRE) Act was intended to provide tax breaks and incentives for American businesses to hire unemployed workers. As a means to provide the US government with additional income to offset the spending required for the HIRE Act itself, the Obama administration introduced a further Act under it: the Foreign Account Tax Compliance Act (FATCA). FATCA was devised to seek out and eliminate tax evasion by American citizens and American businesses that operate, earn or invest taxable income, totalling over $50,000, outside the United States.

What was exceptional about FATCA, as a newly proposed financial regulation that would affect financial institutions of all sizes from nations across the globe, was the way it was ultimately implemented and enforced internationally. Unlike most other international banking and finance regulations promulgated by supranational regulatory bodies such as the Basel Committee on Banking Supervision (BCBS), FATCA was implemented in a far more direct and unilateral manner. While new BCBS regulations commonly take many years to be accepted and successfully implemented in banks across the world, involving significant industry feedback in the form of multi-year quantitative impact studies, for example, the United States' new tax law was enforced on banks with little consideration of industry feedback. FATCA was agreed to and implemented in such a quick and uncompromising fashion through a simple, yet highly effective mechanism.

To implement FATCA effectively, US tax authorities ultimately needed to be able to identify and quantify all taxable assets held by American nationals outside the US. This in itself was an enormously complex task. In countries like Switzerland, the Bahamas, Liechtenstein and Monaco, where their banks' reputations were defined by their focus above all else on client confidentiality, there was no incentive for financial institutions to willingly hand over the names and account details of American citizens who had chosen to bank with them. Without the co-operation of these institutions, the US tax authorities would have no way of gathering all the required information on outstanding taxable assets deposited in foreign bank accounts. FATCA's answer to this dilemma was straightforward, powerful and severe.

In effect, the US imposed a law on its own banks, stating that they would be required to impose a 30% withholding tax on any payment made to a customer account in another country, with a correspondent bank, if that customer was not FATCA-compliant. This withholding tax would be imposed whether the non-compliant entity was an individual or a corporate, and irrespective of whether FATCA had been made a law or not in that country. The correspondent bank would then have to comply with all FATCA regulations, otherwise the US bank would be forced to withhold 30% tax on the payments owed to the non-compliant entity's bank. This amounted to an implicit exclusion from trading with US banks and in dollar-denominated financial products if institutions were not FATCA-compliant – an exclusion from the world's most significant financial market.

To comply with FATCA, banks had to adhere to the reporting of a very specific and complex set of indicia – in effect, the information indicators – that include the nature of the transaction, the nature of the beneficial recipient and its relation to the account in the correspondent bank, whether that correspondent bank was compliant or not, and whether the customer was recalcitrant. This complex combination of indicia tied together financial entities, their customers and their transactions in a way that made the ubiquity of FATCA's reach throughout the financial system nearly impossible to circumvent.

For those banks that wished to comply with FATCA, there was a hard deadline in place for 1 July 2014, at which time financial institutions were required to complete a search of their records and report the specific personal information laid out by the FATCA regulations. This included, among other details, a US citizen's place of birth, identification number, residential address, telephone number, power of attorney and joint account holder information. As a result, US citizens with foreign accounts came under significant pressure to report their foreign earnings to the IRS, since there was little likelihood of them going unnoticed once their bank became FATCA-compliant. It proved to be a remarkable strategy, so effective that the European Union would introduce its own version of FATCA, in the form of the Automatic Exchange of Information, in 2014, with financial institutions required to start their reporting by 2017.

Within a few years, more than a hundred nations had signed intergovernmental agreements (IGAs) with the US, agreeing to have their financial institutions report all information required by FATCA to the IRS – either directly from the institution to the IRS, or from the financial institutions to their local regulator, which would then relay the information to the IRS. In 2012, France, Germany, Italy, Spain, the UK, South Africa, Japan and even Switzerland all agreed to co-operate with the

US to implement FATCA in their countries as proposed by the law, allowing their banks to submit information regarding US citizens directly to the IRS.

As of 2021, nations that have not explicitly implemented FATCA, or signed any IGAs, include Russia and China. "China's banking and tax laws and regulations do not allow Chinese financial institutions to comply with FATCA directly," deputy director general of legal affairs of the People's Bank of China, Liu Xiangmin, said in 2012. While FATCA serves as a powerful example of how the banking system and banking regulations can be effectively used to curtail tax evasion, financing of terrorism and money laundering, the effectiveness of such regulations necessitates the fulfilment of a critical caveat – that those regulations are consistently applied across all global jurisdictions.

———————

The G7 summit held in La Malbaie in Canada in 2018 was by all accounts a tense affair. One notable media photograph from the event showed President Donald Trump sitting at a table with his arms defiantly crossed, while the six other leaders from the world's wealthiest nations stood on the other side, visibly frustrated. German chancellor Angela Merkel could be seen leaning forward with her hands placed on the table, staring straight at the American president, who refused to look directly at her.

The summit had been marked by repeated clashes between Trump and the other world leaders on a variety of topics, from climate change to the Iran nuclear deal, but most especially on discussions over international trade. Cognisant of the fact that negotiating changes in trade policy with the EU would require gaining the support of the European Commission (EC), Trump had addressed the majority of his statements on the matter directly to the president of the EC at the time, Jean-Claude Juncker. One issue that was particularly vexatious for Trump was the escalation of financial penalties that had been levied by the EC against American companies for regulatory and tax violations. "Your tax lady, she really hates the US," he remarked to Juncker.

The "tax lady" to whom Trump was referring was Margrethe Vestager, the European commissioner for competition. Since she took up the position in 2014, Vestager's mission to enforce European competition laws has seen her initiate investigations into some of the largest international firms operating in the EU. This has included European companies such as Fiat and Ikea and the Russian state-owned energy giant Gazprom, and also American multinationals such as Starbucks, Amazon and Google. Responding swiftly to Trump's remark at the summit, Vestager told reporters, "I've done my own fact-checking on the first part of that sentence, and I do work with tax and I am a woman, so this is 100 percent correct. But the second half of the sentence is not correct; I very much like the US."

Vestager had long been defending herself against criticism that she was unfairly targeting US firms for tax avoidance, but the particular case that undoubtedly earned the ire of the American president was her recent attempt to claw back more than €13 billion ($14.5 billion at the time) in "unpaid taxes" from technology giant Apple. In August 2016, the EC concluded an investigation into Apple's tax structure, specifically as it pertained to its operations in Ireland, where the Commission determined that the technology firm had been granted undue tax benefits. The EC argued that this was illegal under EU state aid rules because it allowed Apple to pay substantially less tax than other businesses operating in the country, and it subsequently ordered the Irish government to recover the "unpaid taxes".

Apple has been present in Ireland since 1980, when it opened its first manufacturing plant in the town of Hollyhill, near Cork. By the late 1980s, the firm had grown to become the largest employer in the area, hiring roughly 1,000 direct employees and 500 subcontracted employees, and achieving net profit ratios that exceeded that of other Irish businesses operating in the town. It was on this information that Apple representatives drew in 1991 when they negotiated a tax deal with the Irish government, under the unspoken threat that unless the firm received more favourable corporate tax terms, it could withdraw its operations and move elsewhere. A deal was subsequently struck in which the firm became subject to a much lower effective corporate tax rate than it would have faced in the US – home to the highest corporate income tax in the developed world at the time, at 35%.

When Apple began operations in Ireland, the corporate tax rate was roughly the same as that of the US, though manufacturing was subject to a special corporate tax rate of only 10%. To assist Ireland as it transformed from an agriculture-based to a knowledge-based economy, the EU had waived usual state-aid rules that allow EU countries to set their own corporate tax rates but do not usually permit special treatment of individual industries or firms within a country. In the early 1990s, the EU withdrew this waiver, however, and Ireland subsequently decided to drastically reduce its statutory corporate tax rate, applicable to all industries, from 40% to 12.5%, with the passing of the 1997 Taxes Consolidation Act. This legislation also provided the structure within which base erosion and profit shifting (BEPS) tools could be employed extensively by many US multinationals throughout the late 1990s and early 2000s to achieve an effective corporate tax rate of between 0% and 2.5% on their international earnings. Through its carefully negotiated agreement with the Irish government, Apple made maximum use of this structure to achieve an effective corporate tax rate of around, or even below, 1% in the early 2000s.

Apple attained this rate by establishing two Irish incorporated companies – Apple Sales International and Apple Operations Europe – which were fully owned by the Apple group and ultimately controlled by the US parent company. The Irish companies held the rights to manufacture and sell Apple products outside the US. According to the European Commission's official report on the matter, almost all sales profits recorded by Apple Sales International and Apple Operations Europe were allocated to "head offices", which were the official tax entities for the Apple group's international operations. These entities existed only on paper, without physical premises in any country, and were thus not subject to any national corporate tax rate. As a result, only a small percentage of Apple Sales International's and Apple Operations Europe's sales profits were actually allocated to the Irish entities and subject to taxation in Ireland, in accordance with the unique provisions of the Irish tax agreement, while the rest were diverted through the Irish entities to the head offices, where they remained untaxed. In 2011, for example, Apple Sales International recorded profits of $22 billion – roughly €16 billion – but only €50 million of this was taxable in Ireland.

Thus some €15.95 billion of profits went untaxed, and Apple Sales International paid less than €10 million in corporate tax in Ireland, which translates into an effective tax rate of about 0.05% on Apple Sales International's overall annual profits.

Under pressure from the EU, Irish tax laws were changed in 2013 so that it was no longer legal for any Irish incorporated firm to make use of a stateless entity for tax purposes. In accordance with the new law, Apple established a physical entity to act as its official residence for international tax purposes, a subsidiary that was domiciled in Jersey, a UK Crown dependency that has a 0% corporate tax rate for foreign companies. Profits earned from Apple's Irish entities were then funnelled to Jersey, where they were not subject to corporate tax. Over time, as Apple Sales International's profits increased, the amount taxable in Ireland under the agreement remained static, which meant that by 2014 Apple Sales International was only paying an effective corporate tax rate of 0.005%. In exchange, Ireland was able to position itself as an attractive location for large multinationals, especially in comparison to other EU nations such as France and Germany.

To be clear, the strategy employed by Apple was in full compliance with the special tax arrangement that the firm had made with the Irish government. What the EC was arguing in 2018, as represented by its "tax lady" Margrethe Vestager, was that such an agreement should never have been made in the first place, because it gave Apple an unfair advantage over other companies operating in the EU, which is illegal under EU state aid rules. The commission further argued that the Irish tax agreement with Apple had supported an artificial and unjustified internal allocation of profits, and that the sales profits of the two Irish entities should have been recorded and taxed in Ireland. It concluded that the two tax rulings issued by Ireland to Apple had substantially lowered the tax paid by the firm on its non-US sales since 1991, and ruled that Ireland's treatment of Apple was illegal under EU state aid rules as it provided Apple with a significant advantage over other businesses.

Apple was, and still is, one of the world's largest and most profitable companies – earning close to $50 billion in overall annual after-tax profit when the EC concluded its investigation in 2016 – but it was paying almost no tax on its non-US profits. Ireland was ordered by the EC to recover the unpaid taxes from Apple for the period from 2003 to 2014, which amounted to approximately €13 billion, plus interest.

———

When Deutsche Bank announced its third-quarter earnings for 2016 at €278 million, representing a return on tangible equity of a measly 2%, the market counterintuitively rallied. Investors had evidently already priced in an expected loss of €350 million predicted by a range of analysts at the time. With the result more favourable than expected, there followed a stint of buying on the exchanges that was remarkable, considering that the bank's return on equity was far below any acceptable market threshold. Then again, given that the US Department of Justice had levied a fine against Deutsche of $14 billion in September of that year for misleading investors in the packaging, securitisation, marketing, sale and issuance of residential mortgage-backed securities before and during the Global Financial Crisis, it was remarkable that the bank could eke out any profit at all.

It was not entirely clear how the DOJ had arrived at the $14-billion figure, or why it was suddenly singling out Deutsche for recrimination almost a decade after the events of which it stood accused. But it did not escape the notice of more cynical observers that the fine followed closely in the wake of the EC's attempt to claim back more than $14.5 billion in "unpaid taxes" from American technology giant Apple. Indeed, it was difficult not to see the Deutsche Bank fine as a direct retaliatory response to the EC's investigation into Apple's tax-avoidance strategy.

Although it was difficult to argue with the ethical position taken by the EC in the matter, Apple had not technically violated the agreement that the firm had reached with the Irish government, or even US corporate tax laws at the time. Both the Irish government and Apple challenged the EC's ruling, arguing that the firm had not received any special treatment as far as the corporate tax structure of its two Irish subsidiaries was concerned. The Irish government, undoubtedly eager to preserve its country's attractiveness as a location for other multinationals, stated simply that any arrangement that gave undue advantages to any company was illegal under Irish law, and therefore no such agreement could exist. Apple claimed that it had paid every cent of tax legally due.

The US government, meanwhile, criticised the EC, claiming that it was behaving as though it had been elevated to the position of a supranational tax authority, and argued that it was threatening to undermine international tax reform agreements through its inquiries. US Treasury secretary Jack Lew personally appealed to the EC to abandon the investigation into Apple, and the Senate Committee on Finance even suggested prior to the conclusion of the investigation that if Apple was forced to pay unpaid taxes to

Ireland, then Lew should consider retaliating with a double tax rate on European companies operating in the US.

Putting aside the particulars of the Apple Irish tax agreement, the broader strategy of corporate tax inversion used by Apple – where a firm locates its legal domicile for international tax purposes in a lower-tax-rate nation, while retaining its material operations in its home nation – is classified as "tax avoidance" and is not illegal in the US. This is in contrast to the illicit practice of tax evasion, where a company purposely misrepresents information on a tax return or uses illegal activities to hide profits. Since the 1980s, tax inversion has been a common corporate strategy for reducing tax liabilities used by many large American companies that operate internationally, and though it exploits certain loopholes in US corporate tax law, it does not technically violate the law. The most well-known inverted American companies are the major technology firms, with Apple most prominent among the likes of Microsoft, Google, Amazon, Netflix and Facebook, while others include engineering and construction company McDermott International, consulting firm Accenture and fast-food franchise Burger King.

Prior to the introduction of the Tax Cuts and Jobs Act in 2017, which overhauled key aspects of American corporate tax law, tax inversion was an especially popular strategy. This was owing to the unusually high rate of corporate income tax in the US, which was over 45% for much of the early 1980s and remained high compared to other developed nations, at 35%, throughout the 1990s and early 2000s. The US also applies this tax rate to all profits earned from the international subsidiaries of American firms, if these profits are repatriated to the US. These profits are also taxed by the foreign country in which the subsidiary that records the profits operates. By undertaking a formal restructuring, American firms can therefore substantially reduce the amount of corporate tax they pay on their international earnings – which often account for the majority of their overall group profits – by domiciling their official entity for international tax purposes outside the US, in a lower-tax-rate foreign country. This means that only the US earnings of these firms are subject to the US corporate tax rate, while international earnings are taxed at a much lower rate, so long as these profits are held offshore. Popular corporate tax domiciles include Ireland, Cyprus and Liechtenstein, where the corporate tax rate is 12.5%, and Bermuda, Bahamas and the Cayman Islands, where the corporate tax rate is 0%.

According to American tax laws, Apple therefore had not technically committed any crime and, in the end, it would be determined that it had also not violated any European laws. Apple appealed against the EC's ruling in the European Union's General Court, the second-highest court in the EU, which ruled in favour of the American multinational in July 2020. The court stated that the EC had not produced enough evidence to support the claim that Apple had been unfairly advantaged by an illegal arrangement with the Irish authorities, and it ruled that Apple did not owe Ireland anything in unpaid taxes.

Deutsche Bank, in contrast, reached an agreement with the US Department of Justice in 2017 that resulted in the bank paying $3.1 billion in civil penalties and providing $4.1 billion in relief funds to customers. This agreement, according to the DOJ, represents the single largest residential mortgage-backed securities resolution for the conduct of a single entity.

The Apple case was not entirely unusual, especially as tax inversion has become a logical strategy for many of America's largest technology firms, for whom the greatest asset is their intellectual property (IP), which can be classified as an intangible asset on their balance sheets and subsequently recorded as a tax-deductible royalty payment to end-users. The essence of these firms' strategy is to legally register their IP in a lower-tax-rate jurisdiction, while subsidiaries in higher-tax-rate countries are then charged by the IP-holding company for the use of the IP. Because entities in higher-tax-rate countries must pay substantial royalties for using the IP, they realise far less profit and therefore pay far less tax in the countries where they operate. The majority of profits is recorded by the IP-holding company, which receives the royalty payments and which is located in a country that has a low, or even 0%, corporate tax rate.

This process is somewhat complicated by the fact that most higher-tax-rate countries will not sign full tax treaties with tax havens, and therefore do not accept the IP charged from a tax haven as deductible against local taxation. To side-step this problem, technology firms have made use of the "double Irish" tax strategy. In this case, a German subsidiary of an American company would, for example, pay the IP charge to a subsidiary in Ireland, a nation that has a global network of bilateral tax treaties in place. The Irish subsidiary would then send the IP payment on to the domicile where the IP is officially registered, in a tax haven such as Bermuda. The IP payment substantially reduces the profit recorded by both the German and Irish subsidiaries, resulting in very low tax payments in those countries, while the bulk of the profit is realised in Bermuda, where it remains untaxed. In this manner, American firms greatly reduce the local tax charges on their international subsidiaries, and they avoid paying US taxes on international earnings, unless they are repatriated to the US.

Prior to 2010, companies using the double Irish were subject to a 20% withholding tax on transfers from Ireland to non-EU states. To circumvent this, the strategy was extended into what is known as a "double Irish with a Dutch sandwich". This involved establishing a Dutch subsidiary, so that funds could be sent first from the Irish subsidiary to the Dutch subsidiary – incurring no withholding tax, as the transfer was between EU states – and then from the Dutch subsidiary to the entity in a tax haven. This process worked because no withholding tax is levied on royalty payment schemes under Dutch tax law. In 2010, Ireland relaxed the laws on withholding taxes, effectively ending the Dutch sandwich, and while there were certain rules with which the Irish subsidiaries were required to comply, the effective tax rate in a double Irish scenario for non-US profits was nonetheless usually close to 0%. In 2015, however, under pressure from the US and the EU, Ireland amended its tax laws, effectively ending the use of the double Irish for new tax plans. Companies already using this strategy were allowed to continue using it until 2020.

It was a version of this strategy that Apple used to minimise the taxes due on its international sales, which at the time of the European Commission's investigation in 2016 accounted for 65% of the group's total sales. To avoid incurring US taxes on these profits, these funds were held offshore, with Apple even issuing several rounds of bonds in the US between 2013 and 2017 to pay dividends to shareholders, rather than repatriating any of its international earnings to the US, where astonishingly it was cash-constrained. In 2016, the company issued bonds to the value of $12 billion. When questioned about this decision, Apple CEO Tim Cook responded, "We're not going to bring it back until there's a fair rate. There's no debate about it. Is that legal to do or not legal to do? It is legal to do. It is the current tax law. It's not a matter of being patriotic or not patriotic. It doesn't go that the more you pay, the more patriotic you are."

The question of what Apple considers to be a "fair" rate is uncertain, however, for when Congress enacted a temporary repatriation tax holiday in 2004 – allowing multinational companies to repatriate foreign profits to the US at a tax rate of just 5.25%, essentially condoning all previous years' accumulation of funds offshore – Apple repatriated only $755 million of the $132 billion in foreign profits it held at the time. Many of America's largest companies similarly recalled only a small percentage of their international earnings, and overall it was determined that the tax holiday had *cost* the US Treasury $3.3 billion. A proposal for a second repatriation tax holiday in 2009 was subsequently defeated in Senate.

Facebook, Google, Microsoft, Amazon and Netflix have all made use of similar tax inversion strategies based on IP payments, weaving between the varying tax laws of different countries to achieve a 0%, or close to 0%, rate of tax on their global earnings. While these firms are still required to pay taxes on profits earned in the US, their overall effective tax rates are usually well below the average of 23.5% for Organisation for Economic Co-operation and Development (OECD) countries.

Based on data reported by S&P Global Market Intelligence, IT firms in the S&P 500 had an average effective tax rate of 14.5% for 2019, with Netflix and Microsoft reporting an effective tax rate of roughly 10% and Alphabet (the parent company of Google), Apple and Amazon reporting 13%, 15% and 17% respectively. Facebook was the only company to report an effective tax rate above the OECD average rate, at 25%. Meanwhile, a report produced by Fair Tax Foundation, a UK not-for-profit community benefit society, estimates that the "Silicon Six" – Facebook, Apple, Amazon, Netflix, Google and Microsoft – which in 2019 had a combined market capitalisation of $4.5 trillion, collectively paid just 15.9% of corporate tax on their declared profits over the period from 2010 to 2017, and 17.2% for 2018 and 2019.

Most of these firms have also endured a battle with European authorities at one point or another over their tax structures. For example, Facebook agreed to pay the French government €106 million in back taxes in 2020, to settle a dispute over revenues earned in the country. This amount covered a decade of the firm's presence in France, and was topped up with an additional €8.46 million in taxes on revenues earned in France for the 2020 financial year. While the total paid was almost negligible in the context of the social media giant's total annual revenue – about $86 billion for 2020 – it nonetheless joined Google, Apple and Amazon in the process, all having reached similar agreements with France. Conversely, in the same year, in a series of events that mirrored the Apple Irish tax case, the EU General Court overturned a ruling by the European Commission that would have seen Amazon pay over €250 million in back taxes in Luxembourg.

A marked point of similarity in these cases was the public statements made by the firms, which have repeatedly insisted that they uphold all tax laws and always pay every cent due in every jurisdiction in which they operate. Technically, this has been true. But with the World Economic Forum estimating in 2021 that around 40% of multinational profits are shifted to tax havens each year, producing an overall loss of some $200 billion in global tax revenue, the question that inevitably arises is why, for more than four decades, and despite the repeated and apparently widespread disparagement of the practice, tax inversion has nonetheless been allowed to continue with minimal intervention from the global community.

———

"US multinational firms are the global grandmasters of tax avoidance schemes that deplete not just US tax collection but the tax collection of almost every large economy in the world." This was the view of Edward D Kleinbard, a former corporate tax adviser and now law professor at the University of Southern California, in a 2017 interview with *The New York Times*. And indeed, while the benefits of shrewd corporate tax strategies are undeniable from a business perspective, what is deeply troubling from an ethical point of view is the flagrant disregard for any kind of social responsibility and the indifference to the growing problem of global inequality which is baked into ideas such as tax inversion.

Inversions are typically undertaken by the largest and most profitable American corporations, which have benefited in many ways from their home country during their years of establishment, through access to education, a skilled workforce, and government research and grants, among other things. There is something deeply affronting about the idea that once they become successful, these companies should actively work to minimise the contributions they make to the country that helped nurture them to success – and subsequently to the other nations in which they establish their operations and grow their profits. Debates over how to tax companies, and indeed *where* to tax them, have been ongoing for decades, and have only grown more intense as companies have become increasingly internationalised and the products they sell more likely to be treated as intangible assets.

In the US, the general attitude towards tax inversion schemes, tax havens and corporate tax rates has historically been ambivalent. Throughout his presidency, Barack Obama urged Congress to enact changes to the tax law that would close what he referred to as the "unpatriotic tax loophole" that allowed for corporate tax inversions, and in 2012 he put forward a Framework for Business Tax Reform that proposed a set of fundamental changes to the US tax system. Any suggestion of lowering the corporate tax rates was, however, strongly contested in Congress owing to the uncertain effect that this could have on the overall national budget deficit – and no doubt to the influence of lobbyists at various levels and across industries. In keeping with the spirit of the free-market era of the 1990s and early 2000s, the US also maintained a kind of silent support for tax havens, justifying this position through controversial economic research, such as that of economist James Hines Jr, which suggested that the use of tax havens by American companies enabled the US to increase its tax revenues because of the way in which tax credits are allocated.

The move towards tax reform nonetheless gained some momentum in 2015, when multinational pharmaceutical and biotechnology corporation Pfizer announced that it would be undertaking an Irish inversion through a $150 billion merger with the pharmaceutical company Allergan, itself an inverted company. This would have effectively established one of the largest corporate inversions in history. In response, the Treasury Department acted within its authority to make inversions less economically attractive by placing limits on serial inversions – when a company inverts by acquiring a foreign company that itself has inverted or grown larger through acquisitions of American firms – and addressing the practice of earnings stripping, which companies have used to avoid paying US taxes by artificially shifting their profits abroad. In 2016, Pfizer announced that it would not be going through with the inversion. The secretary of the US Treasury at the time, Jack Lew, noted that the only way to effectively address inversions would be through legislative changes, which were difficult to achieve owing to the divided opinions of Republicans and Democrats in Congress on the matter.

More substantial revisions to the American tax system were forced through by Donald Trump. In 2017 Congress narrowly passed the Tax Cuts and Jobs Act (TCJA) with 53% of the votes, even though no Democrats supported the bill. The TCJA introduced changes in both individual and corporate tax. For corporate tax, the most significant changes included lowering the corporate tax rate for domestically earned profits from 35% to 21% and lowering the rate for internationally earned profits repatriated to the US to 15.5% for liquid assets and 8% for nonliquid assets, payable over eight years. Through the Base Erosion and Anti-Abuse Tax provision, the TCJA also placed restrictions on the degree to which companies could deduct interest expenses and royalty payments. This meant that, in certain instances, the effective tax rates for inverted companies were increased, though in most cases not enough to merit moving their international head offices back to the US. Essentially, these companies therefore continued to enjoy the benefits of tax inversion on their international earnings, while also benefiting from a lower corporate tax rate on their US profits.

The Act also instituted a minimum 10.5% tax on all new foreign income earned by American firms under the Global Intangible Low-Taxed Income provision, which would, it was estimated, reduce the amount of profit held by US companies in tax havens by between 12% and 16%. Overall, when the TCJA was passed, Congress further estimated that the base erosion provision would increase tax receipts by $150 billion over ten years, and that the interest-expense cap would achieve a further $253 billion. The issue of what effect the Act would have more broadly on the US budget deficit was widely debated, however. Treasury estimated – based on projections of relatively high GDP growth of roughly 3% per year, compared to the Federal Reserve's more conservative estimate of about 2% per year – that tax revenues would increase by $1.8 trillion over the ten years following the introduction of the TCJA. But the Committee for a Responsible Federal Budget, a non-profit public policy organisation, argued that Treasury's estimates relied on a flawed baseline, and having conducted its own analysis, it provided a far less optimistic projection – that the TCJA could, in fact, increase the budget *deficit* by as much as $2 trillion by 2027.

The results of the TCJA have so far been mixed: very few new inversions have taken place since the Act was passed, while those large companies that had already inverted have generally opted to continue their operations as before. On aggregate, Kim Clausing, deputy assistant secretary of Treasury for tax analysis, suggests that the design of the various aspects of the TCJA created a nullifying effect, resulting in no evidence of any reduction in profit shifting by large corporates. According to Bank of America, over 60% of American multinationals' total reported foreign income in 2021 is generated in seven small low-tax countries, which is about double the share of what it was in 2000. The Congressional Budget Office further highlights that, relative to the size of the economy, corporate tax revenue in 2021 is less than a quarter of what it was in 1967.

———

In April 2021, newly elected President Joe Biden promised to take a harder line against corporate tax avoidance by raising the minimum tax on all new foreign income earned by American firms from 10.5% to 21%, ensuring stricter enforcement of the Global Intangible Low-Taxed Income rate, and leading global efforts to reach agreement on a minimum corporate tax rate for OECD countries. Led by the US, the other wealthy nations that form the G7 – Canada, France, Germany, Italy, Japan and the UK – have apparently come to the realisation that the only way to manage corporate tax avoidance effectively is through global co-operation, and the group reached an agreement in June 2021 to pursue global corporate tax reforms. These countries have agreed that a new international tax regime should seek to increase the amount of tax paid by companies in the countries where they are selling their products or services, as opposed to where they declare their profits, and have proposed the idea of instituting a global minimum corporate tax rate of at least 15% to prevent countries from undercutting one another. Early estimates by the OECD suggest that as much as $81 billion in additional tax revenues could be raised annually through these reforms, and there is much hope, particularly in the West, resting on the power of global convergence to drive more definitive change.

In July 2021, the G7's proposal for a global minimum tax rate was endorsed by G20 finance ministers and central bank governors. This represented a critical first step in achieving global convergence on the matter. Formalising the agreement into an official international corporate tax regime remains an ambitious aspiration, however, given that the G7 agreement was deliberated by national leaders for eight years before consensus was reached. As of writing, the details of the global minimum tax structure are yet to be finalised, and it will undoubtedly be no small challenge to achieve agreement between those who steer the diverse economies of the G7, as well as Argentina, Australia, Brazil, China, India, Indonesia, Mexico, Russia, Saudi Arabia, South Africa, South Korea, Turkey and the EU. Early indications are that there will likely be significant disagreement between nation states regarding how low to set the minimum international corporate tax rate. Gaining support from China, which incentivises manufacturing firms to boost investment through lower corporate tax rates, is also expected to be particularly challenging – not to mention the fact that in the US, the agreement will need to be passed by Congress.

It is also unlikely that such an agreement would be accepted without significant resistance from tax haven countries such as Bermuda, the British Virgin Islands, Panama and Mauritius, which, despite their low or 0% tax rates, generally derive a large portion of their national revenues from the international firms domiciled within their borders. In Bermuda, for example, a quarter of the county's GDP is directly attributable to the activities of international corporates, earned through various fees on business, rather than through corporate tax, while related activities, such as real estate and financial activities, accounted for 15% and 14% of GDP respectively. Bermuda's finance minister Curtis Dickinson has stressed the deleterious effect that a global tax rate could have on his country, which relies on the revenues earned from the activities of the 18,000 international companies domiciled in his country as of 2021 to fund infrastructural and social programmes, including Covid-19 relief packages. He has also indicated a degree of resentment regarding the imposition of a global tax rate by wealthier, more powerful nations on the rest of the world. "Bermuda has a right to determine for itself what it thinks is an appropriate tax system for its jurisdiction," he says. "We have a system in place for 200 years. It's not perfect. It does require some adjustment. But we would like to do that on our own and not have someone tell us to change our system to fit some global initiative."

While in theory the G7 agreement represents a crucial moment in the fight against corporate tax avoidance, there is no telling when, or even if, such a multilateral agreement will come to fruition. As political leaders debate the benefits and drawbacks of such a regime, a critical element that has gone largely overlooked is the banking system that facilitates the movement of money across national borders. This system could potentially be used as a powerful tool for monitoring and limiting the movement of funds into tax havens in much the same way as it already functions to regulate personal income tax avoidance through FATCA and Automatic Exchange of Information agreements. It is not unreasonable to suggest that any changes to the complex landscape of international corporate tax laws could be expedited through the banking system in a similar manner, if there was only the political will to do so.

The urgent need for systems that can function as successfully as FATCA is laid bare when the issue of tax evasion or avoidance, by both individuals and corporates, is set against the background of rising global inequality. It was only a few years ago, in 2016, when one of the largest data leaks in history revealed just how rampant tax avoidance has become. Involving 2.6 terabytes of data comprising 11.5 million confidential documents that detailed the transactions of more than 214,488 offshore entities from the 1970s onwards, the infamous Panama Papers exposed the underbelly of the global financial system by divulging the names of companies and individuals – including prominent politicians, criminals and celebrities – who had moved their money offshore, veiled behind opaque structures, to evade paying taxes.

From the perspective of the public, the actions of these companies and wealthy individuals essentially amount to a deliberate attempt to avoid giving back to the societies that enabled them to flourish in the first place. This has enhanced the general perception that the global financial system is somehow "rigged", and has driven a further wedge between the ultra-wealthy and the average citizen – the 1% and the 99%. Most distressingly, it has worked to magnify the relentless chipping away of trust in Western banks and other institutions since the Global Financial Crisis. Today, this trust has been so severely eroded that many people have begun to seriously entertain the idea of the creation of a world in which they no longer need to trust the international monetary system at all.

17

CRYPTOCURRENCY AND
THE FAILURE OF MONEY

Gold, moulded into an 11-gram coin called a shekel, was first used as a medium of exchange in international trade in Egypt around 1500 BC. Similar coinage emerged over the next few hundred years in Asia and Europe and was eventually brought to England in AD 1066 by William of Normandy, initiating the British system of pounds, shillings and pennies. In 1787 the first American gold coin was produced, and by 1792 the Coinage Act had been passed, establishing a bi-metallic silver-gold standard in the US, which would remain in one form or another at the centre of its monetary system for almost two hundred years.

By the beginning of the 20th century, gold had come to form the basis upon which the entire international monetary system was built. Countries throughout the developed world adopted the gold standard to address the growing problem of settling debts in a global economy that was struggling to define a standardised valuation of the various national currencies in circulation. In this system, rather than exchanging actual gold coins for goods, it was decided that if the US gold price was set at $200 an ounce, for example, a one-dollar note would entitle the holder to 1/200th of an ounce of gold held by the government. Because the government was obliged to hold enough gold to pay out the denominated amount promised by the exchange of notes, this effectively constrained the number of notes a government could print at any given time, bringing much-needed stability to the global financial system.

With the onset of World War I, the gold standard was suspended in America and Europe to enable their central banks to print more money to pay for the war. An attempt was made to return to the standard in the window of peace between the world wars, but by this time support for it was waning as many countries struggled to rebuild their economies and manage high unemployment levels. With the economic shock of the Wall Street Crash of 1929 and the Great Depression that followed in America, the gold standard was abandoned completely. Panicked by the instability of the dollar when the stock market crashed, people clung to gold for safety, exchanging their dollars for the metal and hoarding it at home rather than leaving it in the banks that were failing all around them. In times of peace the gold standard had proved beneficial, but in times of crisis it simply disintegrated.

In response to the run on gold, in 1933 the US government not only suspended the convertibility of dollars to gold but also demanded that citizens return their gold bullion and coins to the state in exchange for dollars. This stimulated the flow of paper money through the economy and shored up America's gold reserves, which would prove critical at the end of World War II, when the desire for a new monetary regime that would ensure greater international economic stability led to a return to gold, albeit in a modified sense. The return was achieved in 1944 through the development of the Bretton Woods Agreement, which established a regulated international foreign exchange system. Owing to the US's large gold reserves, the dollar would be pegged to the price of gold, and all other currencies would be pegged to the dollar. Central banks around the world would maintain a fixed exchange rate between national currencies and the dollar, and thus the gold standard was in effect replaced with a "dollar standard".

From the beginning, France, which also held substantial gold reserves, voiced criticisms about the Bretton Woods System. Resenting the degree of supremacy that it bestowed on America as the dollar became the de facto international currency, French policy-makers became determined to *banaliser le dollar* – to dethrone the dollar. The opportunity to do so presented itself in the early 1970s, when dollars held by other countries began to exceed the US's gold reserves, and it was at this point that French president Georges Pompidou ordered a warship into New York harbour to retrieve his country's gold and deliver it to the Banque de France in Paris. Belgium, the Netherlands, the UK and Germany soon announced their intention to do the same. A temporary suspension of the dollar's convertibility to gold was put in place, and by March 1973 the Bretton Woods System had been dissolved entirely, replaced by a system of floating exchange rates, effectively beginning the era of fiat currency that still exists today.

Whereas in the past a dollar was directly exchangeable for an actual amount of gold, today money is no longer backed by any tangible commodity. The system of fiat currency relies on the trust that an ordinary citizen's deposit will be held safely in a bank, retrievable at any time, and that central banks and governments will guard the value of that money and not inflate it away into something worthless. This trust was, however, severely tested just three decades after the system was established, when the Financial Crisis swept across the globe.

It was in the midst of this crisis, on the 18th of August 2008, that the bitcoin.org domain name was registered, followed a month later by the release of a white paper entitled "Bitcoin: A Peer-to-Peer Electronic Cash System". Authored by one "Satoshi Nakamoto", it outlined the concept of a completely trustless monetary system.

The timing of the release of an article that detailed the technical design of the Bitcoin cryptocurrency was no coincidence. Disillusioned with the failings of the incumbent economic system, the mysterious Nakamoto – whether an individual or an ideologically aligned group of cryptographers – sought to bring into the world a transparent and decentralised form of monetary exchange. While central banks and governments were papering over the cracks of the Global Financial Crisis by printing excessive amounts of money, radically increasing money supply as a result, these cryptographers had created a new, alternative network of exchange. It was a network that relied not on centralised entities to authorise and authenticate transactions, but on a peer-to-peer system, underpinned by the security of cryptography and the proof-of-work concept.

These ideas were not entirely new and had been circulating since the early 1980s, leading to various attempts to develop a secure online currency that would allow for the easy and anonymous transfer of money directly from one person to another, with no need for a financial intermediary. Notable early examples included DigiCash, b-money and Bit Gold, but it was only after 2009, when the first-ever block of bitcoin – known as the Genesis Block – was mined, that the idea of cryptocurrency as a potential alternative currency was truly born.

By 2021, there were more than ten thousand different cryptocurrencies in existence, though Bitcoin remained the most popular. For the purists, at the core of Bitcoin's intrigue is its countercultural ethos – the so-called triumph of being able to bypass official institutions such as banks in transactions – and it is the constant appeal to this philosophical underpinning that has been critical to stoking the popularity of the cryptocurrency and raising its price. For more than a decade, the escalating obsession with cryptocurrency has been built on the notion of its tradability and belief in its potential future value for eliminating other currencies.

When weighing the case for cryptocurrency, it is necessary to differentiate between the idea of it as a speculative asset class and as an alternative form of money. There is no doubt that cryptocurrency should be acknowledged as an asset class, given that so many people are now investing in it, buying it and selling it on exchanges around the world, and since its value is determined directly by the dynamics of demand and supply. That it is a genuine speculative asset that has generated fantastic returns for investors in recent years should not, however, be conflated with its viability as an alternative currency. Demand for any speculative asset is driven by the subjective value placed on it by society, whether it is a work of art that costs very little to produce or a rare car that is highly collectable. The demand for cryptocurrency is similarly driven by its rise in popularity, together with the overall amount of money that is available to invest in it, which is determined by the existing system of money supply.

Technically, the supply of any cryptocurrency is determined by the particular rules that govern its system of release and circulation, and it is only through a sound understanding of these rules that the limitations of cryptocurrency as a legitimate alternative to the existing infrastructure of the international monetary system are revealed. To demonstrate this point, it is illuminating to understand how cryptocurrency functions in a practical sense. In the case of Bitcoin, as the primary example, it is ultimately limited to a total of 21 million bitcoins – with more than 18 million of these in circulation by September 2021 – and this finite scarcity contributes to its perceived value. Bitcoin can be obtained in one of three ways: it can be purchased directly through an exchange or from other users, it can in certain spheres be earned as payment in exchange for a product or service, or it can be obtained by "mining" new coins.

In the Bitcoin system, the process of mining is inextricably intertwined with the way in which transactions are executed. To transfer and store bitcoins, users typically download software that installs a digital wallet on their computers, online in the cloud or on a cryptocurrency exchange. This software generates a public address for the wallet, which is disclosed to anyone who wishes to transfer bitcoins into the wallet, functioning as something akin to an email address where the cryptocurrency can be sent. The software also generates a password, known only to the owner of the wallet, which is used to gain access to the bitcoins inside. In this manner, the wallet, and the bitcoins it holds, are kept secure.

If one user wishes to transfer bitcoins from his or her wallet to another user's wallet, a transaction is generated – but it cannot be immediately completed. First, the critical information pertaining to the transaction is recorded. This record contains the public addresses of the wallets between which bitcoins are being transferred and the specified value that is being sent from one wallet to the other. It will include other important information, such as the date and time of the transaction and unique identifiers for each transaction and each bitcoin, to eliminate the possibility of duplicating transactions or double-spending bitcoins – the equivalent of one person spending the same ten-dollar note multiple times without relinquishing ownership of the note. Once the record of the transaction has been generated by the person who wishes to send bitcoins from his or her wallet to another, it is broadcast to the Bitcoin network, joining a queue of pending transactions that must first be validated before they can be finalised. In the traditional monetary system, this function would be carried out by a bank. In the Bitcoin system, the authentication process is decentralised; that is to say, it is carried out by other Bitcoin users. This process is facilitated by the data structure on which Bitcoin is built, which is known as blockchain.

In this structure, the record of each pending transaction appears as a set of data stored as a "block". Each block contains the details of one megabyte worth of transactions – which might be only a handful of transactions or might be thousands, depending on the amount of data involved in each transaction. This block of data must then be checked to authenticate each transaction within it. Once the block of transactions is verified by the network of Bitcoin users, the transactions can be executed, and the block is effectively sealed off – the data it contains can now not be altered in any way. This ensures that a public record of every transaction is maintained indefinitely. A new block of pending transactions is then created and added to the closed block, so that a chain of blocks is formed, from which the term "blockchain" is derived. This chain of blocks forms the public ledger, which is continuously updated as new blocks of transactions are verified and added to the chain.

The distributed ledger is not owned by anyone and it is autonomous in nature – there is no authority that can lay a legitimate claim to it. This autonomy is at the core of the idea of decentralised finance or DeFi, a term that broadly refers to blockchain-based forms of finance that do not rely on traditional centralised financial intermediaries. For the ledger to facilitate a useful system of exchange, however, it must do more than simply ensure that past transactions are recorded in a manner that eliminates the possibility of their being retrospectively altered or corrupted; it must also ensure that any attempts at fraud in the blocks of pending transactions are continually rejected. This is achieved by having multiple users check every transaction. In other words, it is only through a system of consensus that a transaction can be verified and executed.

One potential problem that arises in this system is that bad actors could theoretically create multiple Bitcoin accounts and then use them to falsely validate their own transactions. To eliminate this problem, the process of validating transactions is made unattractive by being computationally intensive. Specifically, once users have verified the details of a block of transactions, there is one more step that must be completed before the transactions can be finalised and the block can be sealed off and added to the blockchain. This step involves solving a mathematical problem that has been designed in such a way that there is no analytical way of solving it – the answer can only be determined through a tedious process of trial and error. Users are effectively presented with an equation in which certain inputs and the output are known, and they must then determine certain unknown numbers that will solve the equation. In the original cryptographic formulation, these were two prime numbers, but there are other mathematical functions that can be used, so long as they are hard to solve and necessitate "brute force" to find the input factors. It is important to understand just how big these numbers can be; one might, for example, have a prime number with thirty digits multiplied by another prime number with thirty digits, creating a particularly difficult factorisation problem. The method by which the equation must be solved involves testing progressive combinations of ever larger numbers to find the solution to the equation. What made the original cryptographic function so hard to solve, and what made these numbers so intractable and difficult to find in the number system, is that there is no known analytical solution to determine how prime numbers are distributed through the number system. Nor is there any analytical solution to determining whether any given number is prime.

———————

Whether making use of prime numbers or not, the point is that the mathematical problems that provide intrinsic value to cryptocurrency, Bitcoin included, are problems that involve the use of brute force computing, making the process of mining difficult, and energy- and time-consuming. In many respects, they simulate the mining of gold from the ground. To put this in perspective, at the time of writing, the computers and software used for normal, everyday tasks, such as Microsoft Excel, can usually handle numbers with a maximum of fifteen digits. Excel is a good example of the limitations of the power of standard computer software: it is able to handle a maximum of 1,048,576 rows, only a seven-digit number. If one tries to find the solution to a three-digit number to the power of another three-digit number, the response is a #NUM! error. In an appendix to Simon Singh's 1999 popular science book *The Code Book*, which explains the history of cryptography before Bitcoin and cryptocurrency became a popular trend, trivially small prime factors, 11 and 17, are used to illustrate the mathematical workings of what is known as the RSA cryptographic function. In short time, Singh arrives at the following conundrum: "Working this out directly on a calculator is not straightforward because the display cannot cope with such large numbers." This is the proof-of-work concept that underlies Bitcoin.

To ensure that there will, nonetheless, be users who volunteer to undertake this tedious process, there is a reward offered to the first user – or miner – who solves the mathematical problem and publishes the block of verified transactions: a quantity of bitcoins. This is how new bitcoins, or parts thereof, enter the system. Not only are users searching for factors in an infinite number series, but they are trying to do this as fast as possible as they compete against one another to be the first to arrive at the correct answer. At any given time, there are multiple users checking the same group of transactions and trying to solve the same mathematical problem. This approach is integral to the system of consensus on which the authentication of transactions in the Bitcoin system relies – and it is why cryptocurrencies are supposedly trustless. But it also means that for every block of transactions added to the blockchain, there are thousands of miners expending huge amounts of computational energy to test potential answers to the mathematical problem.

To demonstrate the scale of this exercise, computers on the Bitcoin network tested roughly 120 quintillion answers per second in 2020. And only one user – or group of users, as miners frequently pool resources in this endeavour – actually achieves the outcome of validating the block and mining new bitcoins. Meanwhile, under the original Bitcoin protocol, the reward offered to miners is decreasing, halving roughly every four years. While miners in 2009 were rewarded with 50 bitcoins for every block mined, as of May 2021 this has been reduced to 6.25 bitcoins, with the next halving due in 2025. This process will continue until all 21 million bitcoins are mined, at which point the volunteers who validate Bitcoin transactions will have to settle for taking transaction fees as payment for their toil.

The energy implications are significant. According to research firm Digiconomist, which specialises in cryptocurrency energy consumption, as of September 2021 a single Bitcoin transaction can expend as much as 1793.40 kWh – the same amount of energy used by an average American family over two months.

Consider, then, a hypothetical future in which Bitcoin has replaced the existing monetary system in its entirety and become a legitimate international currency that does not depend on any government or any financial institutions, such as a bank, and is not controlled by any particular group of technocrats or regulatory bodies, such as the one sitting in Basel, Switzerland. Imagine that the problem of Bitcoin's price volatility has been solved, and that it is stable enough to be used as an effective means of exchange. Now imagine that in a country such as Sweden, with a population of roughly ten million citizens, each person makes on average thirty transactions a month using Bitcoin to buy goods or services. Based on Digiconomist's estimation of the energy consumption associated with a single Bitcoin transaction, this would result in the use of roughly 547TWh of energy, to power a month's worth of transactions. This is four times as much power as the entire country of Sweden used throughout all of 2020.

In terms of energy usage, the cost of having a distributed ledger, which may not rely on government but does require authentication by multiple participants using proof-of-work calculations, would simply be too great.

This is the reason that other cryptocurrencies, such as Ethereum, the second-largest cryptocurrency in terms of market capitalisation in 2021, have started moving away from the proof-of work protocol towards less energy-intensive protocols, such as proof-of-stake. The proof-of-stake system still relies on consensus to validate transactions, but the number of users performing the validation process is reduced. In this case, users volunteer to validate transactions by offering up, or staking, a portion of their own cryptocurrency. The amount staked must meet a minimum pre-set amount, and validators are then chosen randomly from the group that have staked the required amount.

Once a block of transactions is validated through consensus, these users are entitled to retain the amount they staked and earn transaction fees. Should they be found to have added invalid transactions to the blockchain, they lose the amount staked.

This system addresses the energy problem associated with mining cryptocurrency, but it is still ultimately a workaround to creating a trustless monetary system. The proof-of-stake system also threatens to undermine the core idea of decentralised finance, since only those who have enough cryptocurrency to meet the minimum stake will act as transaction validators. It seems that in attempting to achieve the goal of decentralised finance – of not having any centre of authority – there will always be new solutions that bring with them their own contradictions.

———————

The advocates of cryptocurrency generally cite two primary benefits. The first is that it allows for transactions to be conducted anonymously; while every digital wallet has a public address that is known to everyone on the network, the personal details of the legal entity that owns that wallet are not known. The second is that there is no interference in the payments process by a financial intermediary, such as a bank, owing to the structure of the decentralised public ledger; cryptocurrencies are designed specifically to operate outside the formal financial system, without being subject to the market conduct regulations that govern it. These features may, however, also be viewed as structural shortcomings, most obviously because they combine so well to enable illicit activities.

Recall that there was a time when it was much easier than it is now to conceal the nature of certain transactions within the existing financial system and to obfuscate the identities of beneficiaries when transactions were in some way related to illegal activities. That changed after the 9/11 terrorist attacks, when the US and other Western governments realised that they would need to co-opt banks into transaction-level surveillance in order to be effective in tracing terrorist financing. To do so, international market conduct regulations were introduced, specifically anti-money laundering (AML) and combating the financing of terrorism (CFT) regulations, requiring banks to monitor their customers and their transactions at a highly granular level. This has proved a crucial advancement in larger state efforts to prevent terrorism and money laundering. In other words, the existing financial system has developed a key strength since 2001, which cryptocurrencies like Bitcoin radically undermine by eliminating financial intermediaries in the payments process.

Market conduct regulation has become a critical area of oversight in the financial system, considered as important as, if not more so than, the rules governing capital adequacy. Banks are required by law to comply with these regulations, and failure to do so can attract significant fines and reputational damage, as can be seen in the case of banking giant HSBC in the late 2000s, for instance. While the bank did have AML and CFT programmes in place, investigations conducted by a US Senate subcommittee in 2012 revealed that HSBC was routinely ignoring the alerts of suspicious activity that were generated by these programmes and allowing transactions to take place with individuals suspected of criminal activity. Its Mexican branch, in particular, had been facilitating transactions that were clearly related to the laundering of drug-trafficking money. It turned out that one of the bank's biggest clients was the Sinaloa Cartel, responsible for thousands of kidnappings and deaths in Mexico every year. The cartel was also known to be trafficking fentanyl to produce synthetic heroin for sale in the US, where thousands of deaths due to drug overdoses are recorded every year.

The Senate subcommittee that investigated the case ruled that HSBC's failure to comply with AML and CFT standards was too systematic in nature to be the result of negligence. It was, the subcommittee determined, part of a single-minded decision to pursue profits, even if this meant ignoring international market conduct laws. In its report, the subcommittee described the culture of HSBC as being "pervasively polluted" and urged the US Department of Justice to indict the bank. An admission of guilt from HSBC that it had indeed facilitated the laundering of over $881 million of drug-trafficking money enabled the bank to avoid criminal charges, but it was still fined an amount of $1.9 billion, which was unprecedented at the time for an AML violation.

It is precisely because banks are required, by law, to expend substantial amounts of time and money monitoring all transactions that eliminating these institutions from the monetary system is an issue far more complex – and dangerous – than is generally acknowledged. It is because banks must track and record their customers' financial activities at such a granular level that criminal activity on a global scale may be identified and, in many cases, prevented rather than allowed to proliferate unhindered. Converting to a monetary system that is devoid of any kind of regulatory oversight would, therefore, be a societal regression. This has been demonstrated repeatedly in recent years, with the decentralised, unregulated nature of cryptocurrency helping to facilitate money laundering, tax evasion and the raising of funds for terrorist activities. In 2020, for example, the DOJ reported the successful dismantling of three separate terrorist-financing cyber-enabled campaigns involving the al-Qassam Brigades, Al-Qaeda and ISIS. Investigations revealed that as part of their strategies for raising funds, these terrorist groups had sought and received cryptocurrency donations worth millions of dollars from supporters around the world.

Cryptocurrencies are also known to have been involved in the leasing of servers for cybercrimes, and have enabled sophisticated ransomware schemes. More insidiously, they have facilitated the easy buying and selling of everything from drugs and weapons to counterfeit products and child pornography. Prior to its being dismantled by US law officials in 2019, the dark web website "Welcome to Video", as just one example, sold more than 250,000 videos depicting child sexual abuse, using Bitcoin. The website operated on a points system in which users were able to exchange the cryptocurrency for points that could then be spent to download videos or purchase an all-you-can-watch "VIP" account. Points could also be earned by uploading new videos. After apprehending the website's creator, along with more than 300 of the website's users, US state officials obtained information that led to the rescue of 23 underaged victims featured in the videos. Many others remained unidentified. In a separate case, American and European investigators worked together to take down a Dutch-hosted website called "Dark Scandals", which had sold more than 2,000 videos depicting the rape of women and children.

These cases are select examples of a far more pervasive problem: the Internet Watch Foundation in the UK identified 288 new dark web websites selling child sexual exploitation materials in 2019, representing a 238% increase from 2018. Most of these websites accepted payment only in cryptocurrencies. In a separate study, US blockchain analysis company Chainalysis estimated that in 2019 alone, about $930,000 was paid to addresses known to be associated with child sexual exploitation materials using Bitcoin and Ethereum. This represented a 212% increase between 2017 and 2019.

———————

Twenty-nine-year-old Ross Ulbricht was an unlikely villain when he was apprehended by police in October 2013 in a San Francisco library. Somewhat nerdy-looking, he shared a sparsely furnished flat in a good neighbourhood in the city and played djembe drums at house parties. He had excelled at university, graduating from the University of Texas with a bachelor's degree in physics, and later from Pennsylvania State University with a master's degree in materials science and engineering. His roommates weren't sure what work he did, just that it was something IT-related, as he could always be found with his laptop open in front of him, in a library or a local coffee shop or shut away in his bedroom. Nobody would have guessed that this unassuming young man was the mastermind behind Silk Road, a highly successful illicit online marketplace.

Modelled on renowned online marketplaces such as Amazon and eBay, Silk Road operated primarily as a drug bazaar, with anything from cocaine and heroin to prescription drugs, such as Oxycontin and Xanax, readily available for purchase. On occasion, other goods and services would pop up as well – weapons could be bought, hitmen hired and mail-order brides supplied without any questions or interference by official third parties. The website was protected by extensive encryption technology, and to ensure there were no payment records that could be tracked, all transactions were conducted using Bitcoin.

For two years, Ulbricht successfully managed the website before he was caught by a specialised cybercrime unit. By this time, his commission from the site amounted to 144,336 bitcoins – equivalent to roughly $17 million at the time of his arrest, and more than $6 billion in September 2021. In court, he pleaded not guilty, and as he conveyed the story behind the creation of Silk Road, a familiar theme began to emerge. Despite all appearances, the website had not been created solely out of a wish to make money, or out of a twisted desire to buoy the criminal underworld by enhancing the ease and convenience of illicit transactions. Rather, it had been set up from a philosophical belief in the free market.

At university, Ulbricht had been heavily influenced by the philosophies of Austrian economist Ludwig von Mises, who argued that economic freedom was indelibly intertwined with political and moral freedom. It was the same argument that would later be made by one of Von Mises's students, free-market advocate Friedrich von Hayek, in *The Road to Serfdom*, and championed by his friend and ally, the American economist Milton Friedman. In a self-proclaimed bid to "use economic theory as a means to abolish the use of coercion and aggression among mankind", Ulbricht established Silk Road initially to sell psilocybin mushrooms that he had cultivated himself, before opening the marketplace to other vendors. It was a modern underground reincarnation of the free market in the purist sense, where almost anything could be bought, sold and traded free from the watchful gaze of financial institutions and from the international regulators and national governments that require them to police illicit transactions. Full transactional autonomy was only limited by a basic code of conduct that outlawed child pornography, stolen goods or forged degrees. "Our basic rules are to treat others as you would wish to be treated," stated Ulbricht on the website, "and don't do anything to hurt or scam someone else."

The flaw in Ulbricht's thinking was ultimately the naivety at the heart of this pseudo-libertarian plan. Regardless of his original intentions, in Silk Road he had curated the ideal landscape for the worst of human activities to flourish. It was this naivety that also enabled Ulbricht to exempt himself from any moral obligation to consider the potential outcomes of the goods and services being traded on his platform, and this soon led to an escalation in his own criminal behaviour. By the time of his arrest, he had commissioned several murders in the name of protecting the free world he had created.

In 2015, Ross Ulbricht was sentenced to life in prison by a federal jury in New York. This sentence was the result of a litany of hard evidence that had been painstakingly collected by a group of investigators – co-ordinated across different agencies, including Homeland Security, the Secret Service, the FBI and the Drug Enforcement Agency (DEA) – over a period of more than a year. Ulbricht had successfully separated his real identity from his online persona through the opacity and anonymity ensured by dark web encryption and the use of cryptocurrency.

Clues to his identity therefore had to be painstakingly gathered by the cybercrime forensics team, who combed through a large amount of online activity, including transactions that took place through a Bitcoin escrow account used by Ulbricht and a Bitcoin exchange where several Silk Road accounts were held. It was a process not unlike the meticulous and time-consuming analysis of opaque financial transactions undertaken by researchers in the wake of the 9/11 terrorist attacks, and by journalists unravelling mass tax evasion and tax avoidance in the infamous case of the Panama Papers. Several years later, despite the introduction of comprehensive market conduct regulation, brought into existence because of the repeated exploitation of the financial system by criminals, law enforcement officials are essentially faced with the same problem once again.

In the traditional world of money, if one wants to buy a bag of oranges from a local grocer, one might hand over a ten-dollar note to the cashier and perhaps receive some change on the transaction, which takes place immediately. In a world where everyone trusts one another completely, the cashier at the store doesn't even bother looking at the note before placing it in the cash register. In a world where there is some degree of distrust between people, the cashier perhaps holds the note up to the light to check that it does not obviously appear to be counterfeit. In a world where there is a further degree of distrust, the cashier runs the note through a machine installed in the store that can detect counterfeit notes. Finally, in a world defined by total distrust, one might use cryptocurrency to pay for the bag of oranges – it is, after all, called "trustless" for a reason.

In this hypothetical world in which a bag of oranges is purchased from the local grocer using cryptocurrency, funds can only be transferred once the transaction has gone through all the steps required in the validation process facilitated by the decentralised public ledger and the system of consensus. In practical terms, this would be equivalent to handing the ten-dollar note to the cashier, who would then send exact copies of the note to a number of different laboratories where scientists would be required to validate its authenticity. These scientists would then notify the cashier whether the note was authentic or not – but only if all the scientists agreed that it was authentic would the cashier be able to accept the note and complete the transaction. For a cryptocurrency to function as a viable system of exchange, this process would somehow need to happen instantaneously and at no significant cost to the parties involved.

The technical challenges of providing a practical cryptocurrency are widely unappreciated, but even they belie the deeper existential crisis at play: the movement to eradicate trust entirely rather than to restore it. That the idea of cryptocurrency is reaching its zenith in the third decade of the 21st century in a world in which there already exist many functioning currencies operating within a well-established monetary system, and despite its own practical shortcomings as a currency, merits a great deal of reflection. The wealth that cryptocurrencies have generated for so many speculators in recent years goes some way to explaining their popularity at a superficial level, but the genuine ideological support of its true believers is where the deeper problem lies. Distrust in the formal banking system, paired perhaps with a naive belief in the free market in its purest sense, has led to the creation and expansion of an inefficient and impractical ecosystem of financial exchange where criminals thrive unchecked.

While governments and central banks debate how best to regulate this system, which by its very nature resists central oversight, what should be of gravest concern is that there exists significant interest from ordinary citizens in creating a world where there is no trust at all – no trust in the banking system, in any transaction, or even in one another as human beings. The creation of such a world is the logical progression and ultimate expression of the erosion of public trust in the financial system in general, and the banking system in particular – a progression that was catalysed by the Global Financial Crisis, and that does not appear to be dissipating. Instead, it is gaining momentum, more than a decade after the fact.

18

THE CONSEQUENCES
OF PRINTING MONEY

On the 11th of March 2020, the World Health Organization declared the Covid-19 outbreak a global pandemic – and, with that, the world faced unprecedented upheaval. What would follow in the months to come was almost unimaginable. The novel coronavirus would spread to every corner of the globe, killing millions and debilitating tens of millions. In response, governments would implement once-inconceivable lockdown measures to suppress the rapid spread of the virus, ranging from mild social distancing measures to confining citizens to their homes for months at a time. Simultaneously, they began implementing a variety of relief measures to support their economies, as millions of businesses began to struggle and fail under the weight of the severe economic conditions, and as hundreds of millions of individuals suffered financial distress, experiencing a dramatic reduction in income or even losing their livelihoods altogether.

A notable element of the response was the widespread decision to adopt expansionary monetary policy measures:

THE CONSEQUENCES OF PRINTING MONEY

governments collectively injected more than $9 trillion in 2020 to support their economies. The result of these measures, along with social relief spending, was a steep increase in global debt; including government, corporate and household debt, this reached a new peak of $281 trillion by the end of 2020. Of this tally, $24 trillion was added in 2020 alone, representing a significant 9% increase. Although nations from across the world have all contributed to this debt, no other nation has printed more money than or pledged as much to its relief measures in response to the Covid-19 pandemic as the United States.

As of mid-2021, the US had already distributed more than $3 trillion in its Covid-19 relief measures through various channels, most significantly through the $2.2 trillion Coronavirus Aid, Relief and Economic Security (CARES) Act, signed into law on 27 March 2020 under Donald Trump. Among other initiatives, the CARES Act paid out several rounds of $1,200 stimulus cheques directly into the hands of some 90% of the American working population, significantly increased unemployment benefits, and provided forgivable loans to small businesses, cash grants to airlines and loans to local governments. The Act was the single largest stimulus package ever signed into law in the US, three times the size of the Troubled Asset Relief Program created under the Emergency Economic Stabilization Act of 2008, and more than two and a half times the size of the previous record holder, Barack Obama's $831-billion American Recovery and Reinvestment Act of 2009. Ultimately, the magnitude of the pandemic relief measures can only be justified by the US government's belief that the economic fallout of the pandemic would be more than twice as severe as the carnage experienced after the Global Financial Crisis.

This unprecedented government spending was followed by another giant relief package the next year, the $1.9-trillion American Rescue Plan. Its signature into law by President Joe Biden, on 11 March 2021, coincided with the first anniversary of the WHO's declaration of a global health crisis. Key elements of the American Rescue Plan aligned with those set out by the CARES Act, including several more rounds of $1,400 stimulus cheques to all Americans who earned less than $75,000 a year, and expanded the already significant unemployment benefits in place.

Given the unprecedented magnitude of these relief packages, the pressure that has come to bear on the US government's budget deficit has been severe, enlarging it from $984 billion in 2019 to $3.1 trillion in 2020. This represents 14.8% of GDP, the largest deficit as a percentage of GDP since 1945, when defence spending in the US alone reached 37% of GDP because of World War II. In 2021, it is estimated that the deficit will again be in the region of $3 trillion. By comparison, in 2009, following a dramatic increase in government spending to support the economy in the aftermath of the Global Financial Crisis, the budget deficit was recorded at $1.4 trillion, representing 9.6% of GDP; this made the budget deficit in 2020 more than double the size, in dollar terms, of the deficit the year after the Global Financial Crisis.

———————

In traditional monetary theory, as proposed by Milton Friedman in the 1970s, there are three ways in which a central bank can influence the money supply of an economic system. The first of these is by changing the interest rate by means of the central bank's discount rate, the rate at which banks borrow money from the central bank; in the US this is known as the federal funds rate. The second is through the setting of the capital reserve ratio, the percentage of capital reserves a bank must hold in relation to its assets, which affects how much it can lend. And the third is through open market operations (OMO), which involve the central bank buying government securities in the open market. It is only this last option that allows for the creation of "new" money, through the buying of securities such as US Treasuries. Treasuries are government bonds that are issued by the government in order to borrow money, and are bought by the public – individuals and companies, including banks – as assets that pay a fixed coupon to the bond-holder. When the Federal Reserve wishes to increase money supply, it buys these bonds, removing them from the balance sheets of banks and allocating these banks newly created money. In popular terms, this is the concept of "printing money", but in reality new money is simply created digitally, as an electronic transaction. This process has become known as quantitative easing (QE).

Traditional monetary theory proposes that the amount of newly available money in the financial system – the money supply – that is created because of the central bank's open market operations is a function of what is known as the money multiplier effect. This is in turn a function of the capital reserve ratio, which is determined in the US by the Federal Reserve. The money multiplier effect is the way in which banks increase, or multiply, money supply, by increasing their lending in relation to the amount of capital they must legally hold, as determined by the capital reserve ratio. This ratio directly affects how much a bank can lend to its customers – the higher the ratio, the less the banks can lend. Conversely, when the central bank decreases the capital reserve ratio, banks are able to lend more money to customers per dollar of capital they hold. In this way, if the Fed buys $120 billion per month worth of securities, the amount of money supply that is created by this specific open market action is many times larger than $120 billion. If the reserve requirement of banks is 12.5%, for example, the purchase of this amount will theoretically equate to approximately $960 billion of "new" credit becoming available as a result of the money multiplier effect. In simple mathematical terms, the multiplier effect is determined by taking the inverse of the capital reserve ratio and multiplying it by the new money released by the Fed.

The money multiplier effect is a key component of monetary theory, as it underpins the idea that the action of a central bank injecting cash into member banks – by buying securities from the banks, for example – should radically increase money supply. The banks are given more room to extend loans, in terms of their capital reserve levels; therefore more loans should be extended. But this does not always work as the theory suggests, especially during times of economic crisis, when banks become less willing to extend loans. This counterintuitive phenomenon played out in the aftermath of the Global Financial Crisis, when instead of lending freely after the injected large volumes of liquidity into banks from 2008 onwards, banks, in a state of survivalism, chose to hoard the cash. At the peak of the Crisis, banks even refused to lend to *each other*, as fear had reached such a height that not even the most established financial institutions trusted one another as reliable counterparties. In an attempt to remedy the liquidity crunch experienced after the Crisis, the Fed again increased the rate at which it was buying Treasuries and troubled assets, injecting even more cash into banks.

Ultimately, the Federal Reserve's efforts didn't increase the velocity of money – the speed at which money moves from the intermediation process to individuals and businesses and back into the intermediation process – as was intended. Rather, it ended up creating a system that has become addicted to monetary stimulus. For banks, and indeed the financial system as a whole, the unending supply of stimulus is like economic heroin. When the Fed has attempted to slow down this stimulus – which is placing a massive and growing burden on its balance sheet – the market has panicked and gone into shock from withdrawal, thereby forcing the central bank to ramp up bond buying again. This cycle has occurred several times since the Global Financial Crisis, most recently in mid-2020 when, owing to the economic ramifications of the Covid-19 pandemic, the Fed made the decision to increase the size of its asset-buying programmes even further, increasing money supply to extraordinary new heights.

From January 2003 to January 2008, the Federal Reserve of the US held between $700 billion and $800 billion of assets on its balance sheet, largely in the form of US Treasuries. In November 2008, following the collapse of Fannie Mae, Freddie Mac and

Lehman Brothers, the Fed announced that it would significantly expand its asset-purchase programme, increasing the rate at which it would be buying US Treasuries, while taking the unprecedented step to buy toxic debt that had been packaged as corporate paper to help stabilise the embattled financial system. This included the purchase of mortgage-backed securities from financial institutions, not just US Treasuries.

Over the next two years, the Fed almost tripled its balance sheet – from a mostly stable $800 billion to $2.33 trillion in June 2010. This increase of assets was in line with what the government called QE1 – the moniker given to the Fed's initial round of quantitative easing following the Global Financial Crisis. After June 2010, the Fed aimed to maintain a ceiling on its balance sheet of $2.1 trillion by only buying more Treasuries at the same rate as existing securities matured. By November of that year, however, the central bank announced that it would increase its balance sheet again. This second round of quantitative easing was dubbed QE2. Then in September 2012, with the US housing market still reeling from the Crisis – and the velocity of money still very low, as banks and consumers remained cautious in their respective lending and spending – the Fed announced a third round of quantitative easing, QE3, committing itself to purchasing $40 billion of mortgage-backed securities per month for the foreseeable future. In addition, the Federal Open Market Committee stated that it would keep the interest rate near zero until at least 2015, in an attempt to further stimulate the circulation of money through the economy. The next year, in 2013, as the economy started to show signs of heating up, Federal chairman Ben Bernanke announced that the central bank would begin "tapering" its asset-buying programme and would halt purchases by October 2014. In the six years from the start of QE1 to the end of QE3, the Federal Reserve had increased its balance sheet from $800 billion in late 2008 to $4.5 trillion in late 2014 – a compound annual growth rate of 33.3% over the six-year period.

From 2015, the Federal Reserve managed to slightly reduce the size of its balance sheet for several years. But in September 2019, after an unexpected spike in rates in the repo market caused a liquidity crunch, it decided to step in and increase its asset-buying strategy once again. In the next few months, the Fed steadily grew its balance sheet again to just over $4 trillion – and then the Covid-19 pandemic struck, and the strategy changed drastically.

In March 2020, as the global economic shutdown took hold, the Federal Reserve announced that it would be undertaking a multi-billion-dollar asset-purchase programme to support US liquidity. In a single year, from March 2020 to March 2021, the Fed increased the size of its balance sheet by more than $3 trillion and vowed to continue to buy assets at a rate of $120 billion a month. This led to a record 12-month increase of 75% of the Fed's balance sheet. Astonishingly, this represents more than the entirety of the quantitative easing measures in the four-year period that followed the Global Financial Crisis.

As a result of the combination of the radical quantitative easing measures undertaken by the Federal Reserve and the direct stimulus implemented by the US government, including several rounds of stimulus cheques distributed to the US population, M2 money supply in the US rose dramatically from mid-2020 to mid-2021. M2 money supply represents the most highly liquid assets in the economy; it is a slightly broader measure of money supply than M1, which represents only cash and checking deposits, and a narrower measure than M3, which represents all M2 assets and several other less liquid instruments. For the purpose of quantifying the effect of QE on money supply, M2 is an appropriate measure, as it represents a suitable balance of all the most liquid assets in circulation, such as cash, instantly accessible deposits and "near money" in the form of very easily accessible and measurable funds, as opposed to longer-dated and less liquid asset classes.

On 1 February 2020, M2 in the US stood at $15.4 trillion. Twelve months later, it had jumped to $19.4 trillion – a staggering 26% increase in a single year. By comparison, in January 2007, before the peak of the Global Financial Crisis and the introduction of QE1, M2 stood at $7.4 trillion. In January 2010, in the aftermath of the Crisis, M2 reached $8.5 trillion – an increase of $1.1 trillion, representing a total increase of just 5% annual compound growth from early 2007 to early 2010. Then from 2010 to 2020, M2 increased from $8.5 trillion to $15.4 trillion, representing an annual compound growth rate of just over 6%. By comparison, the 26% increase in M2 from mid-2020 to mid-2021 was unparalleled. In fact, the $4 trillion increase in money supply in the twelve months from January 2020 to January 2021 was so steep that it was equivalent to more than the entire $3.8 trillion increase in money supply in the ten years from January 2000 to January 2010 – a decade in history during which the US market experienced the dotcom crash *and* the Global Financial Crisis.

To truly put money supply into perspective, US GDP at the end of 2006 was $13.8 trillion and at the end of 2020 it was $20.9 trillion, equating to an increase of roughly 50%

over those fourteen years, since just before the Crisis. Over the same period, the US population increased by 10%, from 301 million to 331 million people, while M2 has increased from $7.4 trillion to $19.4 trillion, according to the Federal Reserve itself. This means that M2 per person, a hypothetical relative metric, rose from $24,600 to $58,600 per person in the same period, representing an increase of 138%. Incredibly, the increase in money per capita was almost four times greater than the increase in GDP per capita over the same period.

In a sense, the Global Financial Crisis never ended – it was simply papered over by extreme money supply.

"Between March and September 2020, broad equity price indexes around the world experienced a historic rally," according to a research note entitled "The Stock Market-Real Economy 'Disconnect': A Closer Look", published on the US Federal Reserve's website on 14 October 2020. "Although this rally followed a significant decline in stock prices, it appears difficult to explain due to continuing concerns about the global pandemic and national economies running far below their potentials." After some analysis, the research paper curiously concluded that the increase in stock prices had "largely been driven by an increase in the prices of far-dated dividend claims as well as high duration stocks". That the central bank would pose this explanation without mention of the enormous increase in money supply as a possible driving force behind the rise in stock prices is, to say the least, disingenuous.

On 14 February 2020, the S&P 500 – a capitalisation-weighted index of the 500 largest companies listed in the United States, broadly representative of the US stock market as a whole – reached an all-time high of 3,380. The 24-hour Covid news cycle had not yet begun at this point – but it was soon to arrive. In March, when fear and uncertainty around what was now an official pandemic sparked an equity sell-off, the S&P dropped roughly 30% in a month, reaching a low of 2,304. In response to the external shock to the markets, the Federal Reserve dropped the federal funds rate – the rate at which deposit-taking institutions lend money to each other on a short-term basis – from a range of 1.5% to 1.75%, down to a range of 0% to 0.25%. This was the lowest federal funds rate that has ever been recorded, matching the drop in interest rates in the direct aftermath of the Global Financial Crisis. Simultaneously, in mid-March 2020 the Fed announced that, "to support the flow of credit to households and businesses", it would be undertaking a radical programme of open market operations, ultimately pumping trillions of dollars into the financial system through the purchase of US Treasuries and mortgage-backed securities from banks.

Following the introduction of this liquidity into the market, the S&P 500 rocketed from its low on 20 March 2020, well past its pre-pandemic high of 3,380, to reach an astonishing 4,247 by 11 June 2021. This represented an incredible growth of 84% in a matter of fifteen months – compared to a historical annualised compound growth rate, dating back to 1928, of between 9% and 10%. In the same timeframe, the Nasdaq 100 – a capitalisation-weighted index of the 100 largest, most actively traded US companies listed on the Nasdaq stock exchange, which in 2020 largely comprised of technology giants such as Microsoft, Amazon, Google, Facebook and Apple – rose from a value of roughly 7,000 in March of 2020 to an all-time high of roughly 14,000 in June 2021. Thus, two different narratives played out over the course of fifteen months. On the one hand, as the world was beset by a global pandemic, countless companies across all nations were forced to shut down, prompting governments to release trillions of dollars of stimulus to guard against the most calamitous effects of the economic devastation. And on the other hand, the S&P 500 and Nasdaq 100 each roughly doubled in value from their March 2020 lows. This is a paradox worth closer examination.

While the Federal Reserve declared that its decision to open the money supply spigots – this time wider than ever before – was "to support the flow of credit to households and businesses", the reality was that a large proportion of this money found its way into the hands of the wealthiest few in society. This came by means of an increase in speculation and investment in the easiest and most accessible asset class of all, equities, and in more speculative asset classes such as Bitcoin, which repeatedly hit all-time highs during the first half of 2021. While fear-struck banks were reluctant to convert the excess cash flooding the system into loans for the people and businesses that so urgently needed them, stock prices across the board exploded. As a result, a select few corporations in particular – and, indeed, a select few individuals associated with these firms – benefited disproportionately. From mid-2020 to mid-2021, as hundreds of millions of people battened down the economic hatches to make ends meet, the share prices of some of the largest corporations in the world, including Apple, Microsoft and Facebook, doubled. Special mention must be made of Tesla, which experienced a share price jump from a low of $85 in March 2020 to a peak of over $880 in January 2021, an incredible ten-fold increase.

From an investment point of view, Tesla's extraordinary increase in share price was illogical. While the tale of the electric-car manufacturer is no doubt an intriguing one, starring a charismatic founder in Elon Musk, there is no particular technology that the company possesses, even in its battery development, that is sufficiently unique to justify its astronomical valuation. The valuation becomes even more removed from economic reality when considering how Tesla's market capitalisation has, because of its share price, exceeded the market capitalisation of far more established car manufacturers, many of which also now manufacture electric vehicles for mainstream consumption. To illustrate the point, in 2020, Tesla sold roughly half a million vehicles, while VW sold more than nine million vehicles; of these, more than 200,000 were pure electric vehicles and another 200,000 were plug-in hybrids. This means that VW sold almost as many electric and hybrid vehicles as Tesla in 2020, on top of its already enormous base of non-electric vehicles. As of mid-September 2021, VW's market capitalisation stood at $147 billion with a forward price earnings multiple of 5.8 times, whereas Tesla's market capitalisation was $747 billion with a forward price earnings multiple of 101 times. More broadly, the irrational nature of Tesla's share price, beyond any reasonable fundamental market analysis – not unlike other "meme stocks" and cryptocurrencies that have been bid up to stratospheric valuations, including Bitcoin, Dogecoin, AMC and GameStop – is perhaps the most obvious symptom of a financial system that has become disconnected from Main Street reality.

Rising in tandem with the increase of these giant corporations' stock prices has been the wealth of the private individuals at the heart of these organisations. In 2020, for example, the net worth of Jeff Bezos, the founder of Amazon, increased from roughly $110 billion at the beginning of the year to $176 billion by the end. Similarly, the net worth of Elon Musk increased from $24 billion to more than $150 billion in the same period, making him briefly the richest person in the world, ahead of Bezos. While the vast majority of the world was holding its collective breath and trying simply to survive the pandemic, physically and financially, 2020 was a record-setting time for the ultra-rich. As a group, dollar billionaires have not only managed to increase their numbers by 660 members to a total of 2,755 in 2020 – the largest-ever annual increase in history – but their total net worth also increased by a record-breaking 63%, from $8.0 trillion to $13.1 trillion.

Of the 660 new billionaires to join the list in 2021, 238 come from China, now home to 626 of the world's billionaires. That is a 61% increase in billionaires in a country that in the same year experienced its first quarterly decline in GDP growth for more than a quarter of a century. Meanwhile, the US – home of the free market – added "only" 110 billionaires, reaching a total of 724 billionaires as of April 2021, an increase of 18%. Ironically, the Chinese command economy has produced more capitalists than America during the Covid-19 pandemic.

What is evident is that in a period when governments across the world printed more money than ever before to support their economies, a perversely disproportionate amount of that money contributed to greatly enriching already-wealthy individuals, rather than alleviating the suffering of society at large. This extreme concentration of wealth becomes even more disturbing when analysed as a ratio of wealth to GDP, which has increased over time, but specifically in 2020. In Russia, for example, the wealth in the hands of Russian billionaires represented 22% of GDP in late 2019. By the end of the following year, it represented roughly 34% of GDP. Similarly, in India, one of the nations worst hit by the pandemic, the wealth of billionaires as a percentage of GDP doubled to 18% in 2020. Comparable scenarios also played out in the US and China, along with Sweden, France, Germany, Turkey, Taiwan and Brazil.

As a result of the economic slowdown associated with the Covid-19 pandemic in 2020, the productivity of nations throughout the world plummeted, severely diminishing the size of the denominator in the wealth-to-GDP ratio. The net outcome of the rapid accumulation of wealth by already-wealthy individuals, combined with slowing economic growth, has been the acceleration of a trend that has persisted for decades: increasing economic inequality in a number of the world's largest economies.

In his groundbreaking book *Capital in the Twenty-First Century*, French economist Thomas Piketty explores more than 250 years' worth of wealth and income distribution data. Published in 2013, his book argues that, over the long term, there is a tendency for the rate of return on capital to exceed the growth rate of the economy. This thesis is represented in a simple, yet brutal, formulation: $r > g$.

Based on the data analysed in writing his seminal work, Piketty believes that over time, not only does wealth beget wealth (historically at a rate of return on investment of between 4% and 5%), but it does so at a much faster rate than economic growth (historically between 0% and 3%), thereby ultimately concentrating the wealth of the world disproportionately in the hands of very few. This, he argues, is the single greatest driving force of inequality. He suggests that not only has wealth inequality become more pronounced since World War II, but it has been accelerating in more recent decades, especially since the beginning of the 21st century.

"When the rate of return on capital exceeds the rate of growth of output and income, as it did in the 19th century and seems quite likely to do again in the 21st," says Piketty, "capitalism automatically generates arbitrary and unsustainable inequalities that radically undermine the meritocratic values on which democratic societies are based." Piketty paints a bleak picture of inequality, going on to ask his reader the perturbing question: "Will the world in 2050 or 2100 be owned by traders, top managers and the super-rich, or will it belong to the oil-producing countries or the Bank of China? Or perhaps it will be owned by the tax havens in which many of these actors will have sought refuge."

To support such an extreme idea, Piketty argues that in the last few decades the wealthy, and particularly the ultra-wealthy, have been the greatest beneficiaries of rising inequality – a theory that appears to be supported by the rise in the number of billionaires and their combined wealth as a percentage of GDP during the Covid-19 pandemic. "Income inequality has increased significantly in the rich countries, especially the United

States," observed Piketty in 2014, "where the concentration of income in the first decade of the 21st century regained – indeed, slightly exceeded – the level attained in the second decade of the previous century." The latter decade was ultimately witness to the horrors of World War I – initiated by a disaffected teenage peasant shooting dead the Archduke of Austria – from which emerged, first, the tyranny of fascism, and then, the horrors of World War II. Never before or since has the Western world seen such social and economic upheaval.

Piketty argues that this disequilibrium of wealth accumulation over time will ultimately lead to an ever-widening chasm between the ultra-wealthy, representing a tiny fraction of the population, and the rest. Without correction, he concludes, this inequality can only lead to one certain outcome: widespread social unrest.

————

Not only have the ultra-wealthy, particularly those in developed nations, soaked up a disproportionate amount of the excess liquidity that has flooded the markets on the back of the Covid-19 pandemic, largely through the subsequent rise in stock prices and real estate valuations, but simultaneously, the poor have become poorer. The United Nations Development Programme (UNDP) has noted that global per capita income declined by 4% in 2020, and that forty to sixty million individuals could be pushed into extreme poverty as a result. The UNDP also states that their Global Human Development Index – measured as a combination of global education, health and living standards – decreased in 2020 for the first time since 1990 when the index was created. Regarding the effect of the coronavirus on the plight of the poor, UNDP administrator Achim Steiner says, "We risk a massive reversal of gains made over the last two decades, and an entire generation lost, if not in lives, then in rights, opportunities and dignity."

Adding complexity to this already precarious situation is the concern that, because of the trillions of dollars that have been pumped into the financial systems of the US and other nations, there is the very real probability that inflation will begin to rise in the aftermath of the pandemic. This inflationary concern has been exacerbated by significant supply-side shortages that have served to send prices of materials and labour higher, in turn increasing production and operating costs for businesses in various sectors. Evidence of inflation has already surfaced in many different isolated industries, including the used-car market in the US. In that particular market, prices skyrocketed during the pandemic period, coinciding perfectly with the roll-out of stimulus packages by the US government.

Despite the complex combination of factors that contributed to this rise in inflation, the Federal Reserve repeatedly asserted, at any mention that monetary policy was causing inflation, that the higher inflation numbers were "transitory". The Fed argued at the time that once supply, which had been stalled by pandemic shutdowns, caught up with increased demand as the economy opened up again, prices should stabilise. But even if inflation was to be transitory, the fact remains that governments from around the world – and none more so than the United States – made the decision to inject trillions of dollars into the international monetary system from mid-2020 to mid-

2021. The results of this have been drastic and wide-ranging: a ballooning stock market, a massive transfer of wealth into the hands of the ultra-wealthy, an unprecedented level of global debt, and an inevitable rise in inequality. The combination of these phenomena is something the world has never before experienced, and the consequence of the fusion of these forces is yet to be fully realised. No matter the outcome, it is clear there is a limit to which monetary policy can stimulate lending and accelerate the velocity of money in the economy, especially when interest rates have already reached near zero. It is surely evident, then, that the money multiplier effect, and perhaps even the very idea of monetary policy, at best, do not work as well as theorised – and, at worst, are deeply flawed.

In the 1970s, when Milton Friedman advocated the revolutionary idea of monetary policy as a panacea for economic instability, it is unlikely he would have predicted that his ideologies would be pushed to the extremes that are being witnessed at present. Friedman believed that a *gradual* increase in money supply was a healthy method by which to regulate a balance between unemployment and inflation, thereby ensuring steady growth. The measures taken in the US during the Covid-19 pandemic have been anything but gradual. As illustrated, the levels of monetary stimulus injected into the country's economic system are historically incomparable and perhaps irreversible.

Historically, after significant non-financial crises, including pandemics and wars, there has been a trend among societies to descend into political disorder. This pattern is supported by the idea that during times of mass suffering there is increasing pressure to wrest political and economic agendas out of the hands of the elites and into those of the working class – and if this is not managed in a peaceful and democratic manner, history teaches us that it may be delivered by force. Following the cholera epidemic in France in the early 1830s, for example, the working class, hit hardest by the disease, rebelled against the ruling class of elites who had escaped the cities to their holiday homes to avoid infection. Upon their return, the upper classes hoped to continue life as before the epidemic; instead, they were met with an insurrection that became known as the Paris Uprising of 1832 – the event that inspired the story of Victor Hugo's novel *Les Misérables*. Prior to the rebellion, several coincidental factors increased social tensions, including harvest failures, food shortages and a significant increase in the cost of living that especially affected the working class. The catalyst of the revolution, however, was the cholera outbreak in the spring of 1832, which killed more than 18,000 Parisians, especially the working class, and more than 100,000 across France.

It is not inconceivable that the Covid-19 pandemic may bring about similar social upheaval – and there are early warning signs already present, most notably the prolonged protests that occurred in the US throughout 2020 and into 2021. For many years, there has been a steady erosion of trust in institutions and elites, together with ever-increasing suspicion and anger towards mega-corporations and the billionaires at their helms, whose wealth has radically increased as their tax payments decline. Perversely, the consequence of injecting unprecedented volumes of money into the economy, ostensibly for social relief during a global pandemic, has been the disproportionate enrichment of those elites. That they use sophisticated tax structures to enhance this effect only compounds the perversity. Given these facts, the near future – the next five to ten years – does not bode well for the free-market system, which is already in moral crisis.

CONCLUSION

When the leaders of the Group of Seven nations congregated for a photo opportunity on a beach in Falmouth, Cornwall in the clear light of early summer in June 2021, there was something quaint, distinctly British and even uplifting about the scene. Donald Trump may have dismissed the G7 as irrelevant, but for the first time in a long time it appeared, on that clear afternoon, that the ideas of liberal democracy, multilateralism and broad-stroke diplomacy night yet still have a beating heart. All, to be sure, had not been lost in the decade of nihilism that followed the Global Financial Crisis and preceded the Covid-19 pandemic – or so the leaders of the major developed economies of the world may have had us believe.

Notably absent from the upbeat gathering were Vladimir Putin and Xi Jinping. With democratic governance being one of the exclusive group's founding principles, this was no surprise: Russia was expelled from the G8 following its annexation of the Crimea in 2014, and China has never been invited to join the party. Indeed, authoritarian rule may well have been the underlying agenda of the 2021 G7 summit, given the political discord that has rumbled across the United States in recent years, at least in part due to Russian intervention in the presidential elections in 2016 and ongoing tensions with China. Echoing these thoughts on the day of the G7 photo op, Clarissa Ward, the chief international correspondent for CNN, made the remark that for the first time since 2001 there were more countries in the world under authoritarian rule than there were democracies.

Topics covered at the summit included a minimum international corporate tax rate, fast-tracking the international roll-out of the Covid-19 vaccine, defence against cyberattacks, the reinvigoration of climate action, and the alleviation of worsening inequality. In addition, the opportunity was taken to propose a Western alternative to China's Belt and Road Initiative, offering developing nations a new source of infrastructure finance in place of Chinese loans. It would be called, the G7 leaders announced, the "Green Belt and Road Plan", plagiarising not only China's strategy but the name itself. Given the corrosion of the Western agenda to champion liberal democracy over the last two decades, it seemed either disingenuous or incredibly naive to fuse the intractable problem of slowing down climate change with a newly conceived attempt to restrain the relentless march of Chinese economic and social imperialism.

In theory, multilateral development banks will co-ordinate with private sector global banks and institutional investors to provide funding to promote green energy and socially responsible infrastructure. "The G7 has an unprecedented opportunity to drive a global green industrial revolution, with the potential to transform the way we live," Boris Johnson proclaimed. The Chinese Communist Party shot back by arguing that "genuine multilateralism" was only achievable through the UN and not "so-called rules formulated by a small number of countries". Just two days previously, while the G7 leaders were dining with members of the British royal family at Falmouth, a top Chinese foreign policy official had lashed out at the condemnation of the alleged genocide of the Uyghur people in China's Xinjiang region. "The US side has fabricated various lies about Xinjiang in an attempt to sabotage the stability and unity of Xinjiang, which confuse right and wrong and are extremely absurd," the official told international media.

The G7 proposition to simultaneously address climate change and serve as a counterweight to Beijing's geopolitical influence will require a combination of lending and global co-ordination that is unprecedented in size. And even if these particular challenges can be overcome, there remains the surely self-defeating premise of deliberately excluding the world's largest carbon emitter, China, from a grand attempt to reduce carbon emissions and save the planet. The project itself and its underlying ambitions thus aroused the suspicions of political observers – and it was less than three months before world events turned that suspicion to contempt.

"Build Back Better for the World", Boris Johnson's purpose-made slogan for the G7 summit, rang hollow in early June 2021, given the recent geopolitical track record of Western liberal democracies. These were, after all, the same countries, and some of the same leaders, that stood by and watched the annexation of Crimea, the rolling back of democracy in Hong Kong, the murder of journalist Jamal Khashoggi by agents acting on behalf of the Crown Prince of Saudi Arabia, and the steady advance of authoritarian rule all around the world without response. If the evidence was not already in, then in mid-August Johnson's soundbite was reduced to an absurdity almost overnight by the ignominious and sudden withdrawal of US forces from Afghanistan, mirroring the embarrassing exit from Vietnam nearly half a century earlier and signalling the instant defeat of a twenty-year democratic project. As Taliban forces resumed control of the country, armed with American weapons and anti-American ideology, some political observers saw this as truly the end of American hegemony and the end of the belief in the propagation of freedom – and all this barely three decades after the fall of the Berlin Wall at the height of the era of liberal democracy.

Francis Fukuyama, who made the hopeful insight that the events of 1989 and the subsequent failure of communism could represent what he called the end of history – "that is, the end-point of mankind's ideological evolution and the universalisation of Western liberal democracy as the final form of human government" – was compelled to acknowledge the failure of this outcome in witnessing the fall of Kabul in August 2021. Writing in *The Economist*, he described the US withdrawal from Afghanistan as a signal of "the end of the American era". Once the leader of the democratic world, the US has become so distracted by its internal politics that it now lacks the will or the capacity to look outward and continue to lead a global charge against the rise of authoritarianism. "The United States is not likely to regain its earlier hegemonic status, nor should it aspire to," Fukuyama wrote. "What it can hope for is to sustain, with like-minded countries, a world order friendly to democratic values." To do so, however, it will first have to engage in the significant task of recovering some sense of national identity and a cohesive moral response to the external threats that have greatly undermined the hope for a free world. And in doing *that* it will have to regain the trust of its own citizens, just as so many Western governments and institutions need to do.

In China, meanwhile, there would appear, as of the time of writing, to be evidence of an increasing anxiety within the Chinese Communist Party (CCP), which has begun to show a recognition of the country's burgeoning debt problem and an impatience with its own citizens. It is increasingly expressing this through behaviour that is far more aligned with its fundamental political ideology: communism.

Since 2017, the CCP has attempted to take action against growth fuelled by ever-growing debt, and has started to allow large private companies, state-owned enterprises and even entire provinces to default on bond repayments. At the same time, the Chinese state has expressed dissatisfaction with the explosion in number of recently minted local dollar billionaires, and more generally in the number of Chinese millionaires, which was estimated to have reached four million by the end of 2020 – roughly half the population of Switzerland. This rapid accumulation of personal wealth since the turn of the century has, predictably, been accompanied by a broad adoption of Western capitalist ideology and behaviour, mirroring in many respects the infiltration of Western liberal ideals in Chinese thinking that accompanied the country's integration of free-market principles in the 1980s. Back then, this culminated in pro-democratic protests and the subsequent massacre at Tiananmen Square. Once again, the Chinese state is clamping down on such elements, indicating the end of an era of a more open Chinese society. In the period during which this book was being researched, written and readied for print, between mid-2020 and September 2021, the Chinese government implemented a litany of rules and regulations that indicate its intent to govern strictly every part of Chinese life, be it in the social, political or economic sphere.

In early November 2020, Chinese e-commerce giant Alibaba was preparing to take public its financial arm, Ant Group, in what would have been the largest initial public offering (IPO) of all time. But just hours before the company's shares were due to start trading publicly, Chinese regulators put a halt to proceedings, summoning Alibaba CEO Jack Ma to discuss the regulatory shortcomings and risks that the company posed to the stability of the financial sector. On 3 November, Ant Group announced that it would be suspending its IPO indefinitely, stating on its website that the company did not "meet listing qualifications or disclosure requirements due to material matters relating to the regulatory interview".

For the following fifteen weeks, Jack Ma was not seen in public, and when he finally reappeared, he kept a far lower profile as Alibaba came under constant pressure from regulators to reform its business. In April 2021 it was fined the equivalent of $2.8 billion after an anti-trust investigation by Chinese authorities concluded that the company had abused its market dominance and made use of anti-competitive practices. In August, Alibaba undertook to donate more than $15 billion to the CCP's "common prosperity" vision for China, which entails a greater focus on wealth distribution, stronger regulation of "excessively high incomes" and "the encouragement of high-income groups and enterprises to return more to society" – a vision articulated by Xi Jinping at the party's Central Financial and Economic Affairs Commission earlier that month. Not long after the president's speech, China's largest company by market share, the technology giant Tencent, pledged $7.7 billion to the same cause. This act of charity was then followed by a donation of $1.5 billion by Pinduoduo, another large Chinese e-commerce platform. And if charitable obeisance was not enough, the state now insists on having CCP representatives on the boards of Alibaba and other private firms – effectively a corporate political commissar for each.

In contrast to the CCP's rhetoric in the years leading up to the outbreak of the Covid-19 pandemic, the Chinese leadership has reverted to a stricter, more centralised version of control in what appears to be an increasingly chaotic and paranoid manner. The trend of imposing ever more severe and outlandish rules on its citizens and the companies that operate within its borders has escalated recently with a series of new regulations that can only be described as Orwellian. These include the limiting of video gaming time for children to three hours a week; the restriction of private tutoring for profits; the banning of certain songs that encourage young Chinese to "lie flat" and relax; the implementation of arbitrary rules regarding pets, including a limit of one dog, no taller than 35 centimetres, per family in Beijing; and the prohibition of Chinese television and social media from making stars out of "vulgar influencers" and "sissy boys", effeminate male celebrities who the state believes corrupt the morality of its youth. In parallel with this twin barrage of corporate and social regulation, there is the ongoing and escalating pressure being applied to Hong Kong to quell pro-democratic elements on the island. Shortly before this book went to print, Next Daily, the Hong Kong media company that had for decades published strong criticism of the Chinese government, announced its impending closure. Its flagship newspaper, *Apple Daily*, had been forced to close in June, its bank accounts frozen, and its 73-year-old founder, Jimmy Lai, jailed on a number of charges.

Taken together, these are the tell-tale signs of a sea-change in the CCP's thinking, an indication that the socio-economic experiment of running a command economy with capitalist underpinnings may have run its course. Moreover, it is not a coincidence that this economic revolution is occurring at precisely the same time that Chinese growth is struggling to sustain its own debt levels. It would appear that Xi Jinping and his inner circle are particularly concerned about the social fracturing and unrest that may well result when the promise that the CCP has made to its people – that of a better life – does not materialise. Their logic, it seems, is to do the corporal punishment up front, setting the tone, rather than waiting for greater social unrest to occur – but signs of this have already begun to emerge. On 14 September 2021, hundreds of protesters – a mix of nervous homeowners who had made deposits on incomplete buildings, unpaid contractors and concerned investors – gathered at the Shenzhen headquarters of the China Evergrande Group, demanding to be reimbursed by the embattled property developer. The company had recently suspended payments on some of its wealth management products and had even announced that it might default on its bonds. Local police were required to forcibly remove the protesters from Evergrande's premises.

That the CCP has radically changed course is the only rational explanation for its recent behaviour. The signs are manifest that the party has given up on the growth model in the face of overwhelming debt, and has decided to pull back and focus on internal control. The long-run outcome for China is also not positive. As the population ages, the next generation cannot expect as much financial fuel as their parents and grandparents have had over the past thirty years, through ever more grandiose and ever less efficient state-driven infrastructure projects. China has simply run out of money – or, more accurately, it has run out of credit.

———————

While concluding the final edits of this book in August and September 2021, it was impossible to ignore the looming realisation that we would cross paths with the twentieth anniversary of the 9/11 attacks on America and, in effect, on Western civilisation itself. Although it was deeply distressing to recall the tragedy when the day arrived, the passing of a mere two decades had nevertheless conferred a distinct sense of historical and emotional distance on the event. Even the grainy footage, replayed on news channels and in a documentary released for the occasion, seemed archival compared to the rich colour and detail of our modern ultra-high definition screens.

As if to demonstrate how profoundly time had moved on, people around the world turned on their televisions the following day to watch two major international motorsport events, both in high definition. Formula 1 fans took their seats for the Italian Grand Prix held at Monza, the temple of speed, while Moto GP fans tuned in for the Spanish Grand Prix in Jerez. There was plenty of action in both races, but it was the peripheral goings-on that were more illustrative of today's world.

The track at Monza was dominated by the unmistakable green of the Heineken brand, with a marketing campaign focused on its 0.0 non-alcoholic beer to avoid the unwanted implication of promoting drinking and driving. Rolex and Tissot, staple emblems of luxury, were also prominently displayed, along with Aramco, the Saudi state-owned and listed oil producer, which has shortened its name from the original Saudi Aramco in an act of spectacular self-awareness. A more recently birthed brand also had a significant presence: Crypto.com. In Jerez, meanwhile, two advertisers dominated the barriers of the track: PokerStars.com and Bitci.com, Turkey's first prominent cryptocurrency.

If the principal advertisers at these major European sports events may serve as a measure of the state of the Western consumer's psyche, then it is apposite to note that what was on display was a celebration of wealth intertwined with – and perhaps masking – a cacophony of contradictions. Gambling websites and crypto trading platforms appeared alongside oil produced in an authoritarian regime and the non-alcoholic offering of one of the world's most popular beer brands. In the free world anything can be advertised and monetised, and the consumer has freedom of choice. But if the last twenty years can be thought of as a war of ideas, beginning with the war on terror, the pointless search for weapons of mass destruction, and the hunt for Bin Laden in Afghanistan, and if one takes into account the weight of this particular moment – the twentieth anniversary of the 9/11 attacks on freedom and democracy – then, simply observing what consumers have manifested at European tracks in the autumn of 2021, we must reluctantly acknowledge that the war may well have been lost. It has patently been lost in Afghanistan and would appear to be lost in Turkey,

Hong Kong, Saudi Arabia, Belarus and many other countries where authoritarian regimes appear to be thriving, unhindered by any intervention or consequences from democratic nations. And perhaps it is because the West has been so distracted, having bought into an extreme free-market ethos, that anything goes so long as it serves the individual.

In a way, the West has not only ignored but enabled the obvious erosion of democratic values and of freedom, distracted by the project of individual greed and increasing self-containment, the most conspicuous expression of which is the cult of cryptocurrency. This is the ultimate proof of the public's distrust of the monetary system – embracing a new system of money that is no longer backed by, issued by or governed by a state or a bank. It is necessary to ask whether it is logical, feasible and internally consistent with the idea of humanism to wish for a world in which the response to the erosion of trust is to create a system in which, by definition, no person trusts another whatsoever. The only way transactions can take place in such a world is to insist on a highly inefficient process of mass collaboration, underpinned by contrived and impractical consensus methodologies. Ideologically, it amounts to the glorification of chaos and disorder, and it closely aligns with the anarchy that drove the delinquent mob who stormed the Capitol in America in January 2021.

If this ideology of distrust is logically extended to the other organisations that shape society, it would mean that the public should not trust the most fundamental of government establishments or the institutions that represent the higher attainments of human civilisation, from the military and police to schools and universities. It would mean losing all rights to anything offered by the state or by state-regulated institutions, such as a safer living environment, a functioning justice system and a network of medical facilities. All these benefits are part of a societal agreement based on trust. In a world without trust, chaos would be the only constant.

To retrace our steps, the roots of society's great loss of trust can be seen to extend back to the early 1970s and specifically to the abandonment of the gold standard during the Nixon shock. It followed during the 1980s, '90s and early 2000s that free-market thinking – theoretically aligned closely with the ideals of liberal democracy – began to mutate into a system characterised by greed and excess. This was when the underbelly of capitalism was truly exposed, as its ambitions began to diverge ever more obviously from those of the Western democratic project. Gradually, unfettered capitalism and pure individualism proved to be unsustainable. Laissez-faire capitalism did not, as it was theorised, self-regulate effectively, and there began a subsequent infiltration of political agendas into monetary policy. The culmination of this was the 2007/2008 Global Financial Crisis. This event – and the inadequate government responses to it – significantly accelerated the public's distrust of and loss of confidence in the capitalist free-market system, and even in the idea of Western democracy as a way of life.

Governments have attempted to print their way out of the economic downturn, but what were initially planned as small, incremental additions to money supply to regulate the economy quickly became an unstoppable torrent. This problem has only been exacerbated by the Covid-19 pandemic. In 2020 and 2021, relief funds were provided throughout the world, intended theoretically to flow through the banking system to boost international trade and economic activity. But owing to the fear pervading the Western banking system in the aftermath of the Financial Crisis, and to the prospect of entire industries defaulting on their loans, this money has found its way less to those who have suffered from pandemic-related economic devastation and more to known customers who don't actually need it. To put it bluntly, monetary policy relief, worldwide, has found its way into the hands of the super-rich, further crystallising the average citizen's distrust in the monetary system and the institutions that facilitate the system, including governments and banks. The result of this, on aggregate, is a fragmented and fragile international financial system.

In the years following the Global Financial Crisis, journalists, economists and business leaders from across the globe retrospectively acknowledged the warning signs that had gone unheeded. In 2021, the data relating to China's banking system and its debt levels alone should be sufficient to motivate global attention. When combined with runaway monetary policy in the US and elsewhere, which is accelerating already worrying inequality and distrust in the West, this problem becomes even more pressing. During the global pandemic, the monetary system has created a record number of new billionaires, who have profited from ballooning asset prices and whose fortunes are sheltered in both legal and illegal sovereign tax havens. In this state of growing inequality, confusion and distrust, a new form of volatile, inefficient and unregulated monetary exchange has also proliferated in the idea of cryptocurrency, extolled, in cult-like manner, as the natural and rightful end of money. Rather than seeking to rebuild trust in the institutions that have facilitated the greatest gains in human progress, uplifting the bulk of humanity in the process, those who promote the ideals of decentralised finance would prefer to eradicate trust in its entirety.

The most pressing question is how we could have reached such ontological depths. It can be tempting to blame political leadership for the failures of the democratic project, particularly for allowing the growth of authoritarian leadership, and even government-level fascism to re-emerge nearly a hundred years after it last thrived. But that would be naive. The original sin ironically, and somewhat tragically, can be accurately pinpointed to a particular time and place – the Nixon shock – and tracked from there. It is in the imposition of extreme free-market ideology that the true fault lies, in its rewarding of psychopathically self-serving behaviour, both within individuals and within organisations, and in its infection of Western free-market ideology as it was practically exercised towards the end of the 20th century. This extreme ideology was authenticated by the veneer of scientific rigour in complex mathematical economics papers, and sanctified by Nobel prizes and its near-total adoption by the leaders of the free world.

Through the imposition of theoretical models onto real-world marketplaces, the intertwined relationship between the concept of capitalism and the concept of democracy began to unravel. Through the imposition of mathematical models and oversimplified political ideology onto the Western system, capitalism and freedom as ideas have become decoupled. In some authentic ideological sense, one can now say that the end of money has undone the end of history.

GLOSSARY
(AND ABBREVIATIONS)

Select glossary of companies and institutions

1Malaysia Development Berhad (1MDB) Insolvent Malaysian sovereign wealth fund, founded in 2008.

Agricultural Bank of China (ABC) One of the four major state-owned commercial banks in China, founded in 1951. 3rd largest bank in the world, with total assets of $4.2 trillion as of year-end 2020.

American International Group (AIG) American multinational finance and insurance corporation, founded in 1919.

Archegos Capital Management American family office that managed the personal assets of Bill Hwang, founded in 2013. Collapsed dramatically in 2021.

Asset management corporation (AMC) Collective term for Chinese government-established and owned financial asset management institutions, which focus on distressed debt management.

Bank for International Settlements (BIS) International banking regulator established in 1930 through intergovernmental agreement between Belgium, France, Germany, Italy, Japan, Switzerland, the UK and the US. Incorporates the Basel Committee on Banking Supervision (BCBS).

Bank of America American investment bank and financial services holding company, founded in 1998. 9th largest bank in the world, with total assets of $2.8 trillion as of year-end 2020.

Bank of China (BOC) One of the four major state-owned commercial banks in China, founded in 1912. 4th largest bank in the world, with total assets of $3.7 trillion as of year-end 2020.

Bank of England Central bank of England, established in 1694 to act as the government's banker.

Bankers Trust American investment bank, founded in 1903, that pleaded guilty to fraud in a notorious case against Procter & Gamble in the mid-'90s.

Acquired by Deutsche Bank in 1999.

Barings Bank British merchant bank, founded in 1762 and based in London. Collapsed in 1995 after suffering significant losses in fraudulent investments made by "rogue trader" Nick Leeson.

Basel Committee on Banking Supervision (BCBS) International regulator of banking supervisory authorities established by central bank governors of the Group of Ten countries in 1974. Provides a forum for regular cooperation on international banking supervisory matters. Arm of the BIS.

Bear Stearns (Bear) US-headquartered global investment bank, securities trading and brokerage firm, founded in 1923. Failed in 2008 and was sold to JPMorgan Chase.

BNP Paribas French international banking group, founded in 1848. 7th largest bank in the world, with total assets of $3.1 trillion as of year-end 2020.

China Construction Bank (CCB) One of the four major state-owned commercial banks in China, founded in 1954. 2nd largest bank in the world, with total assets of $4.3 trillion as of year-end 2020.

China Evergrande Group China's second-largest property development firm, by sales, founded in 1996. Suffered severe financial difficulties in 2021.

Chinese Communist Party (CCP) Common name for Communist Party of China, founding and sole governing political party of the People's Republic of China since 1949.

Cinda Asset Management AMC for CCB, founded in 1999.

Citigroup American investment bank and financial services company, formed in 1998 by the merger of Citicorp and financial conglomerate Travelers Group. 11th largest bank in the world, with total assets of $2.3 trillion as of year-end 2020.

Deloitte One of the "Big Four" accounting and audit firms, founded in 1845 and headquartered in the Netherlands. Also provides consulting services.

Department of Justice (DOJ) Federal executive department of the US government tasked with the enforcement of federal law and administration of justice.

Deutsche Bank German multinational investment bank and financial services company, founded in 1870 and headquartered in Frankfurt.

Drexel Burnham Lambert American multinational investment bank, founded in 1935, and forced into bankruptcy in 1990 due to its involvement in illegal activities in the junk bond market.

Ernst & Young (EY) One of the "Big Four" accounting and audit firms, founded in 1989 and headquartered in the UK. Also provides consulting services. Name officially changed to EY in 2013.

European Commission (EC) Executive branch of the European Union, founded in 1958. Responsible for proposing legislation, enforcing EU laws and directing the union's administrative operations.

Fannie Mae The Federal National Mortgage Association, founded during the

Great Depression in 1938 to expand the secondary mortgage market by buying home loans from banks, effectively taking those loans off banks' balance sheets to create liquidity for the banks to make more loans.

Federal Bureau of Investigation (FBI) Domestic intelligence and security service of the US, and the country's principal federal law-enforcement agency.

Federal Reserve (Fed) Central bank of the United States, founded in 1913 after a series of financial panics led to a desire for central control of the monetary system to alleviate financial crises.

Financial Stability Institute (FSI) Jointly created in 1998 by BIS and BCBS, and mandated to assist supervisors around the world in improving and strengthening their financial systems.

Fitch Ratings (Fitch) One of the "Big Three" credit rating agencies, founded in 1913 and headquartered in the US.

Freddie Mac The Federal Home Loan Mortgage Corporation, established through the passing of the Emergency Home Finance Act of 1970. This piece of legislation aimed to extend and diversify the rapidly growing secondary mortgage market in which Fannie Mae had, until then, been the only player.

Goldman Sachs (Goldman) American multinational investment bank and financial services company, founded in 1869. 20th largest bank in the world, with total assets of $1.2 trillion as of year-end 2020.

Great Wall Asset Management Co AMC for ABC, founded in 1999.

Group of Seven (G7) Intergovernmental forum, founded in 1975, consisting of Canada, France, Germany, Italy, Japan, the UK and the US. Its members are the world's largest advanced economies and wealthiest liberal democracies as per the IMF.

Group of Twenty (G20) Intergovernmental forum comprising 19 countries and the European Union, founded in 1999 to address major issues related to the global economy, such as international financial stability, climate change mitigation and sustainable development.

Hayman Capital (Hayman) Asset management firm, founded in 2005 and based in the US.

HSBC UK investment bank and financial services company, founded in 1865. 8th largest bank in the world, with total assets of $3 trillion as of year-end 2020.

Huarong Asset Management AMC for Industrial and Commercial Bank of China, founded in 1999.

Industrial and Commercial Bank of China (ICBC) One of the four major state-owned commercial banks in China, founded in 1984. The largest bank in the world, with total assets of $5.1 trillion as of year-end 2020.

Internal Revenue Service (IRS) Revenue service of the US federal government, founded in 1862, and responsible for collecting taxes and administering the Internal Revenue Code, the main body of the federal statutory tax law.

International Monetary Fund (IMF) International financial institution, formed in 1944 at the Bretton Woods Conference along with the IMF, headquartered in the US. Consists of almost 200 countries working to foster global monetary cooperation, secure financial stability, facilitate international trade, promote high employment and sustainable economic growth, and reduce poverty around the world.

J Capital Research American firm, founded in 2007, that publishes highly credible research reports on publicly traded companies.

JPMorgan Chase & Co (JPMorgan) American financial institution formed through the merger of JP Morgan & Co Incorporated and Chase Manhattan commercial banks in 2000, offering investment banking, commercial banking, retail banking, asset management, private banking and private equity businesses. Formerly JPMorgan & Co Incorporated commercial bank (1988-2000), JPMorgan & Co commercial bank (1933-1988) and JPMorgan & Co commercial and investment bank, founded by JP Morgan in 1871. See *Morgan Stanley*.

KPMG One of the "Big Four" accounting and audit firms, founded in 1987 and headquartered in the UK. Also provides consulting services.

Lehman Brothers (Lehman) American investment bank, founded in 1850. 4th largest investment bank in the US prior to its collapse in 2008.

Long-Term Capital Management (LTCM) American hedge fund, founded by high-profile economists in 1994, which used absolute return trading strategies combined with high financial leverage in derivatives instruments. Rescued after near-collapse in 1998.

Malaysian Anti-Corruption Commission (MACC) Government agency in Malaysia, founded in 1967 to investigate and prosecute corruption in the public and private sectors.

Mitsubishi UFJ Financial Group Japanese bank holding and financial services company. 9th largest bank in the world by asset size as of year-end 2020.

Moody's One of the "Big Three" credit rating agencies, founded in 1909 and headquartered in the US.

Morgan Stanley American investment bank, formed in 1935 through the division of the investment and commercial banking divisions of the original JP Morgan & Co. See *JPMorgan Chase & Co*.

Organization for Economic Co-operation and Development (OECD) Intergovernmental economic organisation with 38 member countries, founded in 1961 to stimulate economic progress and world trade.

Organisation of the Petroleum Exporting Countries (OPEC) Cartel of 13 oil-producing countries, founded in 1960 and headquartered in Austria.

Orient Asset Management AMC for BOC, founded in 1999.

People's Bank of China (PBOC) Central bank of China, founded in 1948.

PricewaterhouseCoopers (PwC) One of the "Big Four" accounting and audit firms, founded in 1998 and headquartered in the UK. Also provides consulting services.

Procter & Gamble (P&G) US-headquartered multinational consumer-goods corporation, founded in 1837.

Securities and Exchange Commission (SEC) Independent agency of the US federal government, created in 1934 in the aftermath of the 1929 Wall Street Crash primarily to enforce the law against market manipulation.

Standard & Poor's (S&P) One of the "Big Three" credit rating agencies, founded in 1860 and headquartered in the US.

Wells Fargo American commercial bank and financial services company, founded in 1929. 13th largest bank in the world, with total assets of $2 trillion as of year-end 2020.

World Bank International financial institution, created at the 1944 Bretton Woods Conference along with the IMF, headquartered in the US. Provides loans and grants to the governments of low- and middle-income countries for the purpose of pursuing capital projects.

World Trade Organisation (WTO) Intergovernmental organisation, formed in 1995 to regulate and facilitate international trade between nations. Governments use it to establish, revise and enforce rules that govern international trade.

Select glossary of terms

We recommend and gratefully acknowledge Investopedia, from which many of these definitions are adapted.

Anti-money laundering (AML) Laws, regulations and procedures intended to prevent criminals from disguising illegally obtained funds as legitimate income.

Asset Resource with economic value that an individual, corporation or country owns or controls with the expectation that it will provide a future benefit.

Assets (banking) Bank assets, including loans such as home loans, vehicle loans, business loans and personal loans, as well as securities owned by the bank.

Assets under management Total market value of the investments that a person or entity manages on behalf of clients.

Balance sheet Financial statement that reports a company's assets, liabilities and shareholder equity at a specific point in time.

Bank holding company Corporation that owns a controlling interest in one or more banks but does not itself offer banking services.

Base erosion and profit shifting (BEPS) Tax strategies used to shift profits from higher-tax jurisdictions to lower-tax jurisdictions, thus eroding the tax base of higher-tax jurisdictions.

Best estimated expected loss (BEEL) Equation mandated by the regulator used for calculating credit loss expectations on defaulted assets.

Bond Fixed income instrument that represents a loan made by an investor to a borrower, typically corporate or governmental.

Bond coupons Annual interest rates paid on a bond, expressed as a percentage of the face value, and paid from issue date until maturity.

Call option Financial contract that gives the buyer the right, but not the obligation, to buy an asset at a specified price within a specific time period.

Capital (banking) Represents the value of a bank's equity instruments that can absorb losses and have the lowest priority in payments if the bank liquidates.

Capital reserve ratio Portion of capital that commercial banks must hold in relation to their lending.

Collateral Asset that a lender accepts as security for a loan.

Collateralised debt obligation (CDO) Structured finance product backed by a pool of loans and other assets, and sold to institutional investors.

Command economy Key aspect of a political system in which a central governmental authority dictates the levels of production that are permissible and the prices that may be charged therefor.

Commercial bank Financial institution that accepts deposits, offers checking account services, makes various loans, and offers basic financial products to individuals and small businesses. Compare *Investment bank*.

Compound annual growth rate (CAGR) Measure of an investment's annual growth rate over time, with the effect of compounding taken into account. Compare *Simple average growth rate*.

Cost-to-income ratio Key financial measure, particularly important in valuing banks, that shows a company's operating costs in relation to its income.

Counter financing of terrorism (CFT) Set of regulations intended to restrict access to funding and financial services for those whom the government designates as terrorists.

Counterparty Opposite party participating in a financial transaction. Every transaction must have a counterparty in order for it to go through.

Credit default swap (CDS) Financial derivative or contract that allows an investor to "swap" or offset their credit risk with that of another investor.

Credit rating agency Institution that provides investors with information that assists them in determining whether issuers of bonds and other debt instruments and fixed-income securities will be able to meet their obligations. The "Big Three" credit rating agencies are Fitch, Moody's and S&P.

Decentralised finance (DeFi) Blockchain-based form of finance that does not rely on centralised financial intermediaries such as banks to offer traditional financial instruments.

Derivatives Type of financial contract, the value of which is dependent on an underlying asset, group of assets or benchmark.

Discount window Central bank lending facility meant to help commercial banks manage short-term liquidity needs.

Dividend Distribution of corporate profits to eligible shareholders.

Equity Representation of the amount of money that would be returned to a company's shareholders if all assets were liquidated and all of the company's debt paid off in the case of liquidation.

Escrow Financial instrument whereby money is held by a third party on behalf of two other parties that are in the process of completing a transaction.

Exposure Risk inherent in an investment, indicating the amount of money an investor stands to lose.

Federal funds rate Interest rate that banks in the US charge each other to borrow or lend excess reserves overnight.

Fiat money Government-issued currency not backed by a physical commodity, such as gold or silver, but rather by the government that issued it.

Fintech New technology that seeks to improve and automate the delivery and use of financial services.

Fiscal policy Use of government spending to influence economic conditions, especially macroeconomic conditions, including aggregate demand for goods and services, employment, inflation and economic growth.

Forward price-to-earnings ratio Version of the ratio of price to earnings that uses forecasted earnings for the price-to-earnings calculation.

Forwards Customised derivative financial contracts between two parties to buy or sell an asset at a specified price on a future date.

Free market Economic system based on supply and demand with little or no government control.

Fungibility The ability of a good or asset to be interchanged with other goods or assets of the same type. Cash is the obvious example, with one $100 note being interchangeable with two $50 notes – as opposed to a house or used car.

Futures Standardised exchange-traded forward contracts in which a buyer and a seller are obligated to transact the underlying asset at a predetermined future date and price, regardless of the market price at that time.

Gaussian distribution See *Normal distribution*.

GDP per capita Financial metric that breaks down a country's economic output per person, calculated by dividing the GDP of a nation by its population.

Government-sponsored enterprise (GSE) Quasi-governmental entity, such as Fannie Mae and Freddie Mac, which is publicly traded but retains an implicit government guarantee.

Gross domestic product (GDP) Total monetary or market value of all finished goods and services produced within a country's borders in a specific time period.

Hedge fund Actively managed investment pool, the managers of which use a wide range of strategies, often including buying with borrowed money and trading assets, to beat average investment returns for their clients.

Hedging Investing with the intention of reducing the risk of adverse price movements in an asset.

Indicia Signs, indications or distinguishing marks. In finance, used especially in relation to tax compliance, representing the information connected to persons related to a certain bank account.

Inflation Decline in purchasing power of a given currency over time.

Initial public offering (IPO) Process of offering shares of a private corporation to the public in a new stock issuance.

Interbank market Global network utilised by financial institutions to loan one another money and trade currencies.

Investment bank Financial services company that acts as an intermediary in large and complex financial transactions, such as sovereign bond underwriting. Compare *Commercial bank*.

Invisible hand Concept introduced by Adam Smith as a metaphor for the unseen forces of demand and supply that move the free-market economy.

Junk bonds Bonds that carry a higher risk of default than most bonds issued by corporations and governments.

Know your customer (KYC) Standard in the investment industry that ensures investment advisers know detailed information about their clients' risk tolerance, investment knowledge and financial position.

Laissez-faire 18th-century economic theory that opposed any government intervention in business affairs.

Leverage Results from using borrowed capital as a funding source when investing to expand the firm's asset base and generate returns on risk capital.

Liability Something a person or company owes, usually a sum of money.

Liability (banking) Deposits owed to customers, as well as any debt a bank owes, such as in the interbank market.

Liquidity Ease with which an asset or security can be converted into ready cash without affecting its market price.

Liquidity ratio Important class of financial metrics used to determine a debtor's ability to pay off current debt obligations without raising external capital.

London Interbank Offered Rate (LIBOR) Benchmark interest rate at which major global banks extend short-term loans to one another.

Macroeconomics Branch of economics that studies how an overall economy, market or other systems that operate on a large scale behave.

Margin call Demand for an investor to deposit more funds when the value of the investor's margin account falls below the broker's required amount.

Market share Percentage of total sales in an industry generated by a particular company.

Monetary policy Control, usually by a central bank, of the quantity of money available in an economy and the channels by which new money is supplied.

Nominal amount Unadjusted rate in value, such as interest rates or GDP.

Normal distribution Probability distribution that is symmetric about the mean, showing that data near the mean are more frequent in occurrence than data far from the mean. Also known as Gaussian distribution.

Obligee Person or entity to whom an obligation is owed under a contract or other legal procedure. Also known as creditor.

Obligor Person or entity who is legally or contractually obliged to provide a benefit or payment to another. Also known as debtor.

Open market operations (OMO) Central banks' buying and selling of securities, usually bonds, on the open market to regulate the supply of money that is on reserve in banks.

Option Derivatives contract that gives the buyer the right, but not the obligation, to buy or sell, depending on the type of contract they hold, the underlying asset after a certain period or at a certain price.

Over-the-counter (OTC) How securities are traded via a broker-dealer network, directly between counterparties, as opposed to on a centralised exchange.

Preference shares Shares of a company's stock with dividends that are paid out to shareholders before common stock dividends are issued.

Price-to-earnings ratio (PE ratio) Ratio for valuing a company that measures its current share price relative to its earnings per share.

Producer price index (PPI) Group of indexes published by the US Bureau of Labor Statistics to calculate and represent average movement in selling prices from domestic production over time.

Put option Contract giving the owner the right, but not the obligation, to sell a specified amount of an underlying security at a pre-determined price within a specified timeframe.

Quantitative easing (QE) Monetary policy whereby a central bank purchases longer-term securities from the open market to increase the money supply and encourage lending.

Regulatory arbitrage Corporate strategy that involves using more favourable laws in one jurisdiction to circumvent less favourable regulations elsewhere.

Return on assets (ROA) Indicator of how profitable a company is relative to its total assets.

Return on equity (ROE) Measure of financial performance calculated by dividing net income by shareholders' equity.

Securities Fungible, negotiable financial instruments that hold monetary value and include an ownership position in a publicly traded corporation via stock, a creditor relationship with a governmental body or a corporation represented by owning that entity's bond, or rights to ownership as represented by an option.

Short selling Investment or trading strategy that speculates on the decline in a stock or other security's price.

Simple annual growth rate Average annual growth rate that does not take compounding into account. Compare *Compound annual growth rate*.

Sovereign debt Debt issued by a central government, usually in the form of securities, to finance various development initiatives within a country.

Spread Difference between two prices, rates or yields; gap between the bid and the ask prices of a security or asset, like a stock, bond or commodity.

Standard deviation Statistical measure of the dispersion of a dataset relative to its mean.

Straddle Neutral options strategy that involves simultaneously buying both a put option and a call option for the underlying security with the same strike price and the same expiration date.

Subsidiary Company that belongs to another company (which is known as the parent company or holding company).

Tax arbitrage Transactions that are entered into with the intention of profiting off the spread between tax systems, tax treatments or tax rates.

Tenor Length of time remaining before a financial contract expires.

Troubled Asset Relief Program (TARP) Initiative created and run by the US Treasury to stabilise the country's financial system, restore economic growth, and mitigate foreclosures in the wake of the 2007/2008 Global Financial Crisis.

Underwriting Process through which an institution takes on financial risk for a fee, most typically involving loans, insurance or investments.

Valuation Analytical process of determining the current (or projected) worth of an asset or a company.

Velocity of money Measurement of the rate at which money is exchanged in an economy.

Volatility Statistical measure of the dispersion of returns for a given security or market index.

Warrants Derivatives financial contracts that give the right, but not the obligation, to buy or sell a security – most commonly an equity – at a certain price prior to expiration.

Wealth management Investment advisory service that combines other financial services to address the needs of affluent clients.

Weighted average Calculation that takes into account the varying degrees of importance of the numbers in a dataset.

Yield Earnings generated and realised on an investment, particularly bonds, over a particular period of time.

NOTES

PROLOGUE

Details of Alan Schwartz's request to Jamie Dimon for $29 billion – "Panic: The Untold Story of the 2008 Financial Crisis". HBO (2018)

Details of the stock swap worth $2 a share between Bear Stearns and JPMorgan – Davies, M. and Giannone, J. "JPMorgan to buy Bear Stearns for $2 a share". Reuters (2008)

A loan was provided via the Federal Reserve Bank of New York for Bear Stearns's toxic assets to the value of $29 billion – "NY Fed to provide $29 billion in Bear Stearns financing". Reuters (2008)

Bear Stearns recorded its first ever loss in 2007 – "Timeline: A dozen key dates in the demise of Bear Stearns". Reuters (2008)

INTRODUCTION

There were roughly 13,000 banks in America in 1960 – Federal Reserve Bank of Richmond website, "Changes in the Size Distribution of US Banks: 1960-2005"

The United Nations was created initially with 51 member states but has grown to include 193 states – United Nations website (2021)

This excess lending, if not being converted into economic growth, cannot be leaving China in significant quantities – Read more about China's strict capital controls at: Kuo, M. "China's Capital Controls: Politics or Policy?". *The Diplomat* (2017)

CHAPTER 1

Bear Stearns stock price tumbled to its lowest levels in five years – Giannone, J. "Bear Stearns Stock Plunges Amid Risk Worries". Reuters (2008)

"It's ridiculous, totally ridiculous." – quote from Alan Greenberg: "Bear Stearns' Greenberg: Liquidity Talk Is 'Ridiculous'". CNBC (2008)

"Bear Stearns' balance sheet, liquidity and capital remain strong" – quote from Alan Schwartz: Giannone, J. "Bear Stearns dismisses cash crunch talk". CNBC (2008)

Bear Stearns shares lost about 30% of their value in two months and dropped 11% on 10 March 2008 – Zuill, L. "Bear Stearns Shares Recover After Earlier

Decline". Reuters (2008)

Cost of insuring Bear Stearns debt – "Bear Stearns debt protection costs jump, puts active". Reuters (2008)

Details on Bear Stearns put options – "Bear Stearns unusual option bets gets payoff". Bloomberg (2008)

ING Group suspended short-term funding facility – Kelly, K. "Fear, Rumors Touched Off Fatal Run on Bear Stearns". *The Wall Street Journal* (2008)

Hayman Capital derivatives position with Bear Stearns – "The Financial Crisis Inquiry Report". Govinfo website (2011)

"GS does not consent to this trade." – email from Goldman Sachs to Hayman Capital: "The Financial Crisis Inquiry Report". Govinfo website (2011)

Cost of insuring Bear Stearns's debt through credit default swaps – Kelly, K. "Fear, Rumors Touched Off Fatal Run on Bear Stearns". *The Wall Street Journal* (2008)

Renaissance Technology and Highbridge Capital Management pull-out – Kelly, K. "Fear, Rumors Touched Off Fatal Run on Bear Stearns". *The Wall Street Journal* (2008)

By this stage, the firm had less than $3 billion in cash available – Kelly, K. "Inside the Fall of Bear Stearns". *The Wall Street Journal* (2009)

Bear Stearns was borrowing in the region of $75 billion a day through various repo agreements – "The Financial Crisis Inquiry Report". Govinfo website (2011)

"None of these speculations are true…" – Quote by Alan Schwartz on *Squawk on the Street*. CNBC (March 2008)

"$29-billion mess" – Referring to loan for Bear Stearns's toxic assets via the Federal Reserve Bank of New York to the value of $29 billion

"Communication issues" – Quote by Hank Paulson when interviewed for "Panic: The Untold Story of the 2008 Financial Crisis". HBO (2018)

30% of Fannie Mae's and Freddie Mac's loan purchases must be related to affordable housing – US Code 4562, amended in 1992

Frank Raines's $90 million in salary and bonuses – Feirstein, B. "100 to Blame: Prosperity theologists, Franklin Raines, and more". *Vanity Fair* (2009)

GSEs had purchased $434 billion in securities backed by subprime loans between 2004 and 2006 – Carol, D. "How HUD Mortgage Policy Fed t he Crisis". *The Washington Post* (2008)

The bailout of the two GSEs cost US taxpayers upwards of $187 billion, although this has since been paid back – Levine, M. "Money Stuff: Supreme Court Won't Help GSE Shareholders Much". Bloomberg (2021)

Troubled Asset Relief Program (TARP) made available $700 billion in government funds – Emergency Economic Stabilization Act (2008)

Additional key sources used in the research of this chapter:

Sidel, R., Ip, G., Phillips, M. and Kelly, K. "The Week That Shook Wall Street:

Inside the Demise of Bear Stearns". *The Wall Street Journal* (2008)

Bernanke, B. *The Courage to Act*. WW Norton & Company (2017)

Cohan, D. *House of Cards: A Tale of Hubris and Wretched Excess on Wall Street*. Doubleday (2009)

Holmes, S. "Fannie Mae Eases Credit to Aid Mortgage Lending". *The New York Times* (1999)

CHAPTER 2

Note on *The Banker*'s "Top 1000" list and all future mentions of individual or aggregated figures regarding the financial results of banks, including specifically the mention of total assets: Every year *The Banker* magazine releases its list of the top 1,000 banks in the world on its website. *The Banker* releases its most current list (the "2021 list", for example) using the previous year's annual results (year-end 2020 results, for example). Therefore, when the text refers to *The Banker*'s 2021 list of top 1,000 banks, this will reflect data from year-end 2020. While most of the annual results recorded in *The Banker* magazine's "Top 1000" are year-end 2020 (31 December 2020), some are recorded at financial year-end (31 March 2021), especially in the case of Japanese banks. Beyond this exception, when mention is made of 2020 results, this is always in reference to year-end 2020 results, as is the case when mention is made of 2019 results and so on. The same is true of any other figure associated with a specific year in the book.

Important note on the ranking of banks in the book: While *The Banker* sorts its list of the top banks according to Tier 1 capital levels, in this book's research, the authors have created a list of the world's top banks in terms of total assets (at year-end 2020), which we believe provides for better comparison, especially in terms of comparing asset size to GDP. This list by asset size was created using the data from individual banks' financial statements. When banks' financials were not stated in US dollars, for banks from the UK, China and Japan, for example, conversions were made using the relevant US dollar exchange rate as of 31 December of the financial year in question.

Tier 1 vs total assets: In terms of comparing the top banks by Tier 1 capital (*The Banker*) and by asset size (author's list), there is a large overlap of the banks' rankings – for example, as of year-end 2020, the top five banks in terms of asset size were the same (and in the same order) as the top five banks in terms of Tier 1 capital, namely, ICBC, CCB, ABC, BOC and JPMorgan.

Bank of America total assets $25 billion in 1970 – *The Banker* magazine Top 10 World Banks in 1970. *The Banker* website (2021)

A general note on GDP figures used throughout the book: For all GDP figures, the World Bank database is used as a source, which can be found at data. worldbank.org. When a GDP figure is mentioned for 2020, for example, that figure will be for the year ended 2020 (as is the case with banking results, therefore making these figures more comparable). The GDP figures provided by the World Bank are given in current US dollars. Dollar figures for GDP are converted from domestic currencies using single year official exchange rates, as stated by the World Bank. GDP growth figures, quoted as a percentage (%), are annual percentage growth rates of GDP at market prices based on constant local currency sourced from the World Bank database. Aggregates are based on constant 2010 US dollars, according to the World Bank.

US GDP growth rate of 4.3% between 1990 and 2020 – Compound annual growth rate calculation using World Bank GDP data. Note on compound annual growth rate (CAGR) formula used throughout the book: The formula used by the authors throughout the book is

$$CAGR = \left(\frac{Vlast}{Vfirst}\right)^{1/t} - 1$$

V*last* = last value in period. V*first* = first value in period. t = number of periods. For a ten-year period, for example 2010 to 2020, the first value will be the value at the end of 2010 (e.g. year-end result 2010), the last value will be the value at the end of 2020 (e.g. year-end result 2020), and t will be 10, because there are ten periods of reporting from the end of 2010 to the end of 2020. Conversely, when the authors mention a "simple average" as opposed to a compound average growth rate, this refers to an unweighted, non-compounding average.

US top five bank assets growth rate of 10.4% between 1990 and 2020 – The top five banks referenced here are the top five banks in the US by asset size as per year-end 2020. We then found the total assets of these same banks in 1990 and calculated the CAGR of their total assets over the thirty-year period. Important to note is that these banks have not necessarily retained their place in the top five over the entire period. The banks in question are Bank of America, JPMorgan Chase & Co, Goldman Sachs, Citibank and Wells Fargo. Figures as per individual banks' financial statements.

Figures for total assets of banks in 2020 as per individual banks' financial statements at year-end 2020

ICBC ($5.11 trillion) larger than Citigroup ($2.26 trillion) and Bank of America ($2.82 trillion) combined in terms of total assets as of 2020 – Figures as per individual banks' financial statements at year-end 2020

At year-end 2010, the top five largest banks in terms of asset size were all institutions residing in the global West – Sourced from individual banks' annual statements

The majority of the top 20 banks by asset size were institutions from Western democratic nations, including the US, the UK, France, Germany, Spain and the Netherlands, while China and Japan had only four and two banks in the top 20, respectively – As per individual banks' financial statements

Calculation of top twenty banks' total assets in 2010 and 2020 – As per individual banks' financial statements. These banks were different between 2010 and 2020. Not the same banks in the two periods.

The five largest Chinese banks grew their assets at a compound annual growth rate (CAGR) of 10.3% from 2010 to 2020. Comparatively, the top five US banks have grown their assets by 3.2% (CAGR) in the same timeframe – This comparison involved using the five largest banks by asset size as of 2020 (both in the US and China). We then found the total assets of these same banks in 2010 and calculated the CAGR of their total assets over the ten-year period. Important to note is that these banks have not necessarily retained their place in the top five over the entire period. Assets were sourced as per individual banks' financial statements

Chinese GDP grew by 9.2% (CAGR); US GDP increased by 3.4% (CAGR) – GDP sourced from World Bank database and calculated using compound annual growth rate formula

Pre-tax profits sourced from banks' annual financial results

Operating income is sourced from *Fortune* "Global 2000" list as of 2021

Population figures sourced from World Bank database

GDP per capita sourced from World Bank database

Labour force sourced from World Bank database

GDP per working age is calculated by dividing GDP by working-age population, as sourced from World Bank database

Top five Chinese banks represent roughly 50% of all Chinese commercial banks' assets – "5-Bank Asset Concentration for China". Federal Reserve Bank of St Louis database and World Bank database (2012-2017)

Minimum Capital Requirements as per BCBS regulations – BIS website (2021)

ROE of the five largest banks in the US, by asset size, was 11% – A simple average calculation of the top five bank's ROE as per banks' annual financial results

The average across the entire banking industry in the US was 12% –Return on average equity (unweighted) for all US banks, sourced from Federal Reserve Bank of St Louis database (2021)

In 2019, the simple average of the ROE of the five largest banks in China was 13% – Sourced from individual banks' annual financial results

China's industry average for cost-to-income was lower at 12% – Return on average equity (unweighted) for all Chinese banks, sourced from Federal Reserve Bank of St Louis database (2021)

Top five banks' cost-to-income – Sourced from individual banks' annual financial results (unweighted average)

The economic, financial and regulatory environment of each country can affect cost-to-income ratios – "Cost-to-Income Ratios of Banks Worldwide". S&P Global (2016)

2019 cost-to-income data – LeDonne, G. and Taqi, M. "Most of the world's banks had stable cost-to-income ratios before Covid-19 hit". S&P Global (2020)

Democracy ratings – Provided by the Intelligence Unit's "Global Democracy Index". *The Economist* (2019)

Bank of China and Bank of America figures sourced from the banks' annual financial statements

CHAPTER 3

$8 million was withdrawn from the Knickerbocker Trust on 22 October 1907 – Moen, JR. and Tallman, EW. "The Panic of 1907". Federal Reserve History website (2015)

Trusts held about 5% cash reserves relative to deposits, compared to 25% for commercial banks – Moen, JR. and Tallman, EW. "The Panic of 1907". Federal Reserve History website (2015)

World trade decreased by 12.2% between 2008 and 2009 – "World Trade Report 2009: Trade Policy Commitments and Contingency Measures". World Trade Organization website

$700 billion was granted to buy distressed mortgage-backed securities – Emergency Economic Stabilization Act (2008)

Iceland sentenced 36 bankers to 96 years total prison time – Grettisson, V. "36 Bankers, 96 Years in Jail". *The Reykjavík Grapevine* (2018)

Greece's 2009 budget deficit was 12.5% of GDP – "Report on Greek Government Deficit and Debt Statistics". European Commission website (2010)

Under EU rules, a country budget deficit threshold is set at 3% of GDP – European Union Stability and Growth Pact (1997)

The spread on Greek ten-year bond yields was around 5% between 2007 and 2009 but widened to over 35% between 2010 and 2012 – Greece Government Bond 10Y, Trading Economics website (2021)

The Greek pension system accounted for 14% of GDP in 2010 – "Study on the pension reforms in Greece during the economic adjustment programs: 2010-2018". European Commission website (2020)

Greece's debt-to-GDP in 2015 was 176% – "Greece Preliminary Debt Sustainability Analysis". International Monetary Fund website (2016)

Part of the US's Covid-19 pandemic stimulus involved relief funds for individuals earning below $75,000 per year – "American Rescue Plan". The White House website (2020)

Key studies of political polarisation following financial crises discussed in the chapter, in order of mention:

Doerr, S., Gissler, S., Peydró, J. and Voth, H. "From Finance to Fascism". SSRN e-library (2020)

Halikiopoulou, D. "Economic Crisis, Poor Governance and the Rise of

Populism: The Case of Greece". *Intereconomics* (2020)

Funke, M., Schularick, M. and Trebesch, C. "Going to Extremes: Politics after Financial Crises, 1870-2014". *European Economic Review* (2015)

Additional key sources used in the research for this chapter:

Moen, JR. and Tallman, EW. "The Panic of 1907: The Role of Trust Companies". *The Journal of Economic History* (1992)

Gautney, H. "What is Occupy Wall Street? The history of leaderless movements". *The Washington Post* (2011)

Mukunda, G. "The Social and Political Costs of the Financial Crisis, 10 Years Later". *Harvard Business Review* (2018)

"Europe and right-wing nationalism: A country-by-country guide". BBC (2019)

CHAPTER 4

Fukuyama, F. "Dealing with China". The Working Group on Foreign Policy and Grand Strategy at Stanford University (2014)

70% of all modern industrial enterprises state-owned and 30% under joint public-private ownership – Worden, R., Savada, A. and Dolan, R. *China: A Country Study*. Library of Congress (1989)

30 million deaths in the famine of 1962 – Yang, J. *Tombstone: The Great Chinese Famine, 1958-1962*. Allen Lane (2008)

1.5 million killed during the Cultural Revolution – "China must never repeat Cultural Revolution: People's Daily". Reuters (2016)

Industrial production decreased between 1966 and 1968 by an estimated 12%, although researchers have struggled to determine a definitive figure owing to the opacity of officially reported figures – "Cultural Revolution". History.com website; Field, R. "Industrial Production in Communist China: 1957-1968". *The China Quarterly* (1970)

China GDP growth (according to government statistics) 6.7% per year, 1953-1978 – "China's Economic Rise: History, Trends, Challenges, and Implications for the United States". Congressional Research Service

China GDP growth (other sources) 4.5% per year, 1953-1978 – "China's Economic Rise: History, Trends, Challenges, and Implications for the United States". Congressional Research Service

Japan GDP (PPP basis) over $12 trillion; China GDP (PPP basis) $1 trillion, 1978 – "China's Economic Rise: History, Trends, Challenges, and Implications for the United States". Congressional Research Service

China GDP average growth of 10%, 1979-2018 – "China's Economic Rise: History, Trends, Challenges, and Implications for the United States". Congressional Research Service

Tiananmen Square 200 deaths (Chinese authorities) – "Tiananmen Square protest death toll 'was 10,000'". BBC (2017)

Tiananmen Square 10,000 deaths (UK National Archives) – "Tiananmen Square protest death toll 'was 10,000'". BBC (2017)

20 million migrant workers – Fang, C., Yang, D. and Meiyan, M. "Employment and Inequality Outcomes in China". Institute of Population and Labour Economics, Chinese Academy of Social Sciences, OECD website (2009)

Four trillion yuan (about $586 billion) economic stimulus package – Fang, C., Yang, D. and Meiyan, M. "Employment and Inequality Outcomes in China". Institute of Population and Labour Economics, Chinese Academy of Social Sciences, OECD website (2009)

Package amounted to 12.5% of China's GDP in 2008 – Wong, C. "The Fiscal Stimulus Programme and Public Governance Issues in China". *OECD Journal on Budgeting* Vol. 11/3 (2011)

"The mother of all debt bombs" – Quote from Pei, M. "China's Ticking Debt Bomb". *The Diplomat* (2012)

Between 2008 and 2010, China maintained a compound annual GDP growth rate of 8.1% – GDP data sourced from World Bank database

China's total banking assets in 2010 reach $14.3 trillion – "China banking assets rose 19.7 pct in 2010 – regulator". Reuters (2011)

US total banking assets in 2010 reach $13.4 trillion – Total assets sourced from "Total Assets, All Commercial Banks". Federal Reserve Bank of St Louis (2021)

230% the size of Chinese GDP at the time ($6.1 trillion), while US banking assets equated to 89% of GDP ($15 trillion) in the same year – GDP data sourced from World Bank database

By year-end 2020, the total assets of the Chinese banking sector had grown to $49.45 trillion (a CAGR of 12.9%), equating to 325% of GDP, which stood at $14.1 trillion in the same year – Total assets sourced from China Banking and Insurance Regulatory Commission website: "Supervisory Statistics of the Banking and Insurance Sectors" (2020); China GDP sourced from Trading Economics website: "China GDP" (2020)

The US, in comparison, had grown its total banking assets to $20.6 trillion by the end of 2020 (a CAGR of 4.4%) representing roughly 99% of GDP, which stood at $20.9 trillion – Total assets sourced from "Total Assets, All Commercial Banks". Federal Reserve Bank of St Louis (2021)

While the five large commercial banks have each undergone their own initial public offerings, the government still holds a controlling stake in each of these institutions and effectively controls how they operate. The main shareholders of the largest commercial banks in China are Central Huijin Investment Ltd (the investment arm of the state) and the Ministry of Finance (MOF) itself, in combination owning up to 60% of the banks' outstanding shares in each case as of 2021, according to the banks' individual filings.

Over 4,500 individual banks at various levels of the banking system's hierarchy in 2020 – Woo, R., Leng, C. and Yan, Z. "Chinese banks to feel fund-raising pain as investors fear bad loans". Reuters (2020)

ICBC alone had over 680 million retail customers – "Goldman Forms Wealth
  Venture with China's Largest Bank". Bloomberg (2021)
Twice the size of the US population – US population in 2021 was roughly
  333 million, according to the US Census Bureau website
As of 2020, the big four Chinese banks are estimated to have over two billion
  customers, although it should be noted that many customers hold bank
  accounts at more than one bank – Sourced from individual banks' websites
In 2016, the size of the Chinese banking system had already surpassed the entire
  European Union's banking assets – Cerutti, E. and Zhou, H. "The Chinese
  banking system: Much more than a domestic giant". VoxEU & CEPR website
  (2018)
Chinese banks' pre-tax profits increased by roughly 5% year-on-year, while pre-
  tax profits across banks globally fell roughly 20% – Kemplay, M. "Top 1000
  World Banks 2021". *The Banker* (2021)
Chinese banks held more than a quarter of the world's banking assets and
  generated over a third of all banking profits at year-end 2020 – Kemplay, M.
  "Top 1000 World Banks 2021". *The Banker* website (2021)

CHAPTER 5

Money supply (M1) grew from $228 billion to $249 billion between 1971
  and 1972 in the US – Federal Reserve Bank of St Louis website
Money supply (M2) grew from $710 billion to $802 billion between 1971
  and 1972 in the US – Federal Reserve Bank of St Louis website
Inflation (consumer price index) in the US increased from 3% in 1972 to
  11% in 1974 – World Bank website
Inflation in the US reached just over 13% in 1980 – World Bank website
Paul Volcker quote – Lamoreaux, N. and Shapiro, I. *The Bretton Woods
  Agreements*. Yale University Press (2019)
Annual bank failures in the US remained in the single digits between 1940 and
  1980 but reached over 200 in 1988 – "A Brief History of Deposit Insurance
  in the United States". US Federal Deposit Insurance Corporation (1998)
The price of oil imported from the Middle East to the US almost quadrupled
  between 1973 and 1974, from $2.90 a barrel to $11.65 a barrel – Corbett, M.
  "Oil Shock of 1973-74". Federal Reserve History website (2013)
85% of the world's oil production was owned by the "Seven Sisters" by 1960 –
  "Oil Dependence and US Foreign Policy". US Council on Foreign Relations
  website (2018)
The US federal funds rate increased from 10% in 1979 to just under 20% in
  1981 – Federal Reserve Bank of St Louis website
The US prime rate was over 20% in 1981 – Federal Reserve Bank of St Louis
  website
The US unemployment rate was over 10% in 1982 – Sablik, T. "Recession

of 1981-82". Federal Reserve History website (2013)

Paul Volcker's bibliography – Harper, C. and Volcker, P. *Keeping At It: The Quest for Sound Money and Good Governance.* Hachette UK (2018)

Inflation (CPI) in the UK reached 13% in 1979 – World Bank website

Three million people in the UK were unemployed in 1982 – UK Parliament, Commons and Lords Libraries websites

Inflation (consumer price index) in the UK reached 17% in 1980 – World Bank website

The income tax rate for the top income bracket in the US was reduced to 50% in 1981 – Economic Recovery Tax Act (1981)

The personal income tax rate in the US was lowered to 28% in 1986 – Tax Reform Act (1986)

The US's gross federal debt increased from $900 billion in 1980 to $2.7 trillion in 1988 – Federal Reserve Bank of St Louis website

Additional key source used in the research for this chapter:

"Economic Freedom: Champions of the Free Market". Hoover Institution Library & Archives website

CHAPTER 6

ICBC, CCB, ABC and BOC all recorded the same NPL ratio figure of 1.4% for year-end 2019 – Sourced from individual banks' financial statements

History of alarmingly high NPLs – Lardy, N. "The challenge of bank restructuring in China". Bank for International Settlements (1998)

PBOC estimated that NPLs in the top four Chinese banks were in the region of RMB 2.4 trillion, or $290 billion, representing a 23% NPL ratio – Lou, J. "China's Bank Non-Performing Loan Problem: Seriousness and Causes". *The International Lawyer* Vol. 34, No. 4 (2000)

Credit rating agencies outside of China estimated that the true value of NPLs in the top four Chinese banks in 2003 was closer to RMB 3.5 trillion, or $423 billion – Fung, B., George, J., Hohl, S. and Ma, G. "Public asset management companies in East Asia". Bank for International Settlements (2011)

Transfer of NPLs to AMCs history – Fung, B., George, J., Hohl, S. and Ma, G. "Public asset management companies in East Asia". Bank for International Settlements (2011)

Twice the size of Portugal's GDP in 2007 – World Bank database

AMC bond issuance information – Fung, B., George, J., Hohl, S. and Ma, G. "Public asset management companies in East Asia". Bank for International Settlements (2011)

Pricing of NPLs at book value – Fung, B., George, J., Hohl, S. and Ma, G. "Public asset management companies in East Asia". Bank for International Settlements (2011)

NPL recovery rate 2006 – Fung, B., George, J., Hohl, S. and Ma, G. "Public asset management companies in East Asia". Bank for International Settlements (2011)

Walter, C. and Howie, F. *Red Capitalism: The Fragile Financial Foundation of China's Extraordinary Rise*. John Wiley & Sons (2010)

In 2020, there were over 35 local asset management companies in China – Charoenwong, B., Miao, M. and Ruan, R. "Hidden Non-Performing Loans in China". SSRN (2021)

Between 2016 and 2019, the dollar amount of officially reported NPLs across the Chinese banking system increased from roughly $220 billion to about $340 billion – Isjwara, R. and Garrido, F. "Chinese banks set to clean up balance sheet more quickly in Q4". S&P Global (2020)

The simple average non-performing loan (NPL) ratio across the entire Chinese banking system dropped dramatically from 29.8% in 2001, as reported by the China Banking and Insurance Regulatory Commission (CBIRC), to 0.95% in 2015, before slowly starting to creep up again to 1,96% by 2020 – CBIRC website (2021)

Kauko, K. "The vanishing interest income of Chinese banks". BOFIT Discussion Papers 2/2020, Bank of Finland Institute for Economies in Transition (2020)

"Other research, such as that undertaken by Ben Charoenwong, Meng Miao and Tianyue Ruan, suggests that hidden NPLs in the Chinese banking system may be up to four times higher than officially reported" – Charoenwong, B., Miao, M. and Ruan, R. "Hidden Non-Performing Loans in China". SSRN (2021)

China's five bucket loan classification system – Baudino, P., Orlandi, J. and Zamil, R. "The identification and measurement of nonperforming assets: a cross-country comparison". FSI Insights No 7, Bank for International Settlements (2018)

China's "special mention loans" – "People's Republic Of China Financial Sector Assessment Program, Detailed Assessment of Observance of Basel Core Principles for Effective Banking Supervision". International Monetary Fund (2017)

Instead, as evidenced in a 2017 paper published by the BCBS's Financial Stability Institute, the Committee has deliberately avoided the issue – Restoy, F. and Zamil, R. "Prudential policy considerations under expected loss provisioning: Lessons from Asia". FSI Insights No 5, Bank for International Settlements (2017)

"An oppressive system of mass surveillance, detention, indoctrination, and even forced sterilisation" – Hill, M., Campanale, D. and Gunter, J. "'Their goal is to destroy everyone': Uighur camp detainees allege systematic rape". BBC (2020)

BCBS history – "History of the Basel Committee". BIS website (2021)

Gazprombank was sanctioned by the US Department of the Treasury in 2014, under the presidency of Barack Obama – "US Sanctions on Russia". Congressional Research Service (2020)

In 2013, in a report focused specifically on China's implementation of risk-based capital standards as outlined in the updated Basel III framework – "Basel Committee on Banking Supervision, Regulatory Consistency Assessment Programme (RCAP), Assessment of Basel III regulations – China". Bank for International Settlements (2013)

An update to the report was published in 2019, which showed that no measures had been taken to address these discrepancies – "RCAP jurisdictional assessments: self-reporting monitoring template for RCAP follow-up actions, Jurisdiction: China". Bank for International Settlements (2018)

Quotes from BCBS: "Secure international convergence on revisions to supervisory regulations governing the capital adequacy of internationally active banks"; "Endorsed by the Central Bank Governors and Heads of Banking Supervision" – "International Convergence of Capital Measurement and Capital Standards". Bank for International Settlements (2006)

Additional key source used in the research for this chapter:

Mavroidis, P. and Sapir, A. "China and the WTO: An uneasy relationship". VoxEU (2021)

CHAPTER 7

The US's 1994 $203-billion budget deficit was transformed into a $128-billion budget surplus by 2001 – Congressional Budget Office website

Pets.com paid $1.2 million to air a commercial during the Super Bowl – McNichol, T. "A startup's best friend? Failure". CNN (2007)

Details of Albert Einstein's insights on Brownian Movement – Einstein, A. *Investigations on the Theory of the Brownian Movement.* Dover Publications (1956)

Rentes had a nominal value of about 100 francs and fixed returns typically between 3% and 5% – Davis, M. and Etheridge, A. *Louis Bachelier's Theory of Speculation: The Origins of Modern Finance.* Princeton University Press (2006)

The Chicago Board of Exchange's annual exchange volumes reached 100 million option contracts in 1984 and grew to more than one billion option contracts by 2008 – CBOE website

Fischer Black quote – Black, F. "Noise". *The Journal of Finance* (1986)

Sheldon Cooper quote – *The Big Bang Theory* Season 7/Episode 20: "The Relationship Diremption"

Additional key sources used in the research of this chapter:

Sherman, M. "A Short History of Financial Deregulation in the United States". Center for Economic and Policy Research (2009)

Black, F. and Scholes, M. "The Pricing of Options and Corporate Liabilities". *Journal of Political Economy* (1973)

Greene, B. "Why String Theory Still Offers Hope We Can Unify Physics". *Smithsonian Magazine* (2015)

CHAPTER 8

Chinese economic growth rate has been steadily declining since the 2007/2008
  Global Financial Crisis – Trend calculated using numbers from the World
  Bank database

Xi Jinping announced in November 2020 that the government plans to double
  the size of the Chinese economy by 2035 – "Xi Says Economy Can Double
  as China Lays Out Ambitious Plans". Bloomberg (2020)

The Chinese economy will have to grow at an annual rate of 4,7% for the fifteen
  years between 2020 and 2035 – Calculated using numbers from the World
  Bank database

China GDP grew by 6.1% in 2019 – Sourced from World Bank database

China experienced an annual decline in the growth rate every year for the last
  twenty years, as of 2021 – World Bank database

Yu, S., Mitchell, T. and Hale, T. "China's population grows at slowest rate
  in decades". *Financial Times* (2021)

Japan and Brazil GDP growth – World Bank database

The increased spending has resulted in a total debt level – including government,
  household and corporate debt – that is by most estimates, as of 2020, greater
  than 300% of GDP – Bank for International Settlements database

"China's fiscal policy is bewildering" – "Unraveling the Mysteries of China's
  Multiple Budgets". Bloomberg (2020)

Government spending-to-GDP figures calculated from World Bank GDP figures

US budget deficit 2019 – US Treasury database

Global government deficits 2019 – OECD database

China government debt has more than doubled, from under 2% in 2010
  – "Fitch warns of downgrades for China, Japan". Reuters (2011)

China's government spending has increased from $1.14 trillion in 2009
  to $3.46 trillion in 2019. This represents a compound annual growth rate
  (CAGR) of 11.7% across the period – "Unraveling the Mysteries of China's
  Multiple Budgets". Bloomberg (2020), and OECD database

Federal governmental spending in the US has increased from $3.5 trillion in
  2009 to $4.4 trillion in 2019, representing a CAGR of 2.3%. And in the UK,
  government spending has increased the least of the three nations, from $1.07
  trillion in 2009 to $1.09 trillion in 2019, representing a CAGR of just 0.15%
  – Calculated using budget deficits from OECD database and GDP figures
  from World Bank database

By the end of 2019, the Chinese economy had slowed to its lowest growth rate
  in 28 years – Trend calculated using figures from World Bank database

State-owned enterprises directly constitute more than 40% of China's GDP
  … and which directly employ over 55 million Chinese citizens – Guluzade,
  A. "The role of China's state-owned companies explained". World Economic
  Forum (2020)

CHAPTER 9

On Black Monday, the S&P 500 lost 20.4% on a single day of trading and the Dow Jones Industrial Average dropped by 22.6% – Bernhardt, D. and Eckblad, M. "Stock Market Crash of 1987". Federal Reserve History website (2013)

Arthur Levitt quote – Kirk, M. "The Warning Interviews – Arthur Levitt". *Frontline* Episode 14, PBS (2009)

Details of the first and second five-year interest rate swaps between P&G and Bankers Trust – Macey, J. *The Death of Corporate Reputation*. FT Press (2013)

P&G ultimately paid an interest rate that was 16.4% above the commercial paper rate – Macey, J. *The Death of Corporate Reputation*. FT Press (2013)

Bankers Trust quote – Fromson, B. "Bankers Trust Sued Over Derivatives". *T he Washington Post* (1994)

P&G ultimately paid $35 million of its losses – Hays, L. "Bankers Trust Ends Dispute with P&G". *The Wall Street Journal* (1996)

Bankers Trust employee quote – Holland, K. and Himelstein, L. "The Bankers Trust Tapes". Bloomberg (1995)

The OTC derivatives market had a gross market value of over $3.2 trillion by the end of 1998, and a nominal face value of about $80 trillion – "The global OTC derivatives market at end-December 1998". Bank for International Settlements (1999)

LTCM had $100 billion in assets and annual returns of 40% in 1996 – "Hedge Funds, Leverage, and the Lessons of Long-Term Capital Management: Report by the President's Working Group on Financial Markets". US Treasury website (1999)

LTCM had $129 billion in assets and $4.72 billion equity, implying a leverage ratio of 27:1 – Jorion, P. "Risk Management Lessons from Long-Term Capital Management". *European Financial Management* (2000)

The Dow Jones Industrial Average dropped by 13% in August 2008 – "Dow Jones Industrial Average". S&P Dow Jones Indices

In July 1998, LTCM lost $553 million in one day and $2 billion over the next month – Dungey, M., Fry, R., Ginzalez-Hermosillo, B. and Martin, V. "International Contagion Effects from the Russian Crisis and the LTCM Near-Collapse". International Monetary Fund Working Paper (2002)

LTCM held $400 million in equity and about $100 billion in assets, implying a leverage ratio of roughly 250:1 – Lowenstein, R. *When Genius Failed: The Rise and Fall of Long-Term Capital Management*. Random House (2000)

LTCM was saved with a bailout of $3.65 billion – Partnoy, F. *Infectious Greed: How Deceit and Risk Corrupted the Financial Markets*. Holt McDougal (2003)

Senator Phil Gramm quote – "Over-The-Counter Derivatives: Hearing Before the United States Senate, One Hundred Fifth Congress, Second Session on Over-The-Counter Derivatives". US Congress website (1998)

By late 1998, LTCM had lost $4.8 billion, of which $1.6 billion was related

to swaps – Rimkus, R. "Financial Scandals, Scoundrels & Crises: Long-Term
Capital Management". CFA Institute website (2016)

Alan Greenspan quote – Kirk, M. "The Warning". *Frontline* Ep14, PBS (2009)

Larry Summers quote – Crawford, C. "The Repeal of the Glass-Steagall Act and
the Current Financial Crisis". *Journal of Business and Economics Research* (2011)

Origins of the saying "You can't have your cake and eat it" – An English idiom
meaning that a person cannot have two incompatible things. One of the
earliest records of the use of the phrase is in a letter written in 1538 by Thomas
Howard, Duke of Norfolk, in which he stated that "a man can not have his
cake and eat his cake". The clauses of the phrase appeared reversed in John
Heywood's *A dialogue Conteinyng the Nomber in Effect of All the Prouerbes
in the Englishe Tongue* in 1546, as "wolde you bothe eate your cake, and have
your cake?" While logically the reversal makes more sense – as in, one cannot
eat one's cake and then *still* have it – the order of the clauses has been used
variously in history. From the 1930s onwards, however, the less logical version,
in which one could not have one's cake and eat it, has persisted as the most
widely used variant.

The Hong Kong Monetary Authority ordered its local banks to repay 60% of
the principal amount invested by customers under the age of 65 and 70% to
those over 65 – "Questions and answers about Lehman Brothers Minibonds
Repurchase Scheme by Distributing Banks". Hong Kong Monetary Authority
website

Senator Byron L Dorgan quote – Labaton, S. "Congress Passes Wide-ranging
Bill Easing Bank Laws". *The New York Times* (1999)

Nearly 3,000 people were killed in the September 11 attacks and a further 6,000
were injured – "September 11 Terror Attacks Fast Facts". CNN (2021)

The 9/11 attacks cost Al-Qaeda roughly $500 000, with $300 000 passing
directly through the hijackers' American bank accounts – "The 9/11
Commission Report: Final Report of the National Commission on Terrorist
Attacks Upon the United States (9/11 Report)". (2004)

In the days before the 9/11 attacks, American Airlines' put-to-call ratio reached
6:1 and United Airlines' put-to-call ratio reached 25:1, where it would
ordinarily be around 1:1 – Poteshman, A. "Unusual Option Market Activity
and the Terrorist Attacks of September 1, 2001". *Journal of Business* (2006)

Studies suggesting evidence of insider trading prior to 9/11 include:

> Poteshman, A. "Unusual Option Market Activity and the Terrorist Attacks
> of September 1, 2001". *Journal of Business* (2006)
>
> "Profiting from Disaster?" CBS (2001)
>
> Ryan, K. "Evidence for Informed Trading on the Attacks of September 11".
> *Foreign Policy Journal* (2010)
>
> McDermott, H. "9/11 terrorists made millions on the stock market".
> *Independent Australia* (2011)

In the case of Cantor Fitzgerald, 658 of its 960 New York-based employees were killed in the 9/11 attacks – "Cantor Fitzgerald CEO and the aftermath of 9/11". CBS (2011)

2004 Madrid train bombings – 191 killed (BBC); the 2005 London bombings – 52 killed (BBC); the 2015 Paris attacks – 130 killed (BBC); the 2016 Nice truck attack – 84 killed (BBC); 2016 Orlando nightclub shooting – 49 killed (BBC). Total: 506 people killed

Additional key source used in the research for this chapter:

Smith, D. "Aggressive corporate finance: A closer look at the Procter & Gamble-Bankers Trust leveraged swap". *The Journal of Derivatives* (1997)

CHAPTER 10

Between 2005 and 2019, the bank extended 347 loans to 209 shell companies related to Tomorrow Holdings, totalling over $22 billion – Sweeney, P. "Breakingviews – China bank failure fires quiet warning shot". Reuters (2020)

The government's decision to allow a commercial bank to fail for the first time in twenty years – Sweeney, P. "Breakingviews – China bank failure fires quiet warning shot". Reuters (2020)

In 2019, the bank, which hires over four thousand employees, reported that its NPL ratio of personal business loans had skyrocketed to 14.1%, from 4.7% the year before. Bank of Gansu Co also reported publicly that its profits had dropped 85%, from 3.44 billion yuan in 2018 to 509 million yuan in 2019 – Lee, A. "China's banking system begins to crack at its grass roots as two bank runs take place within a week". *South China Morning Post* (2020)

At the five-yearly National Financial Work Conference, the Chinese president stated that deleveraging at state-owned entities is of the utmost importance – Mitchell, T. "China's Xi orders debt crackdown for state-owned groups". *Financial Times* (2017)

The Federal Reserve of San Francisco, for example, concluded through its own research that China's official growth has been "implausibly smooth since 2013" – "Can China's reported growth be trusted?" *The Economist* (2020)

While the replica town was meant to host over 10,000 residents, by 2013, five years after construction, there were only roughly 2,000 occupants in Tianducheng – Kuo, L. "Welcome to China's beautiful but empty 'little Paris'". *Quartz Africa* (2013)

Many real estate investors from across China and abroad had bought into the vision of the project and purchased over 90% of the apartments by the time construction was completed, but less than a third of the apartments were occupied with residents in the next decade – Barbosa, D. "Chinese City Has Many Buildings, but Few People". *The New York Times* (2010); Rosen, J. "The Colossal Strangeness of China's Most Excellent Tourist City". *The New York Times* (2015)

Once construction was complete, it took more than a decade for 100,000
residents – Barbosa, D. "Chinese City Has Many Buildings, but Few People".
The New York Times (2010)
At the peak of the US property boom in the 2000s, before the crash in 2007,
approximately $900 billion a year was being invested in residential real estate.
In China, in the twelve months before June 2020, roughly 9.66 trillion yuan
($1.4 trillion) was invested in residential real estate – Xie, S. and Bird, M.
"The $52 Trillion Bubble: China Grapples with Epic Property Boom".
The Wall Street Journal (2020)
More funds flowing into residential real estate in June 2020 than in any
other month on record, and with residential sales as measured by floorspace
increasing by 15% in December of 2020 compared with the same period of
2019 – Xie, S. and Bird, M. "The $52 Trillion Bubble: China Grapples with
Epic Property Boom". *The Wall Street Journal* (2020)
Real estate investment in China contributed an estimated 13% of the nation's
entire GDP in 2018. Furthermore, up to a fifth of the entire Chinese economy
is linked to residential real estate through industries such as construction, cement
manufacturing or furniture making, among many others – Rogoff, K. and Yang,
Y. "Peak China Housing". National Bureau of Economic Research (2020)
Evergrande raised its sales target for the year by 23% from its January estimate
– Xie, S. and Bird, M. "The $52 Trillion Bubble: China Grapples with Epic
Property Boom". *The Wall Street Journal* (2020)
China Evergrande debt figures – Fitch Ratings (2021)
Evergrande's debt is larger than the total governmental debts of many nation
states, including, for example, Denmark, Hungary and Romania – World
Bank database
China's government, household and corporate debts which are, in combination,
in excess of 300% of GDP as of 2020 – Bank for International Settlements
database
Since 1998, the Japanese economy has never really recovered to pre-crisis levels,
with no manner of government stimulus managing to boost GDP growth
above 2%, except for a rare spike in 2010 – World Bank database
Japanese GDP growth rate figure of 3% – World Bank database
IMF paper "the loan classification and provisioning requirements" quote – Kanaya,
A. and Woo, D. "The Japanese Banking Crisis of the 1990s". IMF (2000)

CHAPTER 11
Tiger Asia Management accumulated $10 billion in assets under management at
its peak –Schatzker, E., Natarajan, S. and Burton, K. "Bill Hwang Had
$20 Billion, Then Lost It All in Two Days". Bloomberg (2021)
Tiger Asia Management was able to amass approximately $496,000 of
fraudulent management fees – "Hedge Fund Manager to Pay $44 Million

for Illegal Trading in Chinese Bank Stocks". US Securities and Exchange Commission website (2012)

Hwang and associates paid fines and disgorgements to the value of approximately $44 million to the SEC – "Hedge Fund Manager to Pay $44 Million for Illegal Trading in Chinese Bank Stocks". US Securities and Exchange Commission website (2012)

Hwang turned the initial $200 million of his own money, used to fund the creation of his family office, into more than $10 billion by early 2021 – Vardi, N. "How Troubled Trader Bill Hwang Quietly Amassed $10 Billion". *Forbes* (2021)

Hwang amassing ViacomCBS shares via total return swap contracts – Armstrong, R. "Archegos debacle reveals hidden risk of banks' lucrative swaps business". *Financial Times* (2021)

Viacom and Discovery share price movements – sourced from Yahoo Finance

Goldman immediately offloaded almost $4 billion of Archegos related holdings – "Large block trades that caused selling raises questions about cause." Reuters (2021)

Banks' losses from Archegos ties – Makortoff, K. "Bank losses linked to Archegos top $10bn after latest results". *The Guardian* (2021)

Sherrod Brown "I am troubled, but not surprised" quote – Fedor, L. "US Senate banking chair queries Credit Suisse and other banks on Archegos". *Financial Times* (2021)

Elizabeth Warren "all the makings of a dangerous situation" quote – Schwartz, B. "Elizabeth Warren unloads on Archegos meltdown: 'All the makings of a dangerous situation'". CNBC (2021).

Lael Brainard "The potential for material distress" quote – Silverman, G and Politi, J. "Fed warns of hidden leverage lurking in financial system". *Financial Times* (2021)

More about Lehman Brothers' history – Oliver, J. and Goodwin, T. *How They Blew It – The CEOs and Entrepreneurs Behind Some of the World's Most Catastrophic Business Failures*. Kogan Page Publishers (2010)

By 2008, Lehman Brothers had amassed $680 billion in assets, while holding just $22 billion in capital – a leverage ratio of 31:1 – "Valukas Bankruptcy Report". US Senate Committee on Banking, Housing, and Urban Affairs website (2010)

Aurora Loan Services and West Coast subprime mortgage brokers' details – "Valukas Bankruptcy Report". US Senate Committee on Banking, Housing and Urban Affairs website (2010)

In the second quarter of 2008, it was discovered that Lehman had used the Repo 105 technique to move $50 billion off its balance sheet – "Valukas Bankruptcy Report". US Senate Committee on Banking, Housing and Urban Affairs website (2010)

Ending a run of 55 consecutive quarters of profitability – "The Causes and
Effects of the Lehman Brothers Bankruptcy". Hearing before the Committee
on Oversight and Government Reform, House of Representatives, 110th
Congress, Second Session (2008)
Lehman posting a $2.8 billion loss – "The Causes and Effects of the Lehman
Brothers Bankruptcy". Hearing before the Committee on Oversight and
Government Reform, House of Representatives, 110th Congress, Second
Session (2008)
Lehman Brothers filed for Chapter 11 bankruptcy protection just before 01:00
Eastern Standard Time on the 15th of September 2008, reporting bank debt of
$613 billion, $155 billion in bond debt, and assets worth $639 billion – "The
Causes and Effects of the Lehman Brothers Bankruptcy". Hearing before the
Committee on Oversight and Government Reform, House of Representatives,
110th Congress, Second Session (2008)
Lehman shares dropped by over 90% in value and the Dow Jones index lost over
500 points – "The Causes and Effects of the Lehman Brothers Bankruptcy".
Hearing before the Committee on Oversight and Government Reform,
House of Representatives, 110th Congress, Second Session (2008)
One of the biggest single-day drops since the September 11th attacks in 2001
– Bloomberg database
AIG bailout of bailout of $182.3 billion – Massad, T. "INFOGRAPHIC:
Overall $182 Billion Committed to Stabilize AIG During the Financial
Crisis Is Now Fully Recovered". US Department of the Treasury (2012)
TARP made available $700 billion in government funds – Emergency Economic
Stabilization Act (2008)
In November 2008, Fuld sold his $13-million Florida seaside mansion to his
wife for $100 – "Lehman's Fuld sold Florida mansion to wife for $100".
Reuters (2009)

CHAPTER 12
$2.5 billion partnership with the private Saudi oil services company PetroSaudi
International – Ramesh, R. "1MDB: The inside story of the world's biggest
financial scandal". *The Guardian* (2016)
Bandar Malaysia was estimated to cost in the region of $500 million
– "Malaysia to revive multi-billion dollar project linked to China".
Reuters (2019)
Purchase of Tanjong Energy Holdings from Sri Lankan oil tycoon Ananda
Krishnan for $2 billion – "UPDATE 1-Malaysia state firm acquires Tanjong
Energy for $2.8bln". Reuters (2012)
To read more about Tun Razak Exchange, see "Freed of 1MDB taint, Malaysia's
tallest tower opens its doors". Reuters (2019)
$6.5-billion 1MDB bond facilitated by Goldman Sachs – Latiff, R.

"Understanding Goldman Sachs' role in Malaysia's 1MDB mega scandal".
Reuters (2020)

To read more about the Xavier Andre Justo story, see Ramesh, R. "1MDB:
The inside story of the world's biggest financial scandal". *The Guardian* (2016)

By November 2014, it was publicly known that 1MDB had taken on almost
$11 billion in debt from various sources – Wright, T. "Fund Controversy
Threatens Malaysia's Leader". *The Wall Street Journal* (2015)

TIA was transferred to the Minister of Finance Incorporated (MOFI) and the
fund set out to raise five billion Malaysian ringgits – "Executive Summary of
Auditor's Report on 1MDB". National Audit Department of Malaysia (2018)

To read more about Jho Low's 31st birthday, see Wright, T. and Hope, B. "The
Billion-Dollar Mystery Man and the Wildest Party Vegas Ever Saw". *The Wall
Street Journal* (2018)

"Goldman Sachs Charged in Foreign Bribery Case and Agrees to Pay Over
$2.9 Billion". Department of Justice Office of Public Affairs (2020)

Goldman earned over $600 million in fees – "Goldman Sachs Charged in
Foreign Bribery Case and Agrees to Pay Over $2.9 Billion". Department
of Justice Office of Public Affairs (2020)

Leissner was fined $43 million for the illicit payments – "SEC Charges Former
Goldman Sachs Executive with FCPA Violations". Securities and Exchange
Commission (2019)

Razak was sentenced to 12 years in prison and fined $50 million for his
involvement in the 1MDB scandal – "Najib Razak: Malaysian ex-PM gets
12-year jail term in 1MDB corruption trial". BBC (2020)

Aziz's charges were dropped in May of 2020 after he agreed to return $107
million of stolen assets to the fund – Paddock, R. "Malaysia Drops Charges
Against 'Wolf of Wall Street' Producer in 1MDB Case". *The New York Times*
(2020)

Chinese authority's co-operation in the matter has "appeared insincere" – "China
denies harboring 1MDB fugitive Jho Low". Reuters (2020)

Deutsche Bank acted as the correspondent bank for the cross-border transfer of
$6 million from Low's Swiss Bank account to a regional bank in Cyprus – Peel,
M. and Storbeck, O. "Deutsche Bank cleared Cyprus funds for businessman
Jho Low". *Financial Times* (2020)

Deloitte reached a settlement with the Malaysian government to the value
of $80 million for its role as 1MDB's auditors – Shukry, A. "Malaysia Gets
Deloitte's $80 Million 1MDB Settlement Payout". Bloomberg (2021)

CHAPTER 13

Government debt-to-GDP ratios calculated according to IMF database
figures for 2020

In 2008, all three of Iceland's largest banks collapsed – O'Brien, M. "The miraculous story of Iceland". *The Washington Post* (2015)

The Icelandic banking system had leveraged itself by up to ten times the nation's GDP – O'Brien, M. "The miraculous story of Iceland". *The Washington Post* (2015)

To make matters worse, as this was happening, major ratings agencies downgraded Iceland's sovereign and bank debt ratings – S&P, Moody's and Fitch each downgraded Iceland's sovereign credit more than once in 2008

In 2020, Hong Kong's total banking assets stood at $2.95 trillion, representing in the region of 800% of its relatively small GDP of $365.7 billion – Mehra, N. "Hong Kong's banking sector showed resilience in 2020 as total assets grew, finds KPMG". KPMG (2021)

In 2020, China's total banking assets stood at $49 trillion, making it the largest banking system in the world in dollar terms. As a percentage of the nation's gross domestic product, China's banking assets stood at 333% – CBIRC website (2021), and percentage of GDP calculated using figures from the World Bank database

The United Kingdom had total banking assets in the region of $11.5 trillion and in 2010, its banking assets-to-GDP was even higher, at over 500% – "United Kingdom's banking sector: Facts & Figures". European Banking Federation website (2020)

As of 2020, the five largest banks in the United Kingdom in terms of assets held assets that were equivalent to over 280% of the UK's gross domestic product – Sourced from annual financial statements and calculated using GDP figures from World Bank database

GDP per capita sourced from World Bank database

In 2020, HSBC made more than 80% of its profits in Hong Kong and mainland China – Sourced from annual financial statements

Theoretically, by 2030, Chinese banking assets would equate to an astonishing $169 trillion. Comparatively, if the US maintained the same growth rate that it experienced between 2010 and 2020, then by 2030, it would have $36 trillion in banking assets – Calculated using the annual compound growth rates of the US and China between 2010 and 2020, and then growing the current total assets (as of 2020) of each nation by that growth rate into the future to 2030.

Corporate debt levels sourced from Bank for International Settlements database

A research paper published by the World Bank in September of 2020 stated that, as of 2018, China's non-financial corporate debt represented 28% of global corporate debt – Abraham, F., Cortina, J. and Schmukler, S. "Growth of Global Corporate Debt". World Bank Policy Research Working Paper 9394, World Bank (2020)

Government and household debt sourced from Bank for International Settlements database

On the 29th of January 2021, the Chinese government executed Lai Xiaomin, the former head of China's largest asset management corporation, Huarong Asset Management – "Former China Huarong chairman executed after bribery conviction". Reuters (2021)

Apart from corruption, the court also charged the former head of the AMC with bigamy – The precedent for an authoritarian government charging a high-profile detractor or enemy of the state with sexually-charged crimes had been set long before. In 1998, for example, Anwar Ibrahim, the opposition political leader in Malaysia, was charged with corruption and sodomy by the Malaysian government in an attempt to undermine his character.

On the 31st of March 2021, a few weeks after Lai Xiaomin's execution, Huarong announced that its year-end results for 2020 would be delayed because a "relevant transaction" was still being processed – "China's Huarong to delay earnings results again, says auditors need more time". Reuters (2021)

China has become the world's biggest lender to developing nations, lending more to these countries than either the World Bank or the IMF – Horn, S., Trebesch, C. and Reinhart, C. "China's Overseas Lending". Kiel Institute for the World Economy Working Paper 2132 (2019)

China's loans to developing countries data – Horn, S., Trebesch, C. and Reinhart, C. "China's Overseas Lending". Kiel Institute for the World Economy Working Paper 2132 (2019)

Independent research suggesting that Chinese annual GDP may be overstated by up to 12% in recent years – Chen, W., Hsieh, C. and Song, Z. "A forensic examination of China's national accounts". Brookings Papers on Economic Activity, Spring Edition (2019)

Chinese president's call to double the economy by 2035 implies that the economy will grow at an annual compound growth rate of 4.7% from 2020 to 2035 – Growth rate calculated using CAGR over a fifteen-year period from 2020 GDP base

In the last two decades, the growth of the working age population (aged 15 to 64) in China has been steadily declining – Yu, S. "China set to report first population decline in five decades". *Financial Times* (2021)

House prices in Shanghai are twenty-three times median income, twice that of London in 2020 – Xie, S. and Bird, M. "The $52 Trillion Bubble: China Grapples with Epic Property Boom". *The Wall Street Journal* (2020)

The result of this phenomenon is that the working age population in China decreased from about 75% of the total population in 2010 to around 70% by 2020, and this trend is set to continue in the coming decade – Yu, S. "China set to report first population decline in five decades". *Financial Times* (2021)

While it is estimated that the Chinese population will continue to grow steadily in the next fifteen years, it is also estimated that the working population will decrease by some 7% over the same period – Yu, S. "China set to report first population decline in five decades". *Financial Times* (2021)

This means the smaller workforce will have to increase its productivity by a rate of over 5% per year to achieve the required 4.7% compound growth rate to double economic output by 2035 – Calculated as a GDP per workforce ratio using the estimated decline in the workforce in the year as the denominator, and with the GDP increasing by 4.7% per year as the numerator

CHAPTER 14

Confidence in Institutions poll can be found on the Gallup website (2021)

In May 2012, JPMorgan announced losses in excess of $2 billion relating to derivative trading positions – Henry, D. and Horowitz, J. "JPMorgan traders may have hidden derivatives losses". Reuters (2012)

Total estimated losses regarding the London Whale Incident – Hurtado, P. "The London Whale". Bloomberg (2016)

Further details of the London Whale incident can be sourced from Senate Hearing 113-96, Volume 1, Permanent Subcommittee on Investigations of the Committee on Homeland Security and Governmental Affairs (2013)

"First of all, JPMorgan is one of the best managed banks there is. Jamie Dimon, the head of it, is one of the smartest bankers we've got." – Barack Obama quote, sourced from an episode of *The View* that aired on 1 July 2012

"You know, keep in mind, though there are a lot of banks that are actually pretty well managed, JPMorgan being a good example, Jamie Dimon, the CEO there, I don't think should be punished for doing a pretty good job managing an enormous portfolio." – Barack Obama quote, sourced from an interview transcript released on ABC News on 10 February 2009

Bank fine data sourced from Violation Tracker database on GoodJobsFirst website (2021)

This represents – based on JPMorgan's financial statements for the four years ending 31 December 2015 – 26.4% of after-tax earnings on an annual basis – Sourced and calculated from annual financial statement data

The largest bank fine ever handed down by the Chinese banking regulator was a 722-million-yuan (about $113-million) fine against China Guangfa Bank in 2017 – Zhang, S. and Woo, R. "China imposes record fine on Guangfa Bank over guarantees for defaulted bonds". Reuters (2017)

CHAPTER 15

The key source used in the research for this chapter was the "House of Wirecard" series of articles published by the *Financial Times* on its Alphaville blog

Wirecard was processing transactions for 250,000 merchants by 2018 – McCrum, D. "Wirecard: The Timeline". *Financial Times* (2020)

Wirecard's share price reached €191 in 2018, with a company valuation €24 billion – McCrum, D. "Wirecard: The Timeline". *Financial Times* (2020)

SoftBank provided a $1-billion investment in Wirecard in 2018 – McCrum, D., Smith, R. and Massoudii, A. "SoftBank and Wirecard both paid German middleman to broker $1.1bn deal". *Financial Times* (2020)

Wirecard announced that €1.9 billion was missing in 2019 – McCrum, D. and Storbeck, O. "Wirecard says €1.9bn of cash is missing". *Financial Times* (2020)

KPMG quote – McCrum, D. and Storbeck, O. "How the paper trail went cold in KPMG's special audit of Wirecard". *Financial Times* (2020)

Wirecard filed for insolvency in 2019, with €3.5 billion owed to creditors – McCrum, D., Storbeck, O. and Palma, S. "Wirecard collapses into insolvency". *Financial Times* (2020)

Wirecard purchased a package of Indian payment processing businesses for €340 million, including Hermes Tickets, which was valued at €46 million – McCrum, D. "Revisiting Wirecard's big Indian deal". *Financial Times* (2018)

Interview with EY CEO Carmine Di Sibio – "Wirecard auditor EY defends company post-scandal". CNBC (2020)

In 2020, 1,500 Wirecard investors were seeking up to €1 billion from EY – Kinder, T. and Storbeck, O. "EY prepares for backlash over Wirecard scandal". *Financial Times* (2020)

Creditors, shareholders and other aggrieved parties have filed more than €14 billion of claims against Wirecard – Storbeck, O. "Top German asset manager takes Wirecard administrator to court over losses". *Financial Times* (2021)

CHAPTER 16

In 2015, the US Internal Revenue Service (IRS), as part of its whistleblower reward programme, paid Bradley Birkenfeld a total of $104 million, the highest-ever reward for a whistleblower at the time – Saunders, L. and Sidel, R. "Whistleblower Gets $104 Million". *The Wall Street Journal* (2012)

Birkenfeld was charged in 2009 with "conspiracy to defraud the United States" and sentenced to forty months in prison, with a $30 000 fine for not fully disclosing evidence to the state – "Birkenfeld's bonanza". *The Economist* (2012)

On completion of his prison sentence and subsequently receiving a $104 million payout from the IRS, an agreed-upon 26% cut for the $400 million in tax revenue recovered directly because of his evidence against fellow UBS bankers and their customers – "Birkenfeld's bonanza". *The Economist* (2012)

The FBI probe found that over 52,000 US clients held accounts with UBS, and tens of thousands more at other Swiss banks, and that in total, the US was losing out on roughly $100 billion in taxes annually – Cage, S. and Jucca, L. "TIMELINE: UBS pressured by US tax probe". Reuters (2009)

Within a few months, the Swiss Financial Market Supervisory Authority (FINMA), supported by the Swiss government, brokered a deal with the IRS in which UBS required to hand over just 4,450 of the 52,000 names, managing to preserve the anonymity of about 85% of their US customers –

Grimaldi, J. and Ballhaus, R. "UBS Deal Shows Clinton's Complicated Ties". *The Wall Street Journal* (2015)

More on US government vs UBS case can be sourced from the Hearing on Banking Secrecy Practices and Wealthy American Taxpayers, Committee on Ways and Means, US House of Representatives, 111th Congress, First Session. US Congress website (2009)

Scott Michel interview – *The Kudlow Report.* CNBC (2009)

More details on FATCA can be found on the IRS website – Foreign Account Tax Compliance Act (2021)

More details on Automatic Exchange of Information (AEOI) can be found on IECD website – The Automatic Exchange of Information portal (2021)

In 2012, deputy director general of legal affairs of People's Bank of China, Liu Xiangmin, said, "China's banking and tax laws and regulations do not allow Chinese financial institutions to comply with FATCA directly" – "China central bank official slams US tax dodging law". Reuters (2012)

Donald Trump quote – Duncan, M. "Vestager: 'I do work with tax and I am a woman'". Politico (2018)

Margrethe Vestager quote – Duncan, M. "Vestager: 'I do work with tax and I am a woman'". Politico (2018)

The EC ruled that €13 billion in unpaid taxes was owed by Apple – "State aid: Ireland gave illegal tax benefits to Apple worth up to €13 billion". European Commission website (2016)

The US corporate tax rate was 35% between 1993 and 2018 – US Federal Corporate Tax Rate. Trading Economics website (2018)

Ireland had in place a special corporate tax rate of 10% for manufacturing between 1981 and 2010 – Walsh, A. and Sanger, C. "The historical development and international context of the Irish corporate tax system: A report commissioned by the Irish Department of Finance". EY (2015)

Ireland reduced its statutory corporate tax rate from 40% to 12.5% – Walsh, A. and Sanger, C. "The historical development and international context of the Irish corporate tax system: A report commissioned by the Irish Department of Finance". EY (2015)

Apple had an effective corporate tax rate of around, or even below, 1% in the early 2000s – "State aid: Ireland gave illegal tax benefits to Apple worth up to €13 billion". European Commission website (2016)

Apple Sales International paid less than €10 million in corporate tax in Ireland in 2011, translating to an effective tax rate of about 0.05% – "State aid: Ireland gave illegal tax benefits to Apple worth up to €13 billion". European Commission website (2016)

Apple had an effective corporate tax rate of 0.005% in 2014 – "State aid: Ireland gave illegal tax benefits to Apple worth up to €13 billion". European Commission website (2016)

In 2016, Deutsche Bank reported third-quarter earnings of €278 million –
"Deutsche Bank reports third quarter 2016 pre-tax profit of EUR 619 million
and net income of EUR 278 million". Deutsche Bank website (2016)

US Department of Justice fined Deutsche Bank $14 billion – Schuetze, A.
"Deutsche Bank to fight $14 billion demand from US authorities". Reuters
(2016)

Apple had reported net income of $45.687 billion for the financial year ended
24 September 2016 – Apple Annual Report (2016)

US corporate tax rate was above 45% until 1986 and then reduced to 35%
between 1993 and 2018 – "US Federal Corporate Tax Rate". Trading
Economics website (2018)

Ireland, Cyprus and Liechtenstein have a corporate tax rate of 12.5% –
"Corporate Tax Rates around the World". Tax Foundation website (2020)

Bermuda, Bahamas and Cayman Islands have a corporate tax rate of 0% –
"Corporate Tax Rates around the World". Tax Foundation website (2020)

Deutsche Bank paid $3.1 billion in civil penalties and $4.1 billion in relief
funds – "Deutsche Bank Agrees to Pay $7.2 Billion for Misleading Investors
in its Sale of Residential Mortgage-Backed Securities". US Department of
Justice website (2017)

Irish withholding tax was 20% prior to 2010 – Gullver, J. "Ireland Expands
Withholding Tax Exemption On Royalties". Mason, Hayes & Curran website
(2010)

Apple's international net sales accounted for 65% of the company's total net sales
in 2016 – Apple Annual Report (2016)

Apple issued bonds in February 2016 to the value of $12 billion – "Apple goes
green with bond". Reuters (2016)

Tim Cook quote – Fitzpatrick, A. "What Apple CEO Tim Cook Really Thinks
About Corporate Taxes". *Time* (2016)

The US's temporary repatriation tax holiday in 2004 allowed multinational
companies to repatriate foreign profits to the US at a tax rate of just 5.25%
– American Jobs Creation Act (2004)

Apple repatriated only $755 million of $132 billion in foreign profit during the
2004 tax holiday – Marr, C. and Huang, C. "Repatriation Tax Holiday Would
Lose Revenue and is a Proven Policy Failure". Center on Budget and Policy
Priorities (2014)

Organisation for Economic Co-operation and Development (OECD) countries
in 2020 had an average effective tax rate of 23.5% – "Corporate Tax Rates
around the World". Tax Foundation website (2020)

Information technology firms in the S&P 500 had an average effective tax rate
of 14.2% for 2020; Amazon (11.8%), Facebook (12.2%), Netflix (13.7%),
Apple (14.5%), Microsoft (15.5%), Alphabet (16.2%) – S&P Global Market
Intelligence website (June 2021 data)

Facebook, Apple, Amazon, Netflix, Google and Microsoft in 2019 had a
combined market capitalisation of $4.5 trillion and collectively they paid just
15.9% in corporate tax on their declared profits over the period 2010 to 2017,
and 17.2% for 2018 and 2019 – "The Silicon Six and their $100 billion global
tax gap". Fair Tax Foundation website (2019)

Facebook agreed to pay the French government €106 million in back taxes with
an additional €8.46 million for revenues earned during 2020 – "Facebook
agrees to pay France €106m in back taxes". BBC (2020)

Facebook's total annual revenue was $84.169 billion for 2020 – Facebook
Annual Report (2020)

EU General Court overturned the EC's ruling, which would have seen Amazon
pay over €250 million in back taxes in Luxembourg – White, J. "Amazon wins
bid to overturn EU state aid ruling". *International Tax Review* (2021)

40% of multinational profits are shifted to tax havens each year, producing an
overall loss of some $200 billion in global tax revenue – Wier, L. "Tax havens
cost governments $200 billion a year. It's time to change the way global tax
works". World Economic Forum (2020)

Edward D Kleinbard quote – Drukker, J. and Bowers, S. "After a Tax Crackdown,
Apple Found a New Shelter for Its Profits". *The New York Times* (2017)

President Barack Obama quote – Mider, Z. "'Unpatriotic Loophole' Targeted by
Obama Costs $2 Billion". Bloomberg (2014)

Pfizer-Allergan merger was worth $150 billion – Rockoff, J., Hoffman, L. and
Rubin, R. "Pfizer Walks Away from Allergan Deal". *The Wall Street Journal*
(2016)

Congress passed the 2017 Tax Cuts and Jobs Act (TCJA) with 53% of the votes
in favour of the Act – "Actions Overview: HR 1, 115th Congress; Clerk of
the US House of Representatives. Final Vote Results for Roll Call 699". US
Congress website (2017)

The Global Intangible Low-Tax Income (GILTI) provision is estimated to reduce
the amount of profit recorded by US companies in tax havens by between 12%
and 16% – Clausing, K. "Profit Shifting Before and After the Tax Cuts and
Jobs Act". *National Tax Journal* (2018)

The US Treasury estimated that tax revenues would increase by $1.8 trillion over
the ten years following the introduction of the TCJA, based on annual GDP
growth of around 3% – "Analysis of Growth and Revenue Estimates Based
on the US Senate Committee on Finance Tax Reform Plan". US Department
of the Treasury (2017)

The Federal Reserve predicts an annual GDP growth rate of roughly 2% –
"US Federal Reserve Open Market Committee's Summary of Economic
Projections". US Federal Reserve website (2017)

The TCJA could increase the US budget deficit by $2 trillion by 2027 – "Final
Tax Bill Could End Up Costing $2.2 Trillion". Committee for a Responsible

Federal Budget website (2017)

Relative to the size of the economy, corporate tax revenue in 2020 was roughly a quarter of what it was in 1965 – "Trends and Proposals for Corporate Tax Revenue". US Congressional Research Service (2021)

In 2021, American multinationals booked about 60% of their total reported foreign income in low-tax countries, which is about double the share in 2000 – "What could a new system for taxing multinationals look like?" *The Economist* (2021)

Details on US President Joe Biden's proposed changes to the tax system – "The Made in America Tax Plan". US Department of the Treasury website (2021)

The G7 reached an agreement on a minimum corporate tax rate of at least 15% – "G7 tax accord is a game-changing opportunity". *Financial Times* (2021)

A minimum corporate tax rate of 15% could produce an estimated $150 billion in additional tax revenues annually – "OECD Secretary-General Tax Report to G20 Finance Ministers and Central Bank Governors". OECD website (2021)

A quarter of Bermuda's GDP was directly attributable to the activities of international corporates, with real estate and financial activities accounting for 15% and 14% of GDP respectively – Government of Bermuda Department of Statistics (2021)

Details of Bermuda's finance minister Curtis Dickinson's opinions on the proposed minimum tax rate – Silverman, G. "'It's a sovereignty issue': Bermuda digs in against global tax deal". *Financial Times* (2021)

In the case of the Panama Papers, 2.6 terabytes of data was leaked, comprising 11.5 million confidential documents that detailed the transactions of over 214,488 offshore entities from the 1970s onwards – Obermayer, B. and Obermaier, F. *The Panama Papers*. Oneworld Publications (2016)

Additional key sources used in the research for this chapter:

Houlder, V. "What is the Double Irish?" *Financial Times* (2014)

"Paradise Papers: Apple's secret tax bolthole revealed". BBC (2017)

Sherman, E. "New Laws Meant to Close Down Tax Havens and Shut Loopholes Could Have the Opposite Effect". *Fortune* (2020)

CHAPTER 17

By 2021, there were over ten thousand different types of cryptocurrencies in existence – CoinMarketCap website (2021)

18 million of the 21 million bitcoins that will ever exist have already been mined as of 2021 – Haar, R. "What is Bitcoin?" *Time* (2021).

In 2021, Microsoft Excel was limited to 1,048,576 rows and 15 digits – "Excel specifications and limits". Microsoft website (2021)

Simon Singh quote – Singh, S. *The Code Book: The Secret History of Codes and Code-Breaking*. HarperCollins (2002)

In 2020, computers on the Bitcoin network were testing roughly 120 quintillion answers per second – Blockchain.com

Miners in 2009 were rewarded 50 bitcoins for every block mined; as of 2021, this has been reduced to 6.25 bitcoins, with the next halving due in 2025 – Conway, L. "Bitcoin Halving". Investopedia (2021)

As of 2021, a single Bitcoin transaction can expend as much as 707kWh – "Bitcoin Energy Consumption Index". Digiconomist (2021)

Sweden's total population in 2021 was 10,175,760 – Worldometers website

Energy consumption of Bitcoin transactions in the Sweden hypothetical example calculated as follows: 1793.40 kWh x 30 x 10,175,760 = 547TWh

Sweden's total energy consumption in 2020 was 135.6TWh – "IEA Key World Energy Statistics". International Energy Agency website (2020)

Details on the HSBC money laundering case – "HSBC Holdings Plc and HSBC Bank USA NA Admit to Anti-Money Laundering and Sanctions Violations, Forfeit $1.256 Billion in Deferred Prosecution Agreement". US Department of Justice website (2012)

Details on the "Welcome to Video" case – "South Korean National and Hundreds of Others Charged Worldwide in the Takedown of the Largest Darknet Child Pornography Website, which was Funded by Bitcoin". US Department of Justice website (2019)

Details of the "Dark Scandals" case – "Dutch National Charged in Takedown of Obscene Website Selling Over 2,000 'Real Rape' and Child Pornography Videos, Funded by Cryptocurrency". US Department of Justice website (2020)

Internet Watch Foundation (IWF) identified 288 new websites in 2019, up from 85 in 2018. This is an increase of 238% – "Internet Watch Foundation Annual Report 2019". IWF (2019)

In 2019, just under $930,000 was paid to addresses known to be associated with child sexual exploitation materials using Bitcoin and Ethereum, representing a 212% increase between 2017 and 2019 – "Making Cryptocurrency Part of the Solution to Human Trafficking". Chainalysis (2020)

Ulbricht's commission from Silk Road amounted to 144,336 Bitcoin – "Acting Manhattan US Attorney Announces Forfeiture of $48 Million from Sale of Silk Road Bitcoins". US Attorney's Office Southern District of New York website (2017)

This amounted to roughly $17 million at the time of his arrest – LaFrance, A. "US Marshals Are Selling 29,656.51306529 Bitcoin". *The Atlantic* (2014)

This amounted to over $6 billion at the time of writing – calculated using a Bitcoin price of $44,130 on 23 September 2021

Ross Ulbricht quote – Bearman, J. "The Untold Story of Silk Road, Part 1 and 2." *Wired* (2015)

Additional key sources used in the research for this chapter:

World Gold Council website

US National Mining Association website

Cryptopedia website

Investopedia website

Graetz, M. and Briffault, O. "A Barbarous Relic: The French, Gold, and the Demise of Bretton Woods". Columbia Law School website (2016)

Nakamoto, S. "Bitcoin: A Peer-to-Peer Electronic Cash System". Bitcoin.org (2008)

CHAPTER 18

Governments collectively injected more than $9 trillion in 2020 to support their economies –Battersby, B., Lam, W. and Ture, E. "Tracking the $9 Trillion Global Fiscal Support to Fight Covid-19". International Monetary Fund (2020)

Global debt, reaching a new peak of $281 trillion by the end of 2020 – Maki, S. "World Debt Reaches Record $281 Trillion". Bloomberg (2021)

More detail on US relief measures for Covid-19 can be found on the IMF policy tracker – "Policy Responses to Covid-19". IMF website (2021)

More information about the CARES Act – "Policy Issues: Covid-19 Economic Relief". US Department of the Treasury website (2021)

More information on TARP – "Report on the Troubled Asset Relief Program". Congressional Budget Office website (2012)

More information on the American Rescue Plan can be found on the IMF policy tracker – "Policy Responses to Covid-19". IMF website (2021)

More information about Build Back Better – "Build Back Better". The White House website (2021)

US budget deficit – US Department of the Treasury database (2021)

Deficit-to-GDP calculated using GDP figures from World Bank database

Banks hoarding cash following the 2007/2008 Global Financial Crisis – Berrospide, J. "Liquidity Hoarding and the Financial Crisis: An Empirical Evaluation". US Federal Reserve website (2012)

Federal Reserve balance sheet data sourced via Federal Reserve database – "Credit and Liquidity Programs and the Balance Sheet". US Federal Reserve website (2021)

Bernanke announced tapering in 2013 – "Key events for the Fed in 2013: The year of the 'taper tantrum'". Reuters (2019)

This resulted in a record twelve-month increase of 75% of the Fed's balance sheet, and astonishingly, represents more than the entirety of the quantitative easing measures in the four-year period that followed the 2007/2008 Global Financial Crisis – Calculated from Federal Reserve data

M2 Money Supply data sourced from FRED database on Federal Reserve Bank of St Louis database, Series M2 Money Stock (M2SL) (2021)

US GDP sourced from World Bank database (2021)

US population sourced from World Bank database (2021)

More details about billionaires and the pandemic – Sharma, R. "The billionaire boom: How the super-rich soaked up Covid cash". *Financial Times* (2021)

S&P Growth – The authors recognise that we are comparing a fifteen-month period of growth (March 2020 to June 2021) with an annualised (twelve-month) compound growth rate (dating back to 1928). However, we feel the comparison is still useful to provide context.

S&P data sourced from S&P Global website (2021)

Federal funds rate or range sourced from Federal Reserve website database (2021)

Nasdaq 100 data sourced from Nasdaq website (2021)

Tesla share price sourced from Nasdaq website (2021)

As an example, in 2020, Tesla sold roughly half a million vehicles – Tesla financial report (2020)

China experienced its first quarterly decline in GDP growth for more than a quarter of a century – Crossley, G. and Yao, K. "Hobbled by coronavirus, China's first-quarter GDP shrinks for first time on record". Reuters (2020)

VW sold over nine million vehicles, of which over 200,000 were pure electric vehicles and another 200,000 were plug-in hybrids – Inside EVs website (2021)

In mid-September 2021, VW's market capitalisation stood at $147 billion with a forward price earnings multiple of 5.8 times, whereas Tesla's market capitalisation was $747 billion with a forward price earnings of 101 times – Yahoo Finance (2021)

Billionaire data sourced from *Forbes* website (2021)

Billionaires as percentage of GDP – Sharma, R. "The billionaire boom: how the super-rich soaked up Covid cash". *Financial Times* (2021)

Consumer Price Index data sourced from the US Bureau of Labor Statistics website (2021)

Federal Reserve says inflation is "transitory" – Tillier, M. "Fed Chair Powell Still Insists Inflation is Transitory, And the Markets Agree. Why?". Nasdaq (2021)

Piketty quote: "Income inequality has increased significantly in the rich countries, especially the United States where the concentration of income in the first decade of the 21st century regained – indeed, slightly exceeded – the level attained in the second decade of the previous century." – Piketty, T. "Thomas Piketty: New thoughts on capital in the twenty-first century". TED Talk. YouTube (2014).

CONCLUSION

For the first time since 2001, there were more countries under authoritarian rule than there were democracies – Ward, C. "G7 Leaders Meet for First Time in

Nearly 2 Years". CNN (2021)

Boris Johnson quote – "G7 Leaders Commit to Protect Planet and Turbocharge Global Green Growth". G7 UK website (2021)

CCP quote – Faulconbridge, G. "China cautions G7 that 'small' groups don't rule the world". *Japan Today* (2021)

Chinese foreign policy official quote – Xinhua, X. "China's top diplomat Yang Jiechi stressed China's stern position on Xinjiang, HK related issues in phone conversation with Blinken". *Global Times* (2021)

Francis Fukuyama quotes – Fukuyama, F. *The End of History and the Last Man*. Free Press (1992); Fukuyama, F. "Francis Fukuyama on the end of American hegemony". *The Economist* (2021)

Ant Group quote – "Ant Group Announces Suspension of Share Listings". US Securities and Exchange Commission website (2020)

Alibaba fined $2.8 billion in April 2021 – "China Fines Alibaba Record $2.8 Billion After Monopoly Probe". Bloomberg (2021)

Alibaba committed to donate over $15 billion to the CCP's "common prosperity" vision for China – Liu, C. "Alibaba Pledges $15.5 Billion to 'Common Prosperity' Drive". Bloomberg (2021)

CCP's "common prosperity" vision for China – "Xi Jinping's talk of 'common prosperity' spooks the prosperous". *The Economist* (2021)

Tencent pledged $7.7 billion to the CCP's "common prosperity" vision – Li, P. and Munroe, T. "Tencent pledges $7.7bln to support China poverty, environment initiatives". Reuters (2021)

Pinduoduo donated $1.5 billion to the CCP's "common prosperity" vision – Liu, C. "Pinduoduo Pledges $1.5 Billion of Profits to Chinese Farmers". Bloomberg (2021)

CCP has ordered Chinese television and social media to stop making stars out of "vulgar influencers" and "sissy boys" – Lim, S. "China orders local reality shows to stop producing 'sissy boys' and 'vulgar influencers'". *The Drum* (2021)

CCP bans certain songs that encourage young Chinese to "lie flat" – Kynge, J. "China's young 'lie flat' instead of accepting stress". *Financial Times* (2021)

Protests at Evergrande headquarters – Yu, S., Mitchell, T., McMorrow, R. and Hale, T. "China's Evergrande faces investor protests as liquidity crunch worsens". *Financial Times* (2021)

Number of Chinese millionaires estimated to have reached four million by the end of 2020 –"Number of millionaires in China from 2015 to 2020". Statista website (2020)

Population of Switzerland in 2021 was 8,731,673 – Worldometers website

BIBLIOGRAPHY

In the course of researching, writing and fact-checking our manuscript, we inevitably made use of a large number of books and websites. Here follows a selection of those that we found exceptionally useful, provided definitive information or both. The books serve as a recommended reading list by subject matter.

BOOKS

Financial history

Bruner, R. and Carr, S. *The Financial Panic of 1907: Lessons Learned from the Market's Perfect Storm.* John Wiley & Sons (2007)

Davis, M. and Etheridge, A. *Louis Bachelier's Theory of Speculation: The Origins of Modern Finance.* Princeton University Press (2006)

Ferguson, N. *The Ascent of Money: A Financial History of the World.* Penguin Books (2011)

Lamoreaux, N. and Shapiro, I. *The Bretton Woods Agreements.* Yale University Press (2019)

LeBor, A. *Tower of Basel: The Shadowy History of the Secret Bank That Runs the World.* PublicAffairs (2013)

Lowenstein, R. *America's Bank: The Epic Struggle to Create the Federal Reserve.* Penguin (2015)

Stiglitz, J. *The Roaring Nineties.* Penguin (2003)

Wapshott, N. *Keynes Hayek: The Clash That Defined Modern Economics.* WW Norton & Company (2011)

2007/2008 Global Financial Crisis

Baldwin, R. *The Great Trade Collapse: Causes, Consequences and Prospects.* Centre for Economic Policy Research (2009)

Blinder, A. *After the Music Stopped: The Financial Crisis, the Response, and the Work Ahead*. Penguin Books (2013)

Boyes, R. *Meltdown Iceland: Lessons on the World Financial Crisis from a Small Bankrupt Island*. Bloomsbury Publishing PLC (2009)

Cohan, D. *House of Cards: A Tale of Hubris and Wretched Excess on Wall Street*. Doubleday (2009)

Djankov, S. *Inside the Euro Crisis: An Eyewitness Account*. Peterson Institute for International Economics (2014)

Geithner, T. *Stress Test: Reflections on Financial Crises*. Crown (2014)

Lewis, M. *Boomerang*. WW Norton & Company (2011)

Lewis, M. *The Big Short: Inside the Doomsday Machine*. WW Norton & Company (2010)

Sorkin, A. *Too Big to Fail*. Viking Press (2009)

Wolf, M. *The Shifts and the Shocks: What We've Learned – and Have Still to Learn – from the Financial Crisis*. Penguin Books (2014)

General financial

Ahamed, L. *Lords of Finance: The Bankers Who Broke the World*. Penguin Books (2009)

Bernanke, B. *The Courage to Act*. WW Norton & Company (2017)

Bernstein, P. *The Power of Gold: The History of an Obsession*. John Wiley & Sons (2000)

Das, S. *Traders, Guns and Money: Knowns and Unknowns in the Dazzling World of Derivatives*. Financial Times Prentice Hall (2006)

Duncan, R. *The New Depression: The Breakdown of the Paper Money Economy*. John Wiley & Sons (2012)

Hunter, W., Kaufman, G. and Pomerleano, M. *Asset Price Bubbles: The Implications for Monetary, Regulatory, and International Policies*. MIT Press (2001)

King, M. *The End of Alchemy: Money, Banking, and the Future of the Global Economy*. Hachette UK (2016)

Kwak, J. and Johnson, S. *13 Bankers: The Wall Street Takeover and the Next Financial Meltdown*. Knopf Doubleday (2010)

LeFevre, J. *Straight to Hell: True Tales of Deviance, Debauchery, and Billion-Dollar Deals*. Open Road + Grove/Atlantic (2014)

Lowenstein, R. *When Genius Failed: The Rise and Fall of Long-Term Capital Management*. Random House (2000)

Macey, J. *The Death of Corporate Reputation*. FT Press (2013)

Morris, C. *The Two Trillion Dollar Meltdown: Easy Money, High Rollers, and the Great Credit Crash*. PublicAffairs (2008)

Partnoy, F. *Infectious Greed: How Deceit and Risk Corrupted the Financial Markets*.

Holt McDougal (2003)
Rickards, J. *The Death of Money.* Portfolio Penguin (2014)
Stiglitz, J. *Freefall: America, Free Markets, and the Sinking of the World Economy.*
Penguin UK (2010)

China

Beardson, T. *Stumbling Giant: The Threats to China's Future.*
Yale University Press (2013)
McMahon, D. *China's Great Wall of Debt: Shadow Banks, Ghost Cities,*
Massive Loans, and the End of the Chinese Miracle. Mariner Books (2018)
Orlik, T. *China: The Bubble that Never Pops.* Oxford University Press (2020)
Paulson, H. *Dealing with China: An Insider Unmasks the New Economic*
Superpower. Hachette UK (2016)
Walter, C. and Howie, F. *Red Capitalism: The Fragile Financial Foundation*
of China's Extraordinary Rise. John Wiley & Sons (2010)

Cryptocurrency

New Scientist. *The End of Money: The Story of Bitcoin, Cryptocurrencies and the*
Blockchain Revolution. Hachette UK (2017)
Singh, S. *The Code Book: The Secret History of Codes and Code-Breaking.*
HarperCollins Pub Ltd (1999)
Tapscott, A. and Tapscott, D. *Blockchain Revolution: How the Technology Behind*
Bitcoin Is Changing Money, Business, and the World. Penguin Canada (2016)
Vigna, P. and Casey, M. *The Age of Cryptocurrency: How Bitcoin and Digital*
Money are Challenging the Global Economic Order. Macmillan USA (2016)

Other

Collier, P. *The Future of Capitalism.* Allen Lane (2018)
De Soto, H. *The Mystery of Capital: Why Capitalism Triumphs in the West*
and Fails Everywhere Else. Basic Books (2000)
Fukuyama, F. *Identity: The Demand for Dignity and the Politics of Resentment.*
Profile Books Ltd (2018)
Grayling, A. *The Good State: On the Principles of Democracy.*
Simon & Schuster (2020)
Hayek, F. *The Road to Serfdom.* Routledge Press UK (1944)
Phillips, K. *Bad Money: Reckless Finance, Failed Politics, and the Global Crisis*
of American Capitalism. Penguin (2008)
Piketty, T. *Capital in the Twenty-First Century.* Harvard University Press (2013)
Reich, R. *Saving Capitalism: For the Many, Not the Few.* Icon Books Ltd (2015)

Stiglitz, J. *The Great Divide: Unequal Societies and What We Can Do about Them.* WW Norton & Company (2015)

Waterstone, M. and Chomsky, N. *Consequences of Capitalism: Manufacturing Discontent and Resistance.* Haymarket Books (2020)

Zegart, A. *Spying Blind: The CIA, the FBI, and the Origins of 9/11.* Princeton University Press (2009)

WEBSITES

Bank for International Settlements www.bis.org

BBC www.bbc.com

Bitcoin.org www.bitcoin.org

Blockchain.com www.blockchain.com

Bloomberg www.bloomberg.com

CFA Institute www.cfainstitute.org

Chainalysis www.chainalysis.com

Chicago Board Options Exchange www.cboe.com

China Banking and Insurance Regulatory Commission www.cbirc.gov.cn

CNBC www.cnbc.com

CNN www.cnn.com

CoinMarketCap www.coinmarketcap.com

Columbia Law School www.law.columbia.edu

Committee for a Responsible Federal Budget www.crfb.org

Commons Library commonslibrary.parliament.uk

Congressional Budget Office www.cbo.gov

Congressional Research Service crsreports.congress.gov

Cryptopedia www.cryptopedia.com

Deloitte www2.deloitte.com

Deutsche Bank www.db.com

Digiconomist www.digiconomist.net

European Banking Federation www.ebf.eu

European Commission ec.europa.eu

Fair Tax Foundation fairtaxmark.net

Federal Reserve Bank of Richmond www.richmondfed.org

Federal Reserve Bank of St Louis www.stlouisfed.org

Federal Reserve History www.federalreservehistory.org

Financial Times www.ft.com

Forbes www.forbes.com

Fortune www.fortune.com

G7 United Kingdom www.g7uk.org

Gallup www.gallup.com

GoodJobsFirst www.goodjobsfirst.org

Govinfo www.govinfo.gov

Harvard Business Review www.hbr.com

History channel www.history.com

Hong Kong Monetary Authority www.hkma.gov.hk

Hoover Institution Library & Archives www.hoover.org

Inside EVs www.insideevs.com

International Energy Agency www.iea.org

International Monetary Fund www.imf.org

Investopedia www.investopedia.com

Kiel Institute for the World Economy

www.ifw-kiel.de
KPMG www.kpmg.com
Lords Library
  lordslibrary.parliament.uk
Mason, Hayes & Curran www.mhc.ie
Microsoft www.microsoft.com
Nasdaq www.nasdaq.com
National Audit Department of
  Malaysia www.audit.gov.my
Organisation for Economic
  Co-operation and Development
  www.oecd.org
Politico www.politico.com
Quartz Africa www.qz.com
Reuters www.reuters.com
S&P Global Market Intelligence
  www.spglobal.com
South China Morning Post
  www.scmp.com
Statista www.statista.com
Tax Foundation
  www.taxfoundation.org
The Atlantic www.theatlantic.com
The Banker www.thebanker.com
The Economist www.economist.com
The Guardian www.theguardian.com
The New York Times
  www.nytimes.com
The Wall Street Journal www.wsj.com
The Washington Post
  www.washingtonpost.com
The White House
  www.whitehouse.gov
Time www.time.com

Trading Economics
  www.tradingeconomics.com
US Attorney's Office Southern
  District of New York
  www.justice.gov/usao-sdny
US Bureau of Labor Statistics
  www.bls.gov
US Census Bureau www.census.gov
US Congress www.congress.gov
US Council on Foreign Relations
  www.cfr.org
US Department of the Treasury
  home.treasury.gov
US Federal Deposit Insurance
  Corporation www.fdic.gov
US Federal Reserve
  www.federalreserve.gov
US Internal Revenue Service
  www.irs.gov
US National Mining Association
  www.nma.org
US Securities and Exchange
  Commission www.sec.gov
US Senate Committee on Banking,
  Housing and Urban Affairs
  www.banking.senate.gov
World Bank www.worldbank.org
World Economic Forum
  www.weforum.org
World Gold Council www.gold.org
World Trade Organization
  www.wto.org
Worldometers
  www.worldometers.info

ACKNOWLEDGEMENTS

David Buckham

It is my opinion that there is no way that a single person could produce this book. It took Robyn, Chris and me just over a year to write, but we have needed the help of many to bring it to completion. Firstly, it is important to thank Derrick Loades, a Monocle consultant who helped to prepare the database on which the figures that appear in this book are based. Thank you also to Jeanette Taylor, a manager at Monocle, whose experience and attention to detail was invaluable in checking all the numbers and calculations that were used. Thank you to all my colleagues and friends who were kind enough to indulge us by reading various versions of the book as it was being produced. In this respect, I would especially like to thank Benson Joubert, also a Monocle consultant, who read several early versions of these chapters, and who has been one of our most indispensable readers over the years during the production of various issues of the *Monocle Quarterly Journal*. I would also like to thank the Monocle technical readers, Skye Wallace and Guy Wilding, who were co-opted at the last minute to do a review, and who worked after hours to ensure the veracity of the content.

I would like to thank my friends Tom Schultz, Rob Sim and Mick Landi, all three of whom have had to individually endure non-stop diatribes on the topics that make up this book for the last several years, if not for the last decade. I would also like to thank Toby Venter, who of his own volition read the manuscript twice and gave very valuable feedback, and my father Brian Buckham, who has been a great inspiration to me in business and who carefully read through the details of this book and gave me great encouragement. Special mention must be made of Jeremy Goldkorn, a friend of mine from schooldays who spent twenty years living in China. I am very appreciative of the way in which he applied his mind to the project, providing us with incredibly valuable feedback in terms of the direction that China is going in and what the economic environment is like on the ground, and for suggesting a reading list that helped us tremendously.

I would also like to extend my gratitude to Vanessa Wilson from Quickfox Publishing, who has an amazing ability to create publishable content out of our manuscripts and who has been along with us on this journey for a long time, through the publication of all nine issues of the *Monocle Quarterly Journal*. I would also like to give credit to Monocle's marketing wizard Steven Mitchell, who made the impossible possible, who helped enormously in transforming our manuscript into a book, and who introduced us to Burnet Media's Tim Richman. I would like to extend my very sincere gratitude to Tim who believed in us from the beginning and who worked tirelessly to produce this book, adding a very balanced and humane perspective to how we see the future, and who calmed us down at the right times. His experience as a publisher and editor has been invaluable.

It would not be possible to write this book if we were not part of a company that encouraged all three of us to allocate significant portions of our work time to creating a book that is not necessarily directly relevant to our immediate business. For their support in this, I would like to thank the entire Monocle executive team and particularly Willie Ehlers and Jaco van Buren-Schele, who work extremely hard to make all of this possible. It is essential to me as a human being that I also acknowledge the incredible mind and efforts of my wife, Natalie Buckham, whose attention to detail and breadth of knowledge is equivalent to an entire editorial team. Finally, I would like to thank my two favourite colleagues, Robyn and Chris, who have worked with me now for four years on hypotheticals and what-ifs and did-you-knows and whatever else came across my brain.

Christiaan Straeuli

To Monocle, thank you for allowing us the scope and opportunity to undertake such an ambitious project. To David, it is a testament to your vision and creativity that this piece of work has come to fruition as wonderfully as it has. To Robyn, you are an amazing writer, colleague and friend, and we couldn't have done this without you. It is an honour to work with you all.

To my family, particularly my mom, Linda, my dad, Eugen, and my brother, Sasha, thank you for all your love and support and every opportunity, of which there are many, you have provided. To my fiancée and soon-to-be wife, Jess, thank you for your unending patience and kindness throughout this journey. I love you all.

Robyn Wilkinson

This project would not have been possible without the special network of people who have supported us through every step of what has been an enormously challenging, but rewarding, process. Thank you to the Monocle executive team who backed this book from its inception, and to all those who played an active role in producing it. Thank you also to my close friends, my family, especially Darrel, Jayne and Kate, and my boyfriend, Wesley, for cheering us on from the sidelines and unreservedly believing in us.

My greatest respect and thanks go to my fellow writers. To David, thank you for providing us with the opportunity to achieve the ultimate dream of any writer – that is, to become an author – and for all you have taught us in the process. To Chris, I could not ask for a better teammate and friend. Thank you for keeping me laughing and keeping me sane.

INDEX

THE END OF MONEY